D0287086

Heavenly love?

BROOKDALE COMMUNITY COLLEGE

Heavenly love?

Lesbian images
in twentieth-century women's writing

Gabriele Griffin

MANCHESTER UNIVERSITY PRESS
Manchester and New York

distributed exclusively in the USA and Canada by St. Martin's Press

Copyright © Gabriele Griffin 1993

Published by Manchester University Press
Oxford Road, Manchester M13 9PL, UK
and Room 400, 175 Fifth Avenue, New York, NY 10010, USA

Distributed exclusively in the USA and Canada
by St. Martin's Press, Inc., 175 Fifth Avenue, New York, NY 10010, USA

British Library Cataloguing-in-Publication Data
A catalogue record for this book is available from the British Library

Library of Congress Cataloging-in-Publication Data
Griffin, Gabriele,
    Heavenly love? : lesbian images in twentieth-century women's
writing / Gabriele Griffin
        p.   cm.
    Includes bibliographical references.
    ISBN 0-7190-2880-9 (cloth). — ISBN 0-7190-2881-7 (pbk.)
    1. Literature—Women authors—History and criticism.
    2. Literature—Modern—20th century—History and criticism.
    3. Lesbians' writings—History and criticism. 4. Lesbianism in
literature. I. Title.
    PN810.W66G75   1994
    809'.89206643—dc20   93-14673
                                                                              CIP

ISBN 0 7190 2880 9 *hardback*
ISBN 0 7190 2881 7 *paperback*

Typeset in Scala with Fritz Quadrata
by Koinonia Ltd, Bury
Printed in Great Britain
by Bell & Bain Limited, Glasgow

Contents

In memoriam
J.-M. K. and Esmé Langley

Introduction

'I think things are much easier for lesbians now. We have lesbian clubs, and we've got the Pink Paper, various magazines and lots more books by lesbian writers' (p. 42). Thus writes one of the older lesbians in *Women like us*, celebrating a change in the accessibility and availability of material on and by lesbians heralding from the time of the women's and gay liberation movements of the late 1960s. The extent of this increase is reflected in Dell Richards's comment that in her book *Lesbian lists* she chose to concentrate on 'lesbians prior to 1970' because 'lists that included the whole spectrum of contemporary lesbianism – authors, photographers, and artists – would have filled volumes' (p. 14).

Lesbian cultural production is thriving, so much so that it is no longer possible to survey its entirety within the context of a single piece of writing. *Heavenly love?* is therefore not an exhaustive survey. For those who would like more extensive surveys, a number of excellent volumes are available, starting from the classic in this field, Jeannette Foster's *Sex variant women in literature*, first published in 1956 and still a useful resource book, to Barbara Grier's *The lesbian in literature*, J. R. Roberts's *Black lesbians*, Lillian Faderman's *Surpassing the love of men* and Bonnie Zimmerman's *The safe sea of women*. None of these texts covers *everything* that has been produced about and by lesbians; for one thing, lesbian cultural historians are still in the process of rediscovering lesbian texts which have been silenced within the dominant cultural tradition. Thus, although it is true that lesbian writing has proliferated in the last twenty years, it is also the case that a large volume of such writing which existed prior to the 1960s was marginalised so that it failed to reach a lesbian or, indeed, any other audience. Radclyffe Hall's *The well of loneliness* (discussed in chapter 1 of *Heavenly love?*), for instance, (in)famous because of the obscenity trial to which it was subjected, was published at a time when lesbian writing was flourishing and many texts which featured lesbian protagonists were published. Yet, if one looks at older lesbians' narratives of their early engagement with lesbian culture, the only text which is referred to again and again is *The well*. Anonymous in Marcy Adelman's *Long time passing: lives of older lesbians* relates a funny but telling little episode about attempting to get hold of *The well*:

> Her stern image remains vivid, 44 years after our encounter – the city librarian seated primly at the information desk... I rallied all of my courage to whisper, 'Do you have a book called *The Well of Loneliness*? By Radclyffe Hall?'... 'We do not,' she announced, lips barely parting, 'allow pornography on our shelves.' (p. 67)

Lesbian writing was – and to some degree still is – silenced because of its association with sexuality, a sexuality which is resistant to the normative forces of a heterosexist society. The word 'lesbian' conjures up women loving women, and not just platonically. As Tamsin Wilton suggests in 'Desire and the politics of representation,' constructions of sexuality reflect and perpetuate the power structures of our culture. These decree the dominance and agency of men in the realm of sexuality, as elsewhere, and the submission and passivity of women:

> To grant women sexual agency would be to threaten not merely socially constructed gender norms but the discursive matrix of power itself. If to be powerful is to assume sexual rights over the powerless, then sexual power in women represents not only a challenge to existing gendered relations of power, but a rupture with the discursive constitution of power itself. (p. 77)

This, precisely, constitutes the disruptive force that lesbians represent.

As sex is taboo in Western culture, so any expression of sexuality that explodes the narrow bands of the permissible is bound to find itself fenced off, hedged about with signs that mark and contain its difference or deviance. In this context, lesbian writing has only gradually struggled to the surface of our culture but now, very clearly, it is here to stay.

In the course of this century, attitudes towards sexuality, and with these, attitudes towards lesbians, have undergone a number of changes which register in writings about and by lesbians. In *Heavenly love?* I have attempted to chart some of these changes, so the volume is organised in roughly chronological fashion, although if represented in diagrammatic form it would look more like a tree than a stick. This is because lesbian writing throughout this century has become increasingly diverse, spreading and extending its branches in many different cultural directions. This raises the issue of the appropriateness of using the phrase 'lesbian writing' – as I have done until now – as a unitary concept, an identifiable, fixed body of work with distinct and distinguishing traits.

What *is* 'lesbian writing'? To talk of 'lesbian writing' is to raise the issue of difference, for the adjective 'lesbian' implies both a presence, a mark of distinction, and an absence, something which is *not that*. As I shall suggest, however, the drawing of the boundaries between what is and what is not lesbian writing is a problematic exercise, highlighting the provisional nature of such categorization.

The answer to the question, 'What is "lesbian writing"?' depends, in part, on where the locus of the establishment of meaning in relation to a text is sited. One may consider this meaning, in this instance the 'lesbian identity' of a text, to be determined primarily by the author, by the text itself, or by the reader. This ignores, for the moment, the possibility of a multiplicity of interrelating factors determining meaning. As I shall indicate, each of these ways of determining writing as 'lesbian' has implications which question the category such classification is seeking to construct.

If one argues that lesbian writing is writing by women known to be lesbian, one needs to consider what this implies for work by lesbian writers which does not contain or centralize lesbian subject matter. As Valerie Miner maintains, 'Tensions arise... when we confuse the writing with the writer herself' ('An imaginative collectivity of writers and readers', p. 25). One reason for such tensions may be that the lesbian writer, as Maureen Brady details in 'Insider/outsider coming of age', wants 'wider recognition, not less

3

recognition from the lesbian reader, but a greater validation in the literary world' (p. 55), sought by addressing issues which will take her beyond lesbian subject matter. Or it may be that she, as was the case with Rosemary Manning, is not 'out' and therefore does not focus her work exclusively on lesbian concerns.

As one of its projects, recent lesbian scholarship has attempted to establish the way(s) in which lesbian subject matter and/or a lesbian aesthetic might be uncovered in writings by women known to be lesbian but whose work has not been 'classified' as lesbian. An example of this scholarship is Jill Davis' article '"This be different" – the lesbian drama of Mrs Havelock Ellis'. While Davis's article offers a persuasive reading of Ellis's play *The mothers* as encoding lesbian experience structurally and semantically, the question remains as to what extent this is a viable strategy in all cases of lesbian writers' work not overtly addressing lesbianism. It assumes that a writer's lesbianism is the overriding determinant of her work, and as such discernible. Certainly many lesbian writers would accept the former, if not the latter. In 'Theorizing lesbian : writing – a love letter' Elizabeth Meese asks:

> Why is it that the lesbian seems like a shadow – a shadow with/in woman, with/in writing? A contrastive shape in a shadow play, slightly formless, the edges blurred by the turns of the field, the sheets on which a drama is projected. The lesbian subject is not all I am and it is in all I am. A shadow of who I am that attests to my being there, I am never with/out this lesbian. (p. 70)

Meese here locates difference in the gap between herself as material entity and 'a self I create as I write' (p. 71). Further, she suggests that unless her material self enters the system of signification which language constitutes, it does not mean:

> What is it, after all, to be (a) lesbian without the word, without writing *l-e-s-b-i-a-n* or something like it? It seems like nothing. So I write, and in doing so, I enter metaphor, or metaphor enters me. I take up my grammatical place: the lesbian subject. (p. 79)

As metaphor, according to Meese, the lesbian subject achieves presence in discourse and points to the absence of what it names, indicating 'likeness to the thing but never the thing or the thing-in-itself' (p. 80). As presence in discourse, the lesbian subject is 'both included in and stands against the ... discourse which produces it', thus instigating and maintaining a 'project of subversion' (p. 76) of patriarchal discourse.

Meese's stance does not assume a fixity of lesbian identity:

> 'Lesbian being' is something which is 'there,' when 'there' shifts and ex-changes itself to suit the speaker, who also ex-changes herself (making more of us). (p. 81)

The assumed fixity of identity of the 'lesbian writer' is one of the issues such writers struggle with in discussing their positions. In 'Imitation and gender insubordination' Judith Butler assesses 'the lesbian-signifier' in terms of the demarcations invoked by it, maintaining that 'lesbian' '[suggests] a provisional totalization of this "I"' (p. 15). This provisional totalization is in part determined by what it excludes. The fact that both what is included and what is excluded determine 'lesbian' identity – and thus potentially (re)create forms of oppressiveness and homophobia – as well as the fact that the signification of 'lesbian' is 'to some degree out of one's control' (p. 15) and can, further, be put to uses which one might wish to dissent from, lead Butler to argue very forcefully that 'identity categories tend to be instruments of regulatory regimes' (p. 13) and ought to be regarded with suspicion. For these reasons, Butler 'would like to have it permanently unclear what precisely that sign [– 'lesbian' –] signifies' (p. 14).

The coercive potential of the use of identity categories is also the subject of Mary Meigs' article, 'Falling between the cracks'. She found that 'a writer who has come out as a lesbian, no matter what the subject of a subsequent book or its percentage of lesbian content … is forever sealed in her lesbian identity like an insect in plexiglass' (p. 31). What of writers who are lesbian but who remain in the closet and whose work has not been investigated in terms of its lesbian potential? Can we only find what we seek? If so, what is the status of the category 'lesbian'?

If we consider 'lesbian writing' predominantly in terms of the text itself, its content and style, other concerns regarding the category 'lesbian' arise. Novels that centralize female characters explicitly involved in sexual relationships with other women, such as Sarah Schulman's *Girls, visions and everything*, are easily classified as 'lesbian'; but what of novels such as Iris Murdoch's *An unofficial rose* in which the lesbian characters are relatively marginal? One could suggest that such a text replicates the reality of lesbians' situation in contemporary Western society and should therefore perhaps qualify to be described as 'lesbian'. How central does lesbian subject matter have to be for a text to be regarded as 'lesbian'? It seems, to follow Meigs' point, that if the writer is an 'out' lesbian, her text may be considered 'lesbian', no matter how slight – from her perspective – its lesbian content. But what if the writer's sexuality has not been publicly declared? What kind of a lesbian presence in a text is required then to make it 'lesbian'?

Similar questions can be raised in relation to issues of style. Namascar Shaktini's essay 'Displacing the phallic subject: Wittig's lesbian writing' demonstrates how lesbian writing (by a declared lesbian, with explicit lesbian content) can, in style as well as content, refuse the exchange position (woman as object and commodity, exchanged by men) women inhabit in patriarchal culture, centralize the conventionally marginalized figure and thus displace the 'phallic subject', as well as rewrite and transform myths that have served to contain the female in subordinate, male-centred positions. I would suggest that Djuna Barnes's *Nightwood* as well as Christine Crow's *Miss X or the wolf woman*, for example, can be read in those terms.

But what of the many texts that utilize realist modes of representation, complete with linear plot development, closure, and a hierarchy of discourses suggesting that there is such a thing as '*the* truth'? (See Catherine Belsey for a succinct discussion of realist texts.) How do we deal with texts which seemingly offer no stylistic subversion to dominant modes of representation which exclude all that is 'lesbian'? In 'Ourself behind ourself: a theory for lesbian readers' Jean E. Kennard suggests that one can utilise both what is excluded and what is included in one's definition of self in the reading process. One can identify with *and* offer opposition to the text. As Meese argues:

> I would like to think that lesbianism, like feminism, could position itself 'outside'. There's a comfort in the tidiness offered by the absence of complicity and the certainty of absolute difference. But lesbianism, as an attack on hetero-relations [or their encodings in cultural production], takes (its) place within the structure of the institution of heterosexuality. The lesbian is born of/in it. (p. 82)

Thus it is possible to suggest that a style of writing which disrupts conventional modes of representation, such as Monique Wittig's, assumes its identity through its insistence on difference, simultaneously signaling its relationality to the dominant structure from which it seeks to differentiate itself. Conversely, orthodox modes of representation – for example in some lesbian thrillers – can point to difference by breaking with some of their conventions, by replacing one kind of central protagonist with a lesbian other, for instance.

The lesbian reader has two positions open to her in her engagement with a text: identification and dissociation. Through her reading she can impose on the text a lesbian identity simply by asserting it. Similarly, she can declare a text 'not that'. However she argues her position, it will not inevitably be shared by others. The debates around Lillian Faderman's *Surpassing the love of men* are a case in point. That text and the discussions it provoked reinforce the notion that 'lesbian' as a category is unstable. This recognition leads Sally Munt, for example, to write that though she agrees with Diana Fuss's view that

> there is no eternal lesbian essence outside the frame of cultural change and historical definition... this strictly intellectual definition wouldn't stop me *feeling*, and sometimes behaving, as though the total opposite were true. We need our dream of a lesbian nation, even if we recognise its fictionality. (p. xviii)

The desire for a recognition of the lesbian self, for a sense of belonging to an identifiable lesbian community, informs the stance of the lesbian reader in her identification with or dissociation from a text as lesbian or not. It is also this desire which motivates the search for lesbian images in texts.[1]

What the search itself reveals is twofold: first, lesbian images – images of women positioned in erotically charged relation to other women *and* women's relationships with each other placed at the structural and semantic pivots of narratives,[2] have been produced for a long time. Second, these lesbian images are imbricated in the historical and cultural moments of their constuction.

In the early part of the twentieth century, a sense of lesbianism as sickness or deviance was fostered. One older lesbian relates the sense of relief she felt on reading Freud:

> I read Freud when I was in my twenties, it was *Three Essays Towards a View of Sex* where he said he thought most people were bisexual. I found that quite comforting because it didn't say I was deviant. The other books I'd read implied that there was something wrong, it was a sickness. And so I

tended to look for answers to *why* was I a lesbian, for a while. (Neild and Pearson, p. 121)

One positive answer was provided by Edward Carpenter, who saw homosexuality in its ideal form as a kind of 'heavenly love', following one early twentieth-century German term for homosexuals – *Urning* – derived from *Uranos*, meaning heaven, which suggested 'that the Uranian love was of a higher order than the ordinary attachment' (*The intermediate sex*, p. 20). Carpenter thought this higher order love in its purest form was spiritual rather than sexual (p. 70). The title of *Heavenly love?* presented itself in this context, playing both on the idea of lesbian love as wonderful, 'heavenly', and raising the issue of the 'nature' of lesbian love; is it of a 'higher' order, Carpenter's 'spiritual' love, or is it 'basely' sexual? If it seems as if even asking this latter question is archaic, it should be remembered that the definition of what constitutes a lesbian has surfaced again and again in the course of this century, most recently, perhaps, in debates about Adrienne Rich's term 'lesbian continuum' (see chapter 3) and about female friendship, especially in conjunction with Lillian Faderman's book *Surpassing the love of men* (see chapter 5). It registers in the nature/nurture debate (was she *born* or was she *made* a lesbian?) which persists in the opposition of 'essentialist' *versus* 'social constructionist' positions. One radical lesbian writer, Julia Penelope, resolves this dichotomy by arguing that 'Judging from my own experience, both accounts of Lesbian identity are accurate. It's not an either/or situation.' (*Call me lesbian*, p. 20)

In my pursuit of lesbian images in twentieth-century writings by women, I made a decision to focus exclusively on *writing by women*, for the most part known lesbian writers, rather than discussing, as does, for example, Jeannette Foster's *Sex variant women*, male writing on lesbians as well. There are several reasons for this. First, as this cannot be a survey text of *all* the images of lesbians ever constructed in writing, I had to select texts for inclusion, and one of the advantages of such an openly selective attitude is that it gives one the option to discriminate positively in favour of women. In a world dominated by men I very much support the notion of female mediation, of promoting women's work and their views. It is important that lesbian voices are heard, especially in the context of the construction of lesbian images. Second, the representation of lesbians by male authors raises a number of issues – such as men's

8

attitudes towards lesbians – which may well be worth addressing but which I did not want to address here. Not wanting to engage with these issues was a decision made early on in the process of my research for this book when I was reading Compton Mackenzie's *Extraordinary women* (London, 1928) which I found misogynistic and offensive to lesbians. This is not to say that only men produce texts that lesbians might take exception to. But reading that text brought home to me the fact that discussing men's images of lesbians would mean having to work through a set of issues associated with masculinity, men's perceptions of themselves, the world and lesbians which would reduce the amount of space I could devote to discussing texts by (lesbian) women writers. This is something which in the current cultural climate of the 'backlash' I did not think I could afford to do.

Apart from privileging the work of female writers, a number of criteria influenced my choice of texts included for discussion in *Heavenly love?* I wanted, for instance, to look at well-known novels such as Radclyffe Hall's *The well*, but also at texts that are frequently bypassed such as Hall's short story 'Miss Ogilvy finds herself' or H.D.'s *Her* – of formal as well as semantic interest to its readership. Accepting the critique that lesbian feminist criticism has begun to construct its own 'canon' (a now unacceptable because exclusionary practice in cultural categorization) of lesbian 'classics', I wanted to consider different kinds of representations of lesbians across a range of texts which might come under the labels of 'low' or 'high' culture, 'popular' or 'canonical', and to consider them side by side, as part of particular periods or trends in lesbian writing rather than as discrete entities. I should mention in this context that a number of very interesting images of lesbians have begun to surface in media other than writing, for example music and film. These have begun to be addressed in books such as Sally Munt's *New lesbian criticism*, Diana Fuss's *Inside/out* and a book I edited entitled *Outwrite*.

As part of the refusal of traditional boundaries of textual division which include not only 'low' and 'high' culture but also that of categorizing texts by genre, I decided to offer discussions of texts from a range of genres, often raising particular issues which surface in very diverse kinds of writing. I have done so for several reasons: First, all texts share the position of either reflecting or constructing 'the world' (depending on one's theoretical position) whether they are novels or history textbooks. It therefore does not make sense, from my point of view, to treat them as distinct on the level of their relationship to 'truth'. In other words, I do not think that an autobiography is closer to 'truth' than a biography or a poem. Second, images of lesbians across a range of texts influence how lesbians construct and re-present their sense of themselves as lesbians. Images beget, reinforce, disintegrate images, irrespective of the generic specificity of the text. Fiction will thus be discussed in theoretical texts while images constructed in non-fictional writing may well inform poetry.[3] A number of anthologies about/by lesbians such as Judith Barrington's *An intimate wilderness* place different kinds of writing side by side, thus refusing narrow categories of definition and privileging issue over form. Finally, some writing by lesbians refuses the status of a particular genre through drawing on a number of conventions within a single piece of writing. A typical example is Judy Grahn's *Another mother tongue*, which fuses autobiography with the direct address of the letter or epistolary novel as well as historical and mythological material. Lesbian images occur in a variety of writings by women, not all of which are open to 'literary' classification in conventional ways. One might argue that these writers take their refusal of heterosexist norms into the aesthetic as well as the sexual realm, a phenomenon which has become more pronounced in the latter half of the twentieth century.

I would argue that a series of shifts in representations of lesbians has occurred in the course of this century, occasioned by social, cultural and political changes. Portrayals of lesbians from the early part of this century are informed by the issues of definition which exercised sexologists[4] as much as women writers. Sexologists saw lesbianism as an isolatable psychosexual problem; this recognition and categorization had both liberating and inhibiting consequences. Lesbianism could now be 'spoken about' – but in what and on whose terms?

In the rather complex opening sequence of H.D.'s *Her* (and it has to be remembered that H.D. was psychoanalysed by Sigmund Freud, as relayed by her in *Tribute to Freud*), Hermione, trying to come to terms with her sense of self, finds:

> Her[mione] Gart had no word for her dementia, it was predictable by star, by star-sign, by year.
>
> But Her Gart was then no prophet. She could not predict later common usage of uncommon syllogisms; 'failure complex,' 'compensation reflex,'

and that conniving phrase 'arrested development' had opened no door to her. Her development, forced along slippery lines of exact definition, marked supernorm, marked subnorm on some sort of chart or soul-barometer. (p. 3)

As part of Hermione's attempt to come to terms [sic] with herself, she has to find the words, here culled from science and psychology, that will explain her to herself and to others. Hermione is depicted as needing words to give shape and meaning to herself; the images for her, so the narrative suggests, can – indeed will – be found in psychological texts.

Many women writers of the early twentieth century thought it imperative to determine the cause of lesbianism, but found it difficult to decide what it was. In the attempt to decide between four possible answers to the question of the 'origin' of lesbianism (was it a biologically-based problem, a form of mental illness, an innate predisposition, or the result of early conditioning?), most writers found it difficult to decide in favour of *one* 'cause', and tended to invoke at least two, frequently a mixture of innate predisposition and social conditioning. Such is the case, for instance, with Radclyffe Hall's lesbian characters.

Women writers from the early part of the twentieth century not only grappled with issues of definition; they also had to deal with the problem of an absence of a linguistic and cultural tradition representing lesbians. Further, they were subject to the mores and decorum of their period. The result of these multifarious pressures was that many early representations of lesbians create an image of them as *the only one* in their community, as isolated individuals, 'warped' predominantly through nature and a bit of mis-nurture, defensively pitted against a heterosexual world which regards them as males *manqués*, suffering and essentially unfulfilled, intended to arouse pity rather than condemnation. Lesbian relationships were lived out (as opposed to dreamt about) *abroad* rather than at home. Those lesbian protagonists who did not deracinate themselves and enact their alienated condition by going to a foreign land, (as Hermione decides to do at the end of *Her*), would end up either sublimating their desires or leading miserable unfulfilled lives, like, for example, Joan Odgen in *The unlit lamp*.

Although there were texts during this period which portrayed lesbian *communities* – Renée Vivien's *A woman appeared to me* is a case in point – the dominant image remained that of the isolated lesbian. This did not change until the 1950s and 1960s, when the lesbian community first began to surface in the pulp fiction of that period. Instead of lesbians being presented as extruded from their home community, they were now portrayed as ghettoized within the heterosexual community in metropolitan enclaves such as Greenwich Village. While still segregated from heterosexist society, lesbians now seemed part of the 'enemy within' ideology which was one aspect of the conservatism of the 1950s and early 1960s, threatening the stability of the family and the state. Lesbian images from this period reflect this 'threat': lesbians fall in love with and tempt heterosexual women away from their families, they are presented as more assertive, indeed butch, and sexual desire increasingly plays a part in how they are depicted.

What exploded and changed these representations of lesbians, as discussed in chapter 2, was the advent of the women's liberation, gay and civil rights movements, as well as a growing reaction against sickness models in psychiatry and against the deterministic attitudes of Freudian psychoanalysis. The liberation movements allowed for a new form of cause-oriented female bonding over issues such as equal rights, abortion, and so on. As a result of the associated political campaigns, lesbians became more visible in society at large. Questions began to be raised about sexual politics and the politics of sexuality; women's sexuality, now presented as a matter of social conditioning, a prime source of patriarchal oppression and a site of the inter-sexual battle for the control of the female self, needed to be reviewed in the light of the possibility of *choice*. Lesbianism became a choice and an option, politically inflected, that *all* women could consider. Many texts from this period dealing with lesbian images – Adrienne Rich's poetry is one example here – highlight this issue of women's *choice* in assuming or changing sexual identities.

The cultural and political visibility of lesbians achieved in the late 1960s and early 1970s, coupled with a new assertive and celebratory attitude towards lesbianism, encapsulated in the slogan 'glad to be gay', resulted in a proliferation of lesbian writing and the move from constructing lesbians as 'deviant' to seeing them as 'defiant'. Lesbian heroes like Molly Bolt in *Rubyfruit jungle* were created. Gradually, earlier binarisms such as homo/hetero, fe/male, butch/femme were superceded by writing emphasizing diversity and differences among lesbians. Women no longer defined themselves in opposition to men but rather in relation to each other, with resultant debates concerning differences between lesbian and heterosexual women.

Two areas of writing emerged which particularly addressed these concerns: lesbian/feminist science fiction and writings on female friendship. Once women, as part of their political activism, had begun to demand women-only spaces, this demand surfaced in the cultural representation of women-only worlds. This, together with advances in reproductive technology, resulted in the emergence of women's sci fi during the 1980s. Looking at that writing now, and the critical writing it generated, it is possible to see a merging, in cultural perception, of lesbians and politicised women. This ultimately operated to the disadvantage of lesbians, whose sexual identification with women was obliterated in a generalized de-emphasizing of sexuality in favour of other issues, such as reproduction. Women's sci fi, especially the dystopic variety, thus tends to be heterosexual in base. In the 1980s, lesbian writing envisioning lesbian worlds was effectively side-stepped. In chapter 4 I therefore consider such writing rather than offering the conventional analyses of texts such as Margaret Atwood's *Handmaid's tale* or Suzette Haden Elgin's *Native tongue*, which are important texts but are not, I would argue, specifically concerned with images of lesbians.[5] Other texts like Judy Grahn's *Another mother tongue* do that, and from a position informed by a sense of lesbian cultural history and tradition. The same is true of Monique Wittig and Sande Zeig's *Lesbian peoples*. Lesbian writing dealing with lesbian worlds tends not, as women's sci fi frequently does, to focus exclusively on the future; it operates time shifts into the past as well. Its concern is frequently with the continuity of lesbian traditions, in the recognition that people perpetuate themselves through their culture, and through the sense of a history of a culture. Lesbian sci fi, in the sense of futuristic texts, is thus only *one* way in which lesbian writing envisions a women-only world.

Writings on female friendship became prominent in the second half of the 1970s, again, I would argue, in response to the female bonding afforded by the liberation movements. However, as with women's sci fi, much of the writing on friendship de-emphasized sexuality as a vital component in relations between women, thus marginalizing many lesbians in favour of heterosexual women's emotional bonding. In chapter 5 I argue that many writings on female friendship constituted a re-domestication of women as a renewed political conservatism. Much of this writing showed a familialization of female relations, reflecting the conservative insistence on the primacy of the nuclear family in the light of which many female friendships were recast. Again, as with women's sci fi, the much more threatening representations of lesbians refusing the nuclear family and choosing other models of cohabitation – as detailed in Gillian Hanscombe's *Between friends*, for instance – were side-stepped in the reception of writings on female friendship which focussed on those texts that highlighted romanticism over political and social change. This did not help lesbians – when the government proposed anti-homosexual legislation in the form of Clause 28, it recognized and sought to destroy the image of lesbians and gay men living in 'pretend' families, continuing a tradition established by the Warnock report which privileged the heterosexual nuclear family over any other kind of social formation.

The oppressiveness of current legislation relating to homosexuals has not driven lesbians back into the closet, but has resulted, in some respects, in more militant attitudes towards individuals' rights. Simultaneously, conservative attitudes have begun to affect the ideologies informing lesbian writing. This is particularly noticeable in the contested area of writings on lesbian sexuality, which has undergone a number of changes over time. A diversity of writings on lesbian sexuality exists now, from texts that include sexual scenes, graphically or metaphorically encoded, to erotic and pornographic writing focussing exclusively on depictions of lesbian sex. Such writing raises a number of issues, in relation to AIDS and safer sex campaigns, the representation of power (structures), and the articulacy or otherwise of depictions of lesbian sexuality, some of which I address in chapter 6.

The final chapter in this book is devoted to an increasingly significant but, until recently, frequently ignored aspect of lesbian writing – writings on/by older lesbians. In our society, with the number of older people rising steadily, not enough recognition is given to the fact that older lesbians exist – even within the lesbian community itself. This is unfortunate, because representations of older lesbians not only highlight them as custodians of lesbian history, but also because these representations break many of the taboos of our culture and expose its frontiers. Representations of older lesbians signal the move, threatening to heterosexists in patriarchal societies, that women can make from heterosexuality to lesbianism. They highlight the continuing sexuality and sexual activity of lesbians in old age. They also focus on concerns such as illness (especially cancer) and bereavement, offering information and images often silenced in this culture. Older lesbians represent the future of younger lesbians; their images, against the grain of some other contemporary lesbian writing, construct by and large a very positive image of a caring lesbian community of women who choose to support each other.

In any book one inevitably leaves out texts and areas one would like to have included. A positive effect of the proliferation of lesbian writing has been the emergence of images of lesbians in many different kinds of writings, including popular genres such as detective novels and thrillers, which have not been accommodated here. Essays on these can be found in some of the critical anthologies previously mentioned. There is much work that remains to be done, on images of lesbians in the area of performance arts, and (popular) music, for example. But the start has very clearly been made.

Notes

1 This is evident both in Lee Lynch's 'Cruising the libraries' and Alison Hennegan's 'On becoming a lesbian reader'.
2 See Marilyn R. Farwell's 'Heterosexual plots and lesbian subtexts: toward a theory of lesbian narrative space'.
3 In this context I agree with Virginia Woolf's line that 'books continue each other, in spite of our habit of judging them separately' (*A room of one's own*, p. 77).
4 See Havelock Ellis's *Sexual inversion* in *Studies in the psychology of sex* (vol. 2), and Edward Carpenter's *The intermediate sex*.
5 In *The handmaid's tale* one lesbian character, Moira, appears – she is presented as an outlaw and marginalized figure, acting as a prostitute.

Chapter 1

Becoming visible

Lonely lesbians: Radclyffe Hall's images of lesbians

With the emergence of such studies of lesbian literature as Jeannette H. Foster's *Sex variant women in literature* (1956), Jane Rule's *Lesbian images* (1975), and Lillian Faderman's *Surpassing the love of men* (1981), to name but a few, a tradition of twentieth-century lesbian writing has become visible. Within this tradition a number of women writers and texts have emerged as 'classics'. From an English-speaking, white Western perspective, the early twentieth century is dominated by writers such as Dorothy Baker, Djuna Barnes, Elizabeth Bowen, H.D., Radclyffe Hall, Vita Sackville-West, Edna St. Vincent Millay, Gertrude Stein, and Renée Vivien. Some of these wrote a number of texts dealing with lesbians. Others, like Clemence Dane, Lillian Hellman, or Rosamond Lehmann, produced only one novel or play which centred on lesbianism. What these writers have in common is that they were white, middle or upper class,[1] and either financially independent or at least economically self-sufficient (sometimes with a little help from their friends – in Djuna Barnes's case, Peggy Guggenheim). They were writers who, for the most part, could write of themselves, as Gertrude Stein does in *The autobiography of Alice B. Toklas*, 'I led in my childhood and youth the gently bred existence of my class and kind.' (p. 7).

To a certain extent their lives are reflected in their works. A distinction can be made between those writers who lived abroad, for example, the *Women of the left bank* (as Shari Benstock has called them), and those who stayed at home, whether in North America or in England. I would suggest – though there are some exceptions – that those writers who moved to Paris from the United States and from Great Britain were, by and large, 'freer' in their handling of the subject matter of inversion and more adventurous in their stylistic explorations than the writers who stayed at home and portrayed lesbian existence in their home territory.

Radclyffe Hall, in fact, did not stay at home spending much of her adult life in Paris (see Una Troubridge's biography), but three of her texts overtly dealing with inversion, *The unlit lamp* (1924), 'Miss Ogilvy finds herself' (1926), and *The well of loneliness* (1928) are set predominantly in rural England, the home of the British gentry and the seat of conservatism. The texts display, with some variations, the same basic attitude towards inversion, based, as Sonja Ruehl has demonstrated, on Havelock Ellis's theories on that subject. In each of the texts the social focus is on the gentry (impoverished or landed) among whom an invert is struggling to survive. There is no sense of a lesbian *community*; rather, inversion is represented as an isolated, one-off phenomenon, the nature of which virtually everyone, but most specifically the invert herself, is ignorant of. In *The unlit lamp*, for example, inversion as such remains undiscussed. Joan Ogden's lesbianism is contextualized in terms of an unhappy parental marriage in which Joan's mother, to her husband 'little better than this man's slave...', the victim of his lusts, his whims, his tempers and his delicate heart' (p. 140), uses Joan 'as a healer, as a reason, an explanation' (p. 127) for her sufferings at the hands of her husband. What unfolds is what Alice Miller has called 'the drama of the gifted child' in which the narcissistically deprived parent, whose primary and legitimate need to be respected has been ignored, will use the child – whose dependence makes her defenceless against this sort of manipulation – to compensate for this deprivation.

> Later, these children not only become mothers (confidantes, comforters, advisors, supporters) of their own mothers, but also take over the responsibility for their siblings. (p. 23)

This is precisely how Joan behaves to her younger sister Milly. At the same time the child herself becomes narcissistically deprived; trained to be attuned to the mother's needs, she 'cannot develop and differentiate [her] "true self" because [s]he is unable to live it' (p. 27). As a result the child cannot separate from the parent; gratifying the parent's needs proceeds at the cost of self-realization.

Miller's analysis of the narcissistically disturbed child, victim of a narcissistically deprived parent, both of whom are prevented from self-actualization through the demands of others, provides a theoretical framework for the 'family romance' played out in *The unlit lamp*. It also explains how the novel circumvents the direct exploration of lesbianism. The comments made by Joan's unsuccessful suitor Richard provide the wider model for the dynamic between mother and daughter:

> 'How long is it to go on,' cried he, 'this preying of the weak on the strong, the old on the young; this hideous, unnatural injustice one sees all around one, this incredibly wicked thing that tradition sanctifies? ... In your family it was your father who began it, by preying first on her [Joan's mother], and in a kind of horrid retaliation she turned and preyed on you.' (p. 320)

The problematic relationship between Joan and her mother is compounded by Joan's recognition that 'leaving her mother's home for that of another woman' would mean 'embarking upon the unusual':

> She stopped to consider this aspect carefully. It was *unusual*... She had never heard of any girl of her acquaintance taking such a step, now that she came to think of it. It was quite common for men to share rooms with a friend, and, of course, girls left home when they married. When they married. Ah! that was the point, that was what made all the difference, as her mother had pointed out. (p. 263)

The 'centuries of custom, centuries of precedent' to which Joan succumbs are those of a heterosexist society; without a lesbian herstory – a version of the past which encodes and preserves lesbian experiences from a lesbian perspective – she lacks an enabling framework of reference for the move she contemplates – but never makes.[2]

The unlit lamp emphasizes that for Joan to join Elizabeth would be a *move*. Throughout the novel a contrast is set up between those who stay and those who go away. Early on Richard warns Joan not to 'let yourself be bottled' (p. 59). Emotionally manipulated by her mother, Joan is unable to sustain any geographical distance between them, and her sense of the pointlessness of any attempt to move is reinforced by her sister Milly's return to their home to die of consumption. Despite Joan's increasingly fatalistic attitude, the novel makes clear that only those who go *and stay away* can develop independent selves; *The unlit lamp* is full of 'returners' – both female and male, from ex-colonials to relatives looking after their feebler relations – who manage, at best, a life of partial fulfilment in the face of their inability to cut the cord which ties them to country, society, and family. Interestingly enough, 'returning' is correlated with de/generacy in the text: the term itself, of course, denotes the idea of origin, where something *comes from*, and *The unlit lamp* suggests that to return to where you came from is indicative of an enfeebled self. This is as true of Joan's ex-colonial father as it is of Milly.

Despite this depressing stance, the novel projects some optimism concerning the lesbian as she may exist in the future. Richard thinks of women like Joan as 'fine, splendid and fiercely virginal... the women of the future' (p. 220), and Joan comes to see herself as 'the forerunner who had failed, the pioneer who had got left behind, the prophet who had feared his own prophecies' (p. 301). This position is, in some respects, at odds with the investigation of origins in 'Miss Ogilvy finds herself'. Miss Ogilvy, unlike Joan, makes the moves from her home in Surrey necessary to find herself, first through leading an ambulance unit in France during World War I, and then through choosing, seemingly by instinct, to travel to an island off the coast of Devon which she 'recognizes' without, apparently, having been there before. When shown the skull of a caveman by her landlady, Miss Ogilvy is confronted with the extinct self she is about to become; in a pre-death vision she is transformed into a caveman aware of the impending extinction of his tribe.

Described by Hall as 'an excursion into the realms of the fantastic' (p. 6), the story transports Miss Ogilvy not only through space but also through time in order to explore the notion that the invert hails back to some pre-civilized primitive age in which she was a cave*man*. The assertion of the title, Miss Ogilvy *finds herself*, suggests that there is a 'true self' into which Miss Ogilvy transforms when she appears to become a caveman. The implication of the first few sections of the story, where reference is made to 'many another of her kind' (p. 13) who emerge to help with the war effort, seems to be that inverts like Miss Ogilvy are out of place in female bodies and in the twentieth century alike because, in truth, they are troglodytes. They do not seem to have a future so much as a past. In a final fusion of eros and thanatos in sections six and seven of the story, caveman and invert merge to be represented as out of place and doomed to extinction, the caveman because the human race will evolve into increasingly civilized forms, and the invert because she represents a twentieth-century version of an earlier, primitive, pre-civilised form.

In this context Miss Ogilvy's 'instinctive' return to the island seems to signal both a 'reverting to type' and a return to the womb, as symbol-ized by the cave she had remembered – and at the mouth of which (Janus-like, begging the question whether she is emerging from it or retreating into it) she is eventually found dead. Both returns – to type and to the womb – are impossible and as such signify the death of the self. The patronizing tone adopted towards Miss Ogilvy (the adjective 'poor' features repeatedly), the rather mawkish section six in which the transformation into the caveman takes place, and the story's assertion that Miss Ogilvy can only find her 'true self' in death combine to project an image of the invert as a rather sorry ana-chronistic outsider, a lower-order rather than a higher-order being.

In the author's note Hall contrasts this story with her 'serious study of sexual inversion, *The well of loneliness* which seems to indicate that Hall revised her view of the invert in this novel, where Stephen is ambiguously portrayed as both a higher and a lower-order being. The conceptualization of origins is important in *The well*, too, but it is handled with greater ambivalence than in 'Miss Ogilvy finds herself'. The hint of abnormality in the family, a feature typical of Krafft-Ebing's work on inversion where 'observations' were prefixed with family histories which, as Jane Rule puts it in *Lesbian images*, 'read like something out of a gothic novel, the patient's forebears and relatives suffering from alcoholism, insanity, subnormal intelligence, left-handedness, fits, suicidal desires' (p. 32), is absent in *The well*. Stephen has neither consumptive nor neurotic siblings, as do Joan and Miss Ogilvy. In fact, Stephen Gordon has no siblings at all and the description of her hereditary background is significantly at odds with Krafft-Ebing's and Freud's assumptions. Stephen's parents are described in conventionally positive terms: Sir Philip is 'tall', 'exceedingly well-favoured', 'noble', 'gallant', 'intellectual' and Lady Anna is 'the archetype of the very perfect woman' (p. 7). They show no signs of the possibility of degeneracy – no alcoholism, subnormal intelligence, neurosis, or anything else of the kind. Hall takes great pains to portray the Gordon family as socially well-integrated, respected members of the landed gentry. All the greater, therefore, the affront and shock to readers as Stephen's difference unfolds. It might be argued that one reason[3] why *The well*, in 1928, was singled out for prosecution by the establishment – a series of 'Sirs' just like Sir Philip – was that it 'normalized' inversion by portraying it as occurring in a family which was part of the establishment and apparently untainted by hereditary defects. Implicit in this portrayal is the assertion that if inversion can occur in the Gordon family it can occur in *any* family.

This 'offence' against the establishment is carried further in the text by the representation of Stephen's qualities, such as her sense of honour and responsibility, her love of her family seat, and her willingness to serve society, as derived from the behavioural codes of her genteel family background. The specificity of her heritage is invoked throughout the novel to 'exculpate' Stephen from her 'condition'. Her devotion and loyalty to her family home and her (in)voluntary exile to Paris out of respect for her mother's position in society serve as an index of her 'unsinning' nature, as do the attachments of those who are supposed to respond to people instinctively rather than intellectually: animals and servants. If she were a man, Stephen would and could be the 'perfect gentleman'.[4]

Unlike *The unlit lamp*, which does not discuss the origin of inversion, and 'Miss Ogilvy finds herself' which offers an implicit view on the matter, *The well* deals with inversion in a complex manner which simultaneously pays homage to and subverts the realist form in which the novel is written (see J. P. Stern for a discussion on realism). Such a text seeks to provide 'an intelligible history' (Belsey, p. 72) of a subject whose supposed consistency and coherence guarantees 'a single, unified, coherent truth' (Belsey, p. 81), even if, as is the case in *The well*, that truth amounts simply to recognizing the inexplicable nature of a phenomenon. Hall offers the reader three, to some extent inter-related, explanations for Stephen's inversion: a biological, a social, and an evolutionary one. As Vera Brittain, who in 1928 seems to have preferred a biological explanation (p. 48), states in her original review of *The well*:

> The book... raises and never satisfactorily answers... the question as to how far the characteristics of Stephen Gordon are physiological and how far they are psychological. (p. 50)

The biological explanation of Stephen's inversion centres on the details of Stephen's appearance rather than on an inherited degeneracy. She arrives in the world as 'a narrow-hipped, wide-shouldered little *tadpole* of a baby' (p. 9; my emphasis) with the term *tadpole* placing her into an evolutionary and intermediate context, making her a not fully developed (though upwardly mobile!) form – rather than something *de*formed.

Stephen's masculine appearance (she shares this with Joan and Miss Ogilvy) seems to facilitate the indulgence of her father's desire for a son and heir (p. 8), which becomes the basis for the social explanation of her inversion. There is a clear suggestion that she comes to inhabit the role her father had ordained for a male child; his intra-textually uncriticized desire for a son translates itself into the birth of a female child with male features who is given a male name which she attempts to live up to. The novel thus presents a combination of biological and social factors promoting Stephen's inversion. In so far as parental culpability is invoked, this is where it is situated and where any criticism of a patriarchal society which devalues its female offspring can be located.

The ambiguity concerning the nature of inversion created in *The well* through the offer of both biological and social causes is resolved by utilizing an evolutionary position that functions as a 'holding' explanation, serving as a form of 'reassurance' to the reader of the *potential* intelligibility of inversion. The reader (but not Stephen) is told about her:

> You're neither unnatural, nor abominable, nor mad; you're as much part of what people call nature as anyone else; only you're unexplained as yet – you've not got your niche in creation. But some day that will come.[5] (p. 153)

Elsewhere in the novel, Stephen is described in the same vein as 'grotesque and splendid, like some primitive thing conceived in a turbulent age of transition' (p. 49) who has 'the intuition of those who stand mid-way between the sexes' (p. 81) which as 'the no-man's land of sex' is 'the loneliest place in the world' (p. 77).

Together with this tripartite explanation of Stephen's inversion the reader is offered at least two positions to inhabit in response to it, exemplified by Stephen's parents' differing attitudes. Sir Philip, sympathetically drawn, is the all-comprehending, enlightened, masterly father-figure, whose attitude towards Stephen's situation the reader is, one assumes, to emulate. Lady Anna is also treated sympathetic-ally as the feminine, uncomprehending mother-figure, whom the 'enlightened' reader is presumably meant to forgive for her failure at comprehension. This contrasts with Joan's parents in *The unlit lamp*; both parents are seen as culpable and little sympathy for them is invited.

Initially, Stephen is as confused as her mother about her inverted state;[6] it is through *the word*, bequeathed to her by *her father* that she comes to understand her self. As part of its underwriting of patriarchal society, the text is constructed as a dialogue between Stephen and the embodiments of patriarchy. Framed by the exchange between an initially ignorant, then suffering daughter and an all-knowing, merciful father-figure (Sir Stephen/God) who fails to reveal his knowledge/mercy, the novel constitutes a *Bildungsroman*[7] in reverse. The usual narrative of social integration – wherein the protagonist acquires the knowledge of her psychological and social identity necessary for her ultimate and rightful integration into society – is overturned, as Stephen's originally secure identity is undercut by her gradual acquisition of the knowledge that she is different and cannot be explained. In the 'intelligible because familiar' (Belsey, p. 75) world of the realist novel – and as replicated in the obscenity trials[8] – inversion is outside the familiar. Typically for Hall's texts, Stephen is the only 'true' invert in her community although 'correspondents' (Elizabeth, Mary) exist. *The well* as a realist novel, if it is to fulfil its formal requirements, has to be constructed as a 'narrative of damnation' (Stimpson, 'Zero degree deviancy', p. 100) in which the protagonist's final social isolation, based on her difference from the dominant, is confirmed. Here the protagonist can have no 'rights', only the possibility of appealing to those in power; which is precisely how the novel ends – with an appeal to god. Formally and semantically, Stephen is set up as the victim of a conservative society who 'in her... instinctively sensed an outlaw, and theirs was the task of policing nature' (p. 108).

All of Hall's inverts *suffer*, though in differing ways: Joan Ogden as the victim of a narcissistically deprived mother, Miss Ogilvy because she is out of place and time in early twentieth-century England, and Stephen Gordon because she understands her inversion as the dividing difference between her and the rest of the world. These women's isolation, including that from other inverts, and their general social marginalization, are constructed as part of their suffering which, especially in *The well*, is clad in quasi-Christian terms designed to elicit pity from the reader. Although such a method of attempting to endear the invert to the reader may be questionable, one of its 'saving graces' is that its representation of the lesbian is essentially sympathetic – more than can be said for other texts featuring lesbians from the same period, such as Lehmann's *Dusty answer* or Hellman's *The children's hour*.

Good mothers and bad mothers: lesbianism as arrested development

Another largely unsympathetic portrait of a lesbian occurs in Clemence Dane's *Regiment of women* (1917), one of a whole series of boarding-school novels featuring lesbians.[9] Clare Hartill, the dominant lesbian figure in this novel, is described as 'thin, undeveloped, sallow-skinned' (p. 1), with a '*dompteuse* instinct' and a 'craving for power' (p. 29). Into her clutches fall her fourteen-year-old pupil Louise Denny, whose imaginative nature is ill at ease in her mercantile, pragmatic home life, and the sexually naïve eighteen-year-old Alwynne Durant, 'innocent of her own charm as unwedded Eve' (p. 29). What both 'victims' have in common with Clare, and indeed several other characters in the texts, is that they lost their mothers early in life.

Regiment of women does not offer an explicit discussion of inversion or lesbianism but, in terms not unlike those of *The unlit lamp*, it focusses on mother-daughter relationships as a way of exploring same-sex relationships between women. Through the figure of Louise it suggests that all women have a need to be mothered and that where the mother is absent a substitute is looked for. Clare's passing interest in Louise's 'genius' – a genius, the text indicates, based on the ability to translate personal experience into public expression – results in Louise projecting her idolizing of her dead mother onto Clare. In one of the stylistically and semantically most interesting passages of the novel, Louise's scholarship examination turns into an internal, unconscious attempt to retrieve her hold on her life by dis-integrating the composite image she has created of the absent 'good' (i.e. other-oriented) and the present 'bad' (i.e. egocentric) mother-figures of her biological mother and Clare:

> With patient deliberation she strove to disentangle the two personalities, that combined and divided and blurred again into one. There was Mother – and the Other – one was shape and the other was shadow – but which was real? There was Mother – and the Other – who was Mother? No, who was – who was – The Other was not Mother – but if not, who? – who? – who? – (p. 145)

Louise's inability to answer that question prefigures her death; she kills herself after being rejected by Clare.

Alwynne, on the other hand, is saved from a similar fate through the love of a 'good' mother, her mother's sister, who has reared her and who intervenes on her behalf. Saving Alwynne takes the form of her aunt setting her up in a heterosexual match with Alwynne's distant cousin Roger. One of the aunt's comments to Roger indicates, in classic Freudian style, the notion that children's love of the woman or mother ought to be followed by heterosexual love, this being a matter of training:

> Alwynne has been trained to listen to women. She can't follow men yet. She has been advised that they are grown-up children and that her role is to be superior but tactful. (p. 286)

Alwynne's supposedly 'aberrant' attitude towards men is explained as a function of the single-sex boarding-school system. As the authorial voice informs the reader:

> To developing girls a confidante is a necessity. The present boarding-school system of education ousts the mother from that, her natural position; renders her, to the daughter steeped in an alien atmosphere, an outsider, lacking all understanding. Invaluable years pass before the artificial gulf that boarding-school creates between them, is spanned. And the substitute for the only form of sympathy and interest that is entirely untainted by selfish impulses is usually the chance acquaintance, the neighbour of desk and bed. (pp. 49–50)

The novel projects the assumption that the unselfish, 'good' mother would prepare the daughter for entry into a heterosexual relationship while the selfish woman (as Clare admits herself to be, p. 83), melodramatically described as 'an unmated woman – she's a failure – she's unfulfilled' (p. 335), would seek to retain the daughter. (Precisely as Mrs Ogden does in *The unlit lamp*; and as also occurs in the much later *Oranges are not the only fruit*.) Daughters, the novel indicates, are to be exchanged between women and men, not between women. And where Richard in *The unlit lamp*, as one of the voices of patriarchy, admires the future breed of women – even as he seems to feel that they are 'demanding of him an explanation of themselves' (p. 220) – Roger, the dominant patriarchal voice in *Regiment of women*, is allowed to patronize Alwynne in unashamedly uncritical terms; she is ridiculed by him as knowing nothing about men, and for her 'feminine friendship' (p. 334) with Clare:

> But when [Alwynne], as it were, hoisted herself on the shoulders of the women about her, and from that level peered curiously at an outer, alien world, her insight failed her, her views grew distorted and merely grotesque. He thought he guessed the reason. She was no longer gazing, critical and clear-eyed, at known surroundings, but, still supported by the opinions of the women of her circle, was seeing what she had expected to see, what she had been told by them that she would see. (pp. 227–8)

The stance concerning (sexual) relationships adopted in *Regiment of women* is made clear by Elsbeth, Alwynne's aunt, when she says to Clare, 'Alwynne needs a good concrete husband to love, not a fantastic ideal that she calls friendship and clothes in your face and figure.' (p. 336) The 'truth' of this assertion is textually reinforced by the fact that it takes the first man who comes along Alwynne's path no time at all to deflect Alwynne from her avowed position that 'there can never be any one but Clare' (p. 315). Alwynne's and Roger's relationship is then played out along the lines of the traditional romance plot (see Janice Radway's *Reading the romance*) with her abandoning friendship and career in town to become a wife and mother in the country. Woman gives way to man as, the text suggests, single-sex education will give way to co-education in the interests of undermining same-sex attachments. The final image of the lonely, desperate Clare possibly already plotting the victimization of the next dependent female underlines the notion of the lesbian as a pathetic figure over whom, in the end, heterosexual society will triumph, not least because she cannot even kiss:

> [Roger's] kiss had been comforting too. [Alwynne] remembered the first of Clare's rare kisses – the thin fingers that gripped her shoulders; the long, fierce pressure, mouth to mouth; the rough gesture that released her, flung her aside. (p. 300)

As in Hall's texts so in this one: with the exception of this comment on the kiss[10] lesbian sexuality is neither extensively discussed nor represented. This is typical not only for texts of this period in general but is especially marked in the texts representing lesbians within what I would call the 'domesticated context', i.e. the texts that do not portray lesbian communities but focus on the isolated individual lesbian woman.

'Tainted' wo/men: pacifism and homosexuality

If *Regiment of women* allows the heterosexual man to succeed another woman in a woman's life, *Despised and rejected* (1919) by A. T. Fitzroy (the genderless pseudonym for Rose Allatini) gives the gay man pride of place in the lesbian woman's life. As Roger was destined to 'awaken' Alwynne in *Regiment*, so Dennis is given the role of enlightener in relation to Antoinette. Men rule the roost. Indeed, *Despised and rejected*, one of the very few texts from the period which explicitly engages with political issues of the day, is a curious novel because although it is written by a woman and features an unconsummated lesbian relationship – the adored other woman, Hester, turns out to be heterosexual and unhappily in love with a married schoolmaster whose wife is in a lunatic asylum – the lesbian plot occupies only the opening quarter of the novel. The remaining 250 pages are given over to the development of a homosexual relationship between two men, the relationship between Antoinette and Dennis, and issues of pacifism centring on male characters. Not surprisingly, the text has recently been reissued by the Gay Men's Press.

Three concerns of the novel are of immediate interest: Antoinette's falling in love with Hester and seeming to single her out because she projects an image of aloofness and independence, which, the text suggests, is correlated with lesbian predilections; Antoinette's attitude towards homosexuality relative to Dennis's; and the implicit comparison between being a pacifist and being a homosexual.[11] Hester's 'nimbus of unapproachability that was recognised by everyone' (p. 39) is here one of the stereotypical attributes of the lesbian; it transpires that Hester has been subject to approaches like Antoinette's before (pp. 46, 92). Antoinette, on the other hand, the 'true' lesbian in the novel, is not recognized as such by any of the others, with the exception of Dennis, the gay protagonist in the text, who regards her as a 'square peg in a round hole' (pp. 52, 162), like himself. Antoinette, however, is not at all like Dennis: of

27

B

French stock (p. 60),[12] without the constraints and conventional judgements from which the English characters in the novel suffer, she is portrayed as multiply alienated from the English society in which she moves and cast very much in the role of the innocent abroad. Her innocence concerning the adverse judgements made by society of homosexuality (she finds that she has to admit to Dennis that she has not suffered as a consequence of being attracted to women) provides the narrative basis for Dennis's explanations of the 'taint' attached to same-sex relationships. He is given a 'moral' awareness which she does not possess:

> This, then, was the taint of which he spoke; the taint that they shared, he and she. Only whereas he had always striven against these tendencies in himself, in herself she had never regarded them as abnormal. It had seemed disappointing, but not in the least unnatural, that all her passionate longings should have been awakened by women, instead of any members of the opposite sex. (pp. 217–18)

Understanding Dennis's suffering induces Antoinette to feel, in typical romance fashion, that she wants to 'make up to him for all that he had been through' (p. 218) and she falls in love with him, seemingly 'for real'. Unlike Dennis, who gradually comes to acknowledge and stand by his love for Alan while denying any love for Antoinette, she is not granted another same-sex love within the novel; perpetually at the periphery of events, she has neither a public nor a private role to fulfil by the end – instead, she is left fighting her love of a gay man. Her suffering is not one of trying to be a lesbian in a patriarchal society, but one of spurned love.

In comparing the homosexual male, agonising over his disposition, with a homosexual female who has never questioned her inclinations, the novel sets up a debate about attitudes towards 'nature' and what it means to be 'natural' which recurs in the discussions on pacifism. In a heated exchange with his patriarchal father in which the latter maintains that 'man is a fighting animal' who has to live out this instinct (p. 194), Dennis advances the argument that conquering nature in all its negative manifestations, including human nature and its instinct to kill, is the basis of progress (p. 195). The novel suggests that Dennis has tried to conquer his instinctual liking for members of his own sex; Alan's attempt at reasoning Dennis into accepting their love for each other culminates in the following,

> For people made as we are it's natural and it's beautiful to love as we love, and it's perversion in the true sense to try and force ourselves to love differently. (p. 250)

Implicit in the comparison between how to deal with the instinct to kill and the instinct to love is the question of the social desirability of these instincts and their relationship to the advancement of the human race as a whole. On this, *Despised and rejected* adopts Carpenter's position concerning 'the intermediate sex':

> But perhaps these men who stand mid-way between the extremes of the two sexes are the advance-guard of a more enlightened civilisation... I believe that the time is not so far distant when we shall recognise in the best of our intermediate types the leaders and masters of the race. (p. 348)

This credo is linked to a final celebration of an androgynous whole as the most desirable form of existence which, in the early part of this century, women writers repeatedly 'played' with:[13]

> out of their suffering... will arise something great... the human soul complete in itself, perfectly balanced, not limited by the psychological bounds of one sex, but combining the power and the intellect of the one with the subtlety and intuition of the other; a dual nature, possessing the extended range, the attributes of both sides, and therefore loving and beloved of both alike. (p. 349)

Despised and rejected is an unusual novel for the early part of this century both because a woman writer focusses predominantly on males in her exploration of sexual relationships and because this exploration is embedded in an investigation of contemporary political issues. Perhaps, being of Polish and Italian extraction, Rose Allatini was sufficiently outside British society to make a critical interrogation of the political factions within it.

Family romances

Rosamond Lehmann's *Dusty answer* (1927), by comparison, returns the reader to the privatized, domesticated, gentile world of inter-personal relationships in which English women writers during this period more commonly situate their lesbian characters. Although it shares with *Despised and rejected* a female protagonist, Judith, who falls in love with a gay man, Roddy, it has, at its centre, a 'family romance' and is, in this respect, not unlike *The unlit lamp. Dusty*

answer's 'family romance', however, is predicated upon the absence
of parents – which leads to an intense and excluding bond among five
cousins – one girl and four boys – into which Judith, the only child
next door, desparately wants to break. The five cousins and Judith,
locked into a fairy-tale mode of existence, are emotionally incapable
of breaking away from the magic of this 'oppressive self-sufficient
circle of blood-intimacy with its core of indifference' (p. 47). Described
as 'a barren thing; it could not stretch to enclose new life' (p. 48),
the circle's sterility and its doom ('death, lovely death, lay at the heart
of enchantment' – p. 88) are constructed as inevitable, as the
attachments formed among the cousins and with Judith appear to be
based on emotional needs associated with childhood which cannot
easily encompass the sexual maturity towards which the characters
move.

Both Judith and one of the cousins, Roddy, have relationships with
members of the same sex while at university. In the case of Judith,
however, it is made clear that her friendship with Jennifer is
undermined by the absence of a sexual component within it and their
dyad is broken up by Jennifer meeting an older lesbian, Geraldine,
with whom she has a sexual relationship. Jennifer, whom Judith
thinks of as 'the part of you [herself] which you had never been able to
untie and set free' (p. 113), is incapable of explaining to Judith why she
turns away from her, not only because she lacks the vocabulary and
directness to assert that her desire for Judith is a sexual desire but
also because to her Judith seems 'an innocent baby' who 'used to look
after me and kiss me as if you were my mother' (p. 237). The sense of
a quasi-familial bond indicated here which prevents the sexual
consummation of Judith's and Jennifer's relationship is similar to
the quasi-familial bond that ties Judith to the cousins. Both types of
relationships are constructed as untenable. In a final reassessment of
her situation, Judith comes to think of her 'whole past', meaning her
relationships with the cousins and her friendship with Jennifer, as
'one great circle, completed now and ready to be discarded' (p. 248).
All her involvements are, at the end, read by her as the result of her
'futile obsession of dependence on other people' (p. 248) from which
she considers herself free now. It is unclear at this point whether or
not Judith, in apparently transcending her need for others, has
transcended her potential lesbianism. The novel's indirect
explanation for lesbianism seems to be predicated upon an extension

of a childhood need for emotional attachment that, the text suggests, has to be overcome in order to achieve adulthood. At the same time, the image of another type of lesbian in the shape of Geraldine and Jennifer is offered, that of the sexually active, indeed promiscuous and deracinated woman, the purposelessness of whose life is facilitated by the fact that she has an independent income and can afford to follow her inclinations. But this image remains very sketchy, just as Judith's future, including her ultimate sexual orientation, remains uncertain at the end of the novel.

The happiest representation of a 'family romance' in the early part of this century can be found in *Works and days*, the extracts from the journals of Michael Field, otherwise known as Katherine Bradley and Edith Cooper, aunt and niece. Their 'happy union of two in work and aspiration' (p. 3) was underpinned by their sense that 'if two individuals of exactly the same nature are joined together, they make up a single individual, doubly stronger than each other' (p. 6). Katherine had been the focus of Edith's life from early childhood when the former, to assist her permanently invalid sister, joined the Cooper household. As Edith's mother's sister, Katherine was as close to Edith's mother as is possible without actually being her, and one might suggest that on one level their relationship constituted a version of the ideal mother-daughter dyad, with Katherine in the nurturing role due to her seniority and Edith's tendency towards ill-health. As Edith wrote, 'she has lived with me, taught me, encouraged me and joined me in her poetic life' (p. 3).

The two women were also lovers. They made a conscious and deliberate commitment to each other as evidenced in their poetry (pp. xix-xx) and repeated assertions to that effect in their journals and letters (e.g. pp. 16, 50). This commitment[14] included an 'awareness and strategic practice' (White, p. 206) in their self-representation at the levels of writing and living which denies the 'sexual innocence' ascribed to them by Faderman. In *Surpassing the love of men*, Faderman maintains that 'it is hard to believe that their love was not – as a Victorian would phrase it – innocent ... Their volume of verse, *Long ago* (1889), ... gives little hint of any consciousness about the possibility of sexual expression between women...' (p. 210) Their journals, and I would argue some of their poetry, suggest otherwise. In respect of their writing and choice of male pseudonym they maintained, that 'the report of lady authorship will dwarf and enfeeble our work at every turn... we have many things to say that the world will not tolerate from a woman's lips' and that the only way to avoid being 'stifled in drawing-room conventionalities' was to 'shelter' (p. 3) under their male pseudonym. Concerning their relationship, it is noticeable how rarely in *Works and days* their familial relationship is referred to. Terms of endearment like 'my beloved' and 'my Love' as well as nicknames are the most frequently used forms of address and identification. Only when explaining their relationship to outsiders and in 'official' contexts, such as when talking to the doctor who diagnosed Edith's cancer, do the terms 'aunt' and 'niece' appear. This may be a function of Katherine having been both more mother and lover to Edith than aunt, a dual relationship reflected in the distorting mirror of a German nurse's unwelcome infatuation with Edith, of which Katherine wrote, '[The nurse] has in her eyes a two-fold divineness when she looks at P. [Edith] – that of the mother who has done everything for her babe, and that of the dog who watches for the love of a higher Power.' (p. 62) In a parallel passage (implying a manipulative side to Edith's character) certain of her own superior understanding of the nurse's affection as a 'terrible fleshly love, [which] she does not conceive [of] as such' (p. 63), Edith remarks,

> She makes me shiver, but I play with her passion like a child and she is utterly deceived in it herself – I am her child she has washed and dressed with her piteous clinging hands; and her honest, stern eyes, altered to a mother-hen's, belie the welling-up of all her frustrate nature at the touch of first love for any mortal... I must fight Nurse's unreasonableness. (p. 64)

The incident concerning the nurse does not suggest sexual ignorance on Katherine's or Edith's part. A similar knowing attitude concerning sexual matters is implicit in other sections of the journals,[15] as in the following description by the women of a poetry reading given by Verlaine which aunt and niece attended and where they clearly felt *they* knew what was going on where the rest of the audience did not:

> It was such an English scene – Satan [Verlaine] in a frock-coat, reading religious poetry and darting pitch-spark glances at a company incapable of understanding the tragedies of hell (even the devils believe and tremble), still less its bouts of free revel. (p. 189)

It is worth bearing this description in mind when contemplating the religious poetry written by Michael Field which, as is a tradition for such poetry, fuses sensuality and devotional fervour in an ambiguous blend of sex and religion. Typical examples of this fusion of sensuality and devotional fervour are 'Milia multa' and 'Blessed hands'.

Katherine and Edith's 'self-sufficient blood-intimacy' needed no other woman but, as Freud suggests in 'Family romances', the realization that *'pater semper incertus est'* while the mother is *'certissima'* leads to a position where 'the family romance undergoes a curious curtailment: it contents itself with exalting the child's father, but no longer casts any doubts on his maternal origin, which is regarded as something unalterable' (p. 223). In Michael Field's journals there are no idealized female figures, but men are idolized and appear to function as successive father substitutes. The journals parade a series of relationships with such figures whose approval and attention Katherine and Edith sought, initially famous men of letters (John Ruskin, Robert Browning, George Meredith), later 'spiritual' fathers such as Father Gosscannon and Father Vincent McNabb. These 'fathers', in whom Michael Field confided her 'true' identities (see pp. 7, 66) and her spiritual states (pp. 312–15) appear to have treated both women in a similar manner, represented by the women as combining the paternal with the sensual (see pp. 11, 22, 34, 300). Of Robert Browning, for example, they talk as 'our father poet' whom they love 'devotedly' (p. 11). To them 'his limitless belief in us is appalling. What indeed is so appalling as the "Be ye therefore perfect" of love?' (p. 21) It is, it would appear, for these father figures that Katherine and Edith attempted to be 'perfect'.

Their 'perfection' was associated with an ideal of femininity to which they subscribed:

> We hold ourselves bound in life and in literature to reveal – as far as may be – the beauty of the high feminine standard of *the ought to be*. (p. 8)

This ideal was associated with the worship of the feminine in the Sapphic community of classical Greek culture – and Katherine and Edith delighted in being addressed by Robert Browning as 'his "two dear Greek women"' (p. 20). As White suggests,

> Classical Greek literature and culture provided one way for nineteenth-century homosexual writers to talk about homosexuality as a positive social and emotional relationship. (198)

I would argue that one aspect of the 'happiness' of the union of Michael Field was their sense, derived from Greek classical sources, of continuing a tradition of feminine interaction. This sense of a self-affirming tradition is absent in the novels of Radclyffe Hall, for example, but can be found again in the writings of the 'women of the left bank'– Renée Vivien in *A woman appeared to me*, for example – who, like Michael Field, project a positive image of lesbian relationships.

Michael Field's happiness was further enhanced by the fact that the ideal they embraced offered no open opposition to the heterosexist culture of which they were a part; the femininity they subscribed to was not noticeably at odds with the expectations of contemporary society concerning heterosexual women. Having apparently 'made a desperate fight for the freedom of our privacy' (p. 6) and disliking 'the ill-opinion of men' (p. 46), they aspired 'as women... to lead a quiet life' (p. 7). They had no desire to combat social convention (p. 7). Their belief in the distinctness of the sexes led them to frown upon those who seemed to obscure the differences between women and men such as Vernon Lee and her lover, described as 'tailor-made' county types lacking a 'central unity of purpose' (p. 264), or 'spinsterish' Miss Louise wearing clothes 'a little narrowly designed, to please herself' (p. 266). Of a couple they encountered they noted disapprovingly:

> The husband and wife have outgrown the barriers of sex and become so much alike, they are as brother and sister. I have seen this kind of marriage, *unattractive because it is confusion, the distinctness of sex quality impaired.* (p. 268; my emphasis)

Inherent in the choices Katherine and Edith made may have been the recognition that in their society men inhabited the seats of power and that approval by men could make or break them.[16] *Works and days* projects them not as defiant but as utilizing any forces which could further their cause as writers and social beings. Significantly, the extracts do not suggest that they, persistently and overtly, held radical views, feminist or otherwise. Understanding – with Miss Louise – that England was dominated by 'man's interests' (p. 266), many of the comments on wo/men's roles in society and related issues, which may have coincided with Michael Field's views, are made, in *Works and days*, by persons other than themselves. Thus George Moore is quoted as writing to them, 'nothing is vulgar except the conventional' (p. 196), significant because, in some respects at least, Michael Field's lifestyle was unconventional, an unconven-tionality redeemed by being declared, by another male, as 'more like a fairy tale than ever' (p. 125).

Lesbian self and others

Where Katherine and Edith's happy union is perfected through its sanctification by a series of doting father figures, Hermione Gart's quest for self in H.D.'s *Her* (1927) is predicated upon the rejection of/ by the father and what he stands for. Hermione's linear, non-reflective pursuit of a replication of her father's – and indeed, of her brother's – career as scientists is shattered by her failing her exams at Bryn Mawr. The ensuing identity crisis and its resolution in its resistance to the father's image, in some senses constitute a very straightforward representation of the American dream of self-actualization.

Hermione initially assumes that sameness guarantees identity. The identicalness of her surname with that of her father's – played upon in 'Gart and Gart sat facing Gart and Gart.' (p. 35), for example – does not imply that *she is like him*, and the novel, both thematically and stylistically, refutes this assumption of synonymy by fore-grounding multiplicity of meaning and the idea of selfhood as the assertion of the *principium individuationis*. Hermione has to learn *not* to see herself as part of a tradition, either genetic or literary.

Having failed to live up to her father's expectations she tries to re-establish a sense of identity by living up to the expectations of bourgeois society: she becomes engaged to George Lowndes, who thinks of her as 'decorative' (p. 172) and feels threatened by her writing which he denigrates (p. 167). Trying to negotiate between her own sense of having no identity and living in accordance with other people's expectations of her, Hermione grows increasingly aware of the cliched, artificial existence she seems to be condemning herself to in a marriage with George. Her recognition of her enactment of pre-scribed roles[17] which reinforces her sense of a split self, of one self watching another without being able to engage properly, ultimately leads to a rejection of these roles ('I am not Hermione out of Shakespeare.' p. 192) and the creation of a text of her own, in the snow (pp. 223–4). Genetic and textual patrilineage are likewise rejected in Hermione's quest for selfhood. The males in her life show no interest in Hermione once she has failed to be like them and/or to fulfil their expectations.[18] As Hermione quotes to Fayne, 'the world's division divideth us' (p. 179).

Hermione has three muses, all women (her mother Eugenia, her nurse Amy Dennon, and her lover Fayne Rabb), who act as enabling figures propelling her through her crisis and illness into her writerly self. Eugenia encourages Hermione to write because the latter says 'such odd, pretty things' (p. 80). She shows motherly, unselfish concern for Hermione's situation, and gradually for Hermione 'words of Eugenia' acquire 'more power than textbooks, than geometry, than all of Carl Gart and brilliant "Bertie Gart"' (p. 89). Amy Dennon acts as nurse and mother-confessor to Hermione after her physical and mental breakdown. Attentive and non-judgemental she becomes the receptacle of Hermione's story and thus acts as a restorative. Fayne Rabb 'draw[s] things out of [Hermione]' (p. 143), initially disinterestedly, but later as a means of dividing Hermione from George in whom Fayne becomes interested (p. 161). In an allusion to the figure of Pan she insists,

> Your writing is the thin flute holding you to eternity. Take away your flute and you remain, lost in a world of unreality. (pp. 161–2)

Fayne's diagnosis proves to be correct – Hermione finally feels 'at one with herself, with the world, with all outer circumstance' (p. 234) when she decides to try to be a writer and to leave America for Europe. Feeling 'at one' is the crucial phrase here; *Her* operates on the basis that 'at oneness' is crucial for one's sense of identity. Hermione's first and most intense experience of such 'at oneness' is her lesbian love relationship with Fayne Rabb. She muses:

> Things are not *agaçant* now I know her. Her. I am Her. She is Her. Knowing her, I know Her. She is some amplification of myself like amoeba giving birth, by breaking off, to amoeba. (p. 158)

Through the woman, Hermione comes to the woman, herself. Narcissistic identification quells her longing and sense of failure. It is predicated upon her relationship with her own sex. But Her, like Stephen in *The well*, falls in love with a 'feminine' woman who is not a 'true invert' but merely passing time before attaching herself to a male. Her, like Stephen, is constructed as the potentially lonely but gifted lesbian who finds compensation for the absence of relationships and fulfilment in her role as writer, and that, at least initially, abroad, in Paris. Lesbian love is presented as narcissistic and as providing the 'true invert' with a sense of identity through 'oneness' with someone of the same sex who acts as birther of and mirror to the adult female self. Women, *Her* states unambiguously, need women to achieve a sense of identity. They also need to leave behind the heteropatriarchal traditions in which they were reared and thus deracinate themselves in order to live a life of their own. The narcissistic desires of the lesbian character Hermione are sublimated through the suggestion that the creative self can substitute for the sexual self. This will be an equivalent to the heterosexual union towards which Hermione saw herself propelled prior to her breakdown; 'this will be my marriage' Her thinks (p. 234) when contemplating leaving America to set up as a writer in Europe.

In many respects Hermione's character reflects the lesbian as represented in early-twentieth-century women's writing. These lesbians are competent, highly intelligent, middle-class, white women, isolated from one another unless they leave their home environment and settle abroad. Lesbian relationships are frequently portrayed as transitory, this fleetingness a function of the 'true invert' falling in love with a feminine woman who is constructed as destined for a heterosexual marriage. *Choice*, a factor which plays a significant role in later discussions on lesbianism, does not enter into the equation; each woman appears to play out her 'destined' role, with the precise basis for this 'destiny' remaining unexamined. In the texts fulfilment in lesbian relationships is by and large rejected, as they do not last;[19] the prime sublimatory activity is being an artist, most commonly a writer. It is ironic that in 'real life' during the first half of this century, writers such as Michael Field and Gertrude Stein could combine what was not yet 'granted' in writing of lesbians from the period: creativity and relationality. What could be written about was clearly behind what could be lived.

Notes

1 They frequently share these characteristics with their central protagonists. One exception can be found in a short story written by a man, George Moore, entitled 'The history of Albert Nobbs' in which the two protagonists are working-class

women, a waiter and a painter, passing as men. This short story was subsequently turned into a play, *The singular life of Albert Nobbs*, by the French director Simone Benmussa (published in *Benmussa directs*, London and Dallas, 1979).

2 Hall's representation of Joan Odgen's life resembles some of the 'real life' stories brought together in Marcy Adelman's *Long time passing*. As one of the women in that text says: 'When I was growing up I never heard the word "lesbian," never knew there was anything other than heterosexual sex, and prior to my marriage I had never had a lesbian relationship. I was brought up to grace a man's table... I married because it was expected of me, and to get away from home.' (p. 197)

3 For others, read Vera Brittain's *Radclyffe Hall: a case of obscenity?*

4 Stephen as the 'perfect gentleman' is discussed in Esther Newton's essay, 'The mythic mannish lesbian: Radclyffe Hall and the new woman'.

5 This replicates Edward Carpenter's view of homosexuals as the 'intermediate sex' who occupy a point of transition on the evolutionary scale (*The intermediate sex*, pp. 11, 24, 70).

6 'Real life' stories of lesbians who were young women in the first half of this century tell a similar tale. One woman in *Long time passing* writes: 'I didn't know the name lesbian then. We didn't use that word in 1942. I had never heard the word homosexual. But I knew that Sandy and I had to be very discreet about it.' (p. 59)

7 A *Bildungsroman*, according to M. H. Abrams, is a '"novel of formation" or "novel of education". The subject of these novels is the development of the protagonist's mind and character, as he [sic] passes from childhood through varied experiences – and usually through a spiritual crisis – into maturity and the recognition of his identity and role in the world.' (*A glossary of literary terms*, p. 121).

8 See Vera Brittain's *Radclyffe Hall: a case of obscenity?* for further details.

9 See Martha Vicinus's article, 'Distance and desire: English boarding-school friendships' on this subject. Relevant texts are for example Antonia White's *Frost in May*, Olivia's *Olivia*, Brigid Brophy's *The finishing touch* and Harriet Gilbert's *The riding-school mistress*.

10 In 'Zero degree deviancy: the lesbian novel in English' Catharine Stimpson comments on the significance and treatment of 'the kiss' in lesbian writing (pp. 99–100).

11 The introduction to the Gay Men's Press re-issue of this novel offers an interesting discussion about the banning of this novel, which Jeannette Foster attributes to its homosexual content, but which was actually due to its supposedly detrimental effect on recruiting soldiers for World War I.

12 See the discussion of *Rubyfruit jungle* in chapter three of this book for further comments on the invocation of the 'foreign' in the context of lesbian sexual identity.

13 Examples are Olive Schreiner's *Story of an African farm* and Dorothy Cowlin's *Winter solstice* as well as Virginia Woolf's *Orlando*.

14 I agree with Chris White that 'there is in the journals very little explicit analysis of the relationship between Katherine and Edith' ('Poets and lovers evermore', p. 207) by which I take it White means that the two women themselves do not comment directly on their relationship. One therefore has to draw conclusions predominantly from the vocabulary they use in relation to themselves and to others.

15 See, for instance, the comments on Ellen Terry (p. 83), on sex mania (p. 90) and on Walter Pater (p. 120).

16 This is evident in Katherine's letters to Robert Browning where she talks of wanting 'real criticism, such as man gives man' (p. 7).

17 Hermione constantly sees her interactions with George as taking part in a play the

text of which she has not written (e.g. pp. 65, 117, 163).

18 This is particularly evident when Hermione goes to tell her father that she will marry George and he, preoccupied with his work, fails to take her in (p. 100).

19 Many 'real life' lesbians during this period had long-term relationships. They included the Michael Fields, of course, but also Gertrude Stein and Alice B. Toklas, and Sylvia Beach and Adrienne Monier, for example.

Chapter 2

From twilight to limelight: writings on lesbians in the 1950s and 1960s

Coming out and moving in: the lesbian as a threat to the nuclear family

Once lesbianism – described but not 'named' as such – had emerged as a subject for representation in texts of the early twentieth century, its portrayal remained fairly static until the late 1960s/early 1970s. In texts such as Eveline Mahyère's *I will not serve* (1958), Brigid Brophy's misogynistic satire *The finishing touch* (1963) or Rosemary Manning's autobiography *A time and a time* (1971), lesbians were persistently portrayed as isolated women without a strong womanist or political commitment, stereotyped in gender terms as butch and femme and defensive of their position in society. The extent to which lesbians 'in real life' in the 1950s and 1960s promulgated butch-femme role-playing is evident in some of the autobiographical texts by older lesbians such as those of Suzanne Neild and Rosalind Pearson's *Women like us*, in which statements such as the following occur fairly regularly: 'In those days, the early sixties, one just accepted that there was this butch-femme divide. I never thought of myself as either butch or femme, although people used to try and push me into the butch category, but I never felt that I really belonged there. I didn't feel I belonged in the femme category either' (p. 102). Rethinking the representation of lesbians was not an option in the period from 1940 to 1960, which was conservative in its politics and therefore constituted, as Sheila Jeffreys writes in *Anticlimax* 'a particularly bleak period for lesbians and gay men' (p. 50).

Jeffreys relates this anti-homosexual stance to the postwar desire to reinforce the family as the basic unit of the dominant social order, and to re-establish men returning from the war in their 'rightful' roles as heads of households and controllers of economic power. 'Danger to the family was seen as danger to the state, since the male-supremacist state was based upon the subordination of woman in the family.' (*Anticlimax* p. 51) The conflation of homosexuality and left-wing politics as an intertwined threat to familial and governmental stability resulted in attacks on homosexual men. Women, were still supposed to live predominantly 'private' lives, and lesbianism was constructed as a private affair, reinforced by the fact that only men were prosecutable for offences related to homosexual practices. Citing the anecdote of Queen Victoria's intervention concerning the Labouchère Amendment of 1885 (which laid the legal foundation for the prosecution of men committing homosexual acts) centring on Victoria's disbelief in women having sex with one another, Bryan Magee in *One in twenty* (1966) maintains that it 'is still a fact... that society does not acknowledge the existence of lesbianism' (p. 62). One might argue that this denial constitutes one means by which women's ability to be independent of men, manifest as it is in woman-to-woman relationships, is suppressed.

The literature of this period bears this out. In line with some earlier portrayals of lesbians, homosexual women are still frequently presented as falling in love with women who have either only a fleeting sexual interest in another woman or who are already committed to a heterosexual relationship.[1] In Ann Bannon's so-called Beebo Brinker series, for instance, her protagonists Laura and Beebo both fall into this trap of entering into relationships with women whose heterosexual orientation turns out to be dominant and the reason for the lesbian heroine ultimately being deserted. Thus in *Beebo Brinker* (1962), the threat of Beebo's affair with the married film star Venus Bogardus being made public leads to its demise, initiated by Venus's husband and manager. Significantly, Venus denies the accusations of a lesbian affair with Beebo by offering to her public a counterimage – the nuclear family:

She appeared in public at Leo's side emphasizing the duration of their life together. Both of them swore that their marriage had never been

> stronger... The official story was that Beebo was a young woman who had taken a job on the household staff and subsequently became a close friend of Toby's [Venus's son]. Nobody was aware that she was harboring a feverish crush on Venus. When the situation blew up in their faces, Venus and Leo were as startled and shocked as the rest... They expressed their sympathy for their unfortunate friend and hoped she could find a happier life somewhere else. (p. 200)

Beebo is here projected as the unsuspected 'enemy within' who needs to be expelled to resurrect the family as an 'undefiled' unit. Her 'feverish crush', the mark of her desire, turns her into the other whom Leo, Venus's husband, describes as intrinsically alien and alienated:

> 'The world was made for normal people,' he said. 'The abnormal in this world have a tough go. If they keep their abnormality secret, they're damnably lonely. If they broadcast it, they're damnably hurt. You were born with that and you'll have to live with it.' (p. 167)

Beebo is cast as the stranger who threatens to destroy the fabric of the family, not only because of the statement her sexuality makes about the possibilities of experiences other than 'compulsory heterosexuality'[2] but also because she awakens in Venus a sexuality which, temporarily, carries with it the threat of Venus's desertion of her family. There are numerous instances in lesbian writing, not just in the 1950s and 1960s, which portray relationships between a lesbian and a married woman or a woman who is also interested in and eventually carried off by a man: for example, Katherine Mansfield's short story 'Bliss', Radclyffe Hall's *The unlit lamp*, Gale Wilhelm's *We too are drifting* and, more recently, in Anne Leaton's *Good friends, just* and Jeanette Winterson's *Oranges are not the only fruit*. Women responding to women, emotionally and sexually, raise the question of the nature of sexual desire, its object(s) and modalities. They make manifest, as Julia Kristeva puts it in a different context, the notion that what threatens the stability and presumed fixities in a society 'lives within us: ... is the hidden face of our identity, the space that wrecks our abode, the time in which understanding and affinity founder' (*Strangers to ourselves*, p. 1). Thus heterosexual (male) understanding founders in the face of lesbian love. Venus's husband Leo is a case in point. Admitting that his response is 'mostly emotional and irrational' (p. 163), he says, 'Christ, I never could understand why a woman would want anything to do with another woman that way, anyway.' (p. 187)

It is precisely this failure of understanding on the part of the dominant – literally and metaphorically – heterosexual male which promotes the construction of Beebo as a 'strange' individual (and it is worth noting that in the Beebo Brinker series the word 'queer' is used with a decided *double entendre* to mean both 'homosexual' and 'strange'). The discursive exchange about this 'strangeness' is conducted predominantly between the lesbian woman and *men* rather than between women. The Beebo Brinker series suggests that it is *men* who need to be addressed on the issue of lesbianism which, given their dominance in all institutions of political, legal, social and economic significance, is not surprising.

Bannon's novels utilize words such as 'strange', 'odd', and 'queer' to signpost the 'unfamiliar'. Significantly, the first volume of that series is entitled *Odd girl out*, a quasi-Bildungsroman in which one of the protagonists, Laura, learns to conceive of herself as lesbian – to recognize the strange as the familiar.[3] Initially, knowledge of the existence of lesbianism does not facilitate an understanding of her own feelings:

> She knew that there were some men who loved men and some women who loved women, and she thought it a shame that they couldn't be like other people... Her own high school crushes had been on girls, but they were all short and uncertain and secret feelings and she would have been profoundly shocked to hear them called homosexual. (p. 24)

As Laura becomes increasingly emotionally committed to a fellow student, Beth, a sense of disorder begins to overwhelm her:

> Her family was falling apart, and she was falling in love with Beth. The world was inside out, all wrong. She didn't understand it, she hardly even realized what was happening to her. She couldn't stop and she didn't know where she was going. (p. 39)

The lesbian is (still) portrayed as unfamiliar to herself, ignorant of her state and status. Laura finds her responses to Beth and other women 'strange', while considering relations with men as 'normal': 'Charlie stood for Laura-likes-men, men-like-Laura, everything-is-right-with-Laura-so-look-no-further.' (p. 61) In its casting of the male-as-norm/al, the Beebo Brinker series, of course, reflects the reality of Western culture as it exists even now. It is in relation to this 'norm' that lesbian identity and imaging is constructed. When Laura awakens to herself as lesbian she, not unlike Stephen in *The well of loneliness*, 'beg[s] God for an answer' (p. 64). But, significantly, the (hetero-sexual) males – god included – to whom she appeals can provide no answer to her questions about her sense of self. They are presented as ignorant concerning her lesbianism, as rivals for the female affection Laura seeks and therefore as unsympathetic to her plight. It is worth pointing out that the desires of heterosexual men, too, are cast as problematic – woman, to them, is the 'unknown'. This is emblem-atized in *Odd girl out*, as the character Charlie tries to fathom the triangle of himself, Beth and Laura when he finds himself

> in the shade of a statue and leaned against the base. Above him drooped a lush woman in rough stone, rich with female curves. Some feet away a sister statue straddled her pedestal with muscular thighs. Charlie glared at the two women of rock, so warmly shaped that he never passed them without wanting to reach out and touch them. He knew them today for their cold, hard, unknowable selves. (p. 180)

Women are presented as strange both to themselves and to men. But they can come to know themselves. In Bannon's presentation of lesbians, desire predates the ability to name that desire.[4] But whereas sexual initiation for the lesbian occurs through the female, her dis-cursive initiation into her social status remains a male prerogative.[5]

In their male-as-norm/al world, the lesbian protagonists of these novels spend their lives negotiating with men rather than with women. The first male in the lesbian's life, and one constantly haunting the protagonists, whether absent or present, is the father. In line with a long tradition of literary presentations of familial structures, ranging from Shakespeare's plays to the Brontës' novels, Bannon's texts abound with motherless females who need to work out their relationships with their fathers, whether the latter is cast as 'bad' as in Laura's case or as 'good' as in Beebo's (Beebo's living in Cordelia Street is one neat and very literary touch in this context). In an interesting contrast to Radclyffe Hall's novels, where the fathers die and the mothers are the long-term survivors who haunt (and ruin) the lesbian protagonists' lives, in Bannon's texts it is the father who lives on to become the focus of familial constraints.

Thus both Laura and Beebo love their fathers and have problems reconciling this love with their need to live their lives as they feel impelled to (i.e. as a lesbian). For both, the desire to declare their 'true' sexual proclivities to their male parent becomes a major preoccupation. It is this negotiation that governs both women's life choices – where they live, what they do to earn a living and so on. Both women feel that the only way to live their desires is to make themselves outcasts from their families, to break – against their emotional needs – the ties with their fathers.

Bannon juxtaposes the focus on the father as the dominant influence on the lesbians' lives with another, equally antagonistic relationship with a further set of males: heterosexual males who act as sexual rivals. In each of the Bannon volumes there is at least one such antagonistic heterosexual male, who feels threatened by the lesbian and reacts with verbal and/or physical violence against her.

This antagonistic heterosexual male is counterpointed by a third male who is also cast as a central character, a 'good' father and homosexual called Jack Mann, who initiates the lesbian into her lesbianism by introducing her to potential objects of desire and by introducing the relevant vocabulary and social codes to her. His support of the lesbian is determined by a number of factors. One of these is that he, following an established convention in cultural representation, is cast as the older experienced male, whose very age and experience, precisely as is the case in Jane Austen's novels, validate his role as guide, mentor and protector of the young, inexperienced, virginal female. Further, Jack Mann's own status as an outsider to heterosexual society aligns him with Laura and Beebo. In *Beebo Brinker*, his projection of a sense of shared identity with lesbians extends to a circularity of desire when he falls in love with a boy who has fallen in love with Beebo, and is marked by the fact that at different points throughout the five novels he and a lesbian protagonist share a living space, that they are geographically united in a flat and, in a wider context, in Greenwich Village. One point Bannon's novels thus make is that only homosexual men or heterosexual men who suffer from some form of emotional or sexual 'abnormality' will sympathise with and be supportive of the lesbian.

The lesbian as the worm in the bud

In the context of sexual desire, territory represents in spatial form the relationship between the homosexual and heterosexual world. In many of the novels of the first three decades of this century, homosexual desire is cast as something which is acted out in foreign parts (pun intended), 'on the continent' or abroad in Greece or North

Africa, for example in H.D.'s poetry and *Her*, Renée Vivien's *A woman appeared to me*, and later, Mary Renault's novels. The 'enemy' to the heterosexual world does not yet reside 'within' – homosexual relationships enacted on home soil are frequently presented as thwarted.

However, from the 1940s onwards, the literal division of space into foreign and homosexual versus home and heterosexual is increasingly collapsed. (This may be a function of World War II and its consequent movement of people (plus rising tourism and workers' migration) and also of women doing 'men's jobs' for the first time and raising the issue of gender boundaries.) Homosexuals begin to reside on home territory, in an 'inner' but still discrete space such as Greenwich Village or the Chinese garden which forms part of the school grounds of the boarding-school, in which Rosemary Manning's *The Chinese garden* (1962) is set.

As Greenwich Village, in Bannon's novels, acquires the status of a haven for the lesbian, an enclosure within the wider heterosexual world where the lesbian can act out her desire, so in *The Chinese garden*, the garden of the title acts as a refuge – within the grounds of an all-girls' boarding-school – for Margaret and Rena, where they can live their sexual desire. In contrast to Bannon's depiction of Greenwich Village, which is by and large positive, in terms of the fulfilment and release it affords for the lesbian protagonists, Manning invests the Chinese garden with an aura of 'dreadful corruption and soft decay' (p. 23). Lesbian desire, as in René Vivien's earlier *A woman appeared to me*, is given an oriental setting, but whereas Vivien highlights the artificiality and theatricality of this setting, Manning 'naturalizes' it by making it an outdoor rather than an indoor setting, by placing the garden within the park that is part of the school. Both Vivien and Manning invest the setting with all the stereotypes critics such as Edward Saïd have pointed out as typical of Western writings on the Orient. And, significantly, in both instances the setting functions as a means of foregrounding the notion of 'the enemy within'. Lesbians become this enemy within, the alien otherness that is both contained and established within the wider world of heterosexual dominance. Not only are lesbians a threat to this world – they are also a threat to each other, competing for approval in the heterosexist world, competing for sexual objects and for territory in which to exist.

The Chinese garden is permeated by an ambiguity concerning the source and 'nature' of the corruption the garden represents. It is unclear whether the judgements implied are a comment on lesbian love *per se* or on the corrupting effect a heterosexist society has on that love and on lesbians. Offering no direct critique of the socio-economic heterosexist conditions under which its lesbian characters exist, it portrays an absence of bonding and support between the adult and the adolescent lesbians. This almost destroys the integrity of the central protagonist, Rachel, who ends up roundly condemning her lesbian teachers for deserting their lesbian pupils.

This absence of lesbian bonding is elsewhere explained by Manning in terms of the secrecy that governed her own life[6] and that of many lesbians in the first half of this century.[7] In the introduction to the second edition of her autobiography *A time and a time*, Manning states:

> I was myself an 'outsider'. I had spent my adult life ... concealing the fact that I was a lesbian, a habit of secrecy which was to continue for another thirty years.
>
> Young gay women with whom I talk today find it hard to understand that such a defensive secrecy could have been necessary as late as the sixties, still less in the seventies, though when I say that I was a teacher, they become more comprehending.

The result of being an 'outsider' within, a lesbian trying to negotiate a living in a heterosexually constructed world, is a sense of division and split which finds expression in the portrayal of the lesbian as loner, described by Magee as 'the occupational disease of homosexuals' (p. 146). Her private and her public or professional lives being separated, the closeted lesbian leads a life divided into discrete spheres, with a potentially empty private half as she may be too fearful to associate with other lesbians and find socializing with heterosexuals too stressful. Manning's *A time and a time* explores this loneliness both in terms of individual personality (the desire to be solitary) and lesbian existence (the problem of living as a childless homosexual couple). The split between private lesbian self and public persona detailed in *A time and a time* informs most of Manning's writings, in the shape of an unresolvable conflict between allegiances to worlds (heterosexual and lesbian) that are presented as, in many respects, antagonistic, without any analysis of this antagonism and its effects.

Significantly, survival of the lesbian in Manning's texts tends to depend on the heterosexual world, whereas destruction is initiated by problems in her lesbian existence. Thus the suicide attempt which is discussed in the first part of *A time and a time* is a function of the end of a lesbian relationship. Overcoming the aftermath of being rescued is achieved through emotional attachment to a woman who is not interested in a sexual relationship with the protagonist and through the reading of seventeenth-century male authors such as Montaigne. The lesbian community, in so far as it is described, is represented as a 'gay scene', 'the claustrophobic world of homosexuals, seedy, it seemed to me, hectic and endlessly malicious' (p. 136). However, *A time and a time* allows the possibility of reading Manning's non-engagement with a lesbian community not merely in terms of that community's 'shortcomings' but also in terms of her essential desire for solitude.

Bannon's novels, by comparison, are more positive in their depiction of a lesbian community and, significantly, much more celebratory of lesbian sex. What these novels offer is an affirmation of lesbian sexual desire and an explicitness concerning sexual encounters between women, absent from much of lesbian writing until then and even in that period. It cannot be denied that the portrayal of lesbian sex in the novels is clichéd. Phrases such as 'She felt like a column of fire, all heat and light, impossibly sensual, impossibly sexual. She was all feeling, warm and melting, strong and sweet.' (*I am a woman*, p. 94) could come from any romantic pulp writing. However, the assertion of lesbian sexual desire and of the need to have it fulfilled is made over and over again in ways designed to support the validity of these desires, their urgency and power. Similarly, the joy and sexual release women find in having sex with each other is repeatedly emphasized. This, in fact, may be considered to be one of the differences between lesbian pulp fiction of this period and the writing such as *The Chinese garden* that presents itself as 'high culture'. Nonetheless, the Bannon novels are very deliberately crafted, more so than has been acknowledged.[8] It seems as if some lesbian writing of this postwar period, wishing to align itself with the mainstream literary tradition, does so at the cost of its lesbian subject – turning her into an object of pity, exactly as was the case in the first thirty years of this century. Absence of 'literary pretense', by contrast, seems to free the author from the constraint to construct lesbian characters exclusively as victims.

Into the limelight through politicization

Lesbian existence, lived 'microcosmically' (see Maureen Duffy, *The microcosm*), that is in a defined but relatively enclosed space within the macrocosmic world of heterosexual life, changed in some respects with the onset of the gay and women's liberation movements in the second half of the 1960s and early 1970s. (See Susan Cavin's *Lesbian origins* for more on the importance of 'liberation' for lesbians.). Perhaps the most important aspect of these movements was that they created a public forum where women visibly organized themselves, that they 'legitimated' and, indeed, institutionalized women's political action around concerns such as the legalization of the right to abortion, equal opportunities and equal pay. Women as an organizing, politicized group of people thus became visible.[9]

> For many lesbians, feminism in the 70s became a more important political identity than gayness, and women began to split off from GLF [Gay Liberation Front] to fight for the political acknowledgement of lesbians in the Women's Liberation Movement. (Cherry Smyth, *Lesbians talk queer notions*, p. 14)

Both in the gay and in the women's liberation movements intersexual differences were a source of conflict between lesbians and non-lesbians.[10]

Initially, the concerns of the women's liberation movement, focussed as they were on notions of 'equality',[11] were constructed within a frame that centred on a dualist view dividing the world into a female and a male domain in which the female was consistently underprivileged and undervalued. The primacy of this inter-sexual division in women's consciousness is reflected in Juliet Mitchell's *Women: the longest revolution* (1966), in which 'woman's biological destiny as mother [becoming] a cultural vocation in her role as socialiser of children' (p. 39) is extensively debated, as is the issue of women's sexual liberation. Liberation is here taken to mean women's liberation from their enslavement to men which is a function of a seductive acculturation into the notion of romantic love. (See Rich's 'Compulsory heterosexuality' and Radway's *Reading the romance*.) In its discussion of literary texts, and in this respect, typical of its time (consider Kate Millett's *Sexual politics*), *Women: the longest revolution* focusses predominantly on writings by men, juxtaposing the discussion of one text by a woman, Charlotte Brontë's *Wuthering heights*, with an analysis of *three* texts by male authors. The focus is on men's views of women.[12]

In consequence, the debate offered is one of pitting a woman's (the author's) view of women's lives against men's views of women's lives. In this debate lesbians are absent, unmentioned. But the relationship between politics and culture, between the public and the private is manifested in Mitchell's subtitle *Essays in feminism, literature and psychoanalysis*, in which 'feminism' signals the political and the public, 'literature' the intersection of the public, education and the personal, and 'psychoanalysis' the conjunction of gender and private history.

This relationship between public and private, politics and culture, is explored in another book from that period, edited by Elaine Showalter and now virtually forgotten, *Women's liberation and literature* (1971). This text reveals a shift *from* women analysing their position in relation to men *to* women investigating writing by women. It is in this context that the possibilities of the lesbian emerging as visible among women begin. Showalter's book does not overtly discuss lesbianism, but it features, indirectly, as the 'other' awaiting its turn. Thus Hortense Calisher's witty piece entitled 'No important woman writer' points to the absence of a discussion of female sexuality and (resultant) female specificity in women's writing, suggesting that 'heterosexual' in America means 'male' and that women have not come to grips with their sexuality at the level of cultural production.[13] She writes:

> Looking abroad, it can be seen what happens to women who do ride their femininity in the literary races: Doris Lessing, tied to psychiatry, suffragettism, and the vaginal reflex; Simone de Beauvoir, tied in the inimitable French way to the coattails of a man. But the American artist has sometimes avoided that, by getting her mental hysterectomy early. She will often not speak for female experience even when the men do; she will be the angel-artist, with celestially muted lower parts. (p. 229)

Calisher's celebration of feminism that 'comes straight *[sic]* from the belly, from the bed, and from childbed' (p. 230), epitomizing specifically feminine experience (which lesbians of the 1990s may well want to take issue with) may, in part, be problematic; nonetheless, it puts female sexuality and desire on the cultural map and as such moves (slightly) closer to a debate which might include lesbians as a significant body of women, expressive of female sexuality and desire.

In *Women's liberation and literature* Showalter includes one piece whose title points to lesbians, Sylvia Plath's poem 'Lesbos'. But, like Calisher's article, that poem is concerned with women struggling in the context of a heterosexual marriage, motherhood, the kitchen sink. If one considers Lesbos as a women-only domain, the title might be read in two ways. It either relates to the kitchen in which the (one assumes female) persona spews out her venom against the noise, demands, violence and rejection which appear to surround her in a kind of domestic hell, or it suggests an all-female haven, a utopia which would be the very opposite of what the persona inhabits but which remains a fantasy for her. In contrast to Showalter (p. 146), I would suggest the second person's identity is ambiguous, could be interpreted in a multiplicity of ways (not all of which would make that 'you' female or a separate entity from the persona, or indeed, unitary throughout the poem), and does not suggest female bonding, mutual empathy among women, or, more importantly from the point of view of a lesbian, women's (sexual) desire for each other. Its central preoccupation is the violent rejection of what the persona feels confronted with in her heterosexual domesticity. It is important to remember though, in looking at this poem from a 1990s perspective, that it prefigures a stance adopted by, for instance, Radicalesbians, who defined a lesbian as 'the rage of all women condensed to the point of explosion' (*For lesbians only*, p. 17).

Sappho was a right-on woman

In parallel to heterosexual women's critical engagement with patriarchy, which dominates the early writings of women's liberation feminists, lesbians were beginning to demand inclusion and visibility within the liberation and civil rights movements. This demand, inevitable in the context of women organizing themselves for the purposes of political action, was not seen as unproblematic by heterosexual women, who felt threatened by 'their' causes being aligned with lesbians. This fact, and the emergence of lesbians within the women's liberation context, is documented in Sidney Abbott and Barbara Love's *Sappho was a right-on woman* (1972) which offers itself as 'a liberated view of lesbianism'. *Sappho* sought to chronicle the changes that have occurred in the public profile of lesbians in the context of the women's liberation movement. Divided into a 'before' and an 'after', it comes in two parts: 'What it was like' and 'Living the future'. The first half is a rather curious read describing the life of the lesbian prior to women's liberation in terms reminiscent of wildlife programmes. It might as well be sub-titled: 'Lesbians – their habitats, habits, haunts'. This is, in part, a function of the *style* of writing employed (which, in fact, differs to some extent from the style used in the second part of the book). Thus the term 'lesbian' is used as a unitary concept, generically, frequently combined with the definite article and in the singular. Verb forms tend to be in the present tense and indicative (the favoured form for indicating 'universality'). Sentences are delivered as incontestable statements. A typical paragraph reads as follows:

> Perhaps dressed in dark tones or in black, in the fashion of old gay custom, the Lesbian blends into the environment, camouflaged like other life forms that develop protective coloration in hostile environments. By day she must contain her feelings in a dark closet; but protected by the night she feels she can allow her lightest moods to emerge. (p. 70)

Sappho was a right-on woman sets out to present 'the Lesbian' as an endangered species ('Less is known about her – and less accurately – than about the Newfoundland dog.' p. 13) whose every aspect of life is a hazardous fight for survival. The conflict between 'nature' and 'culture' concerning lesbian identity remains unresolved. Indeed, on p. 174 they write, 'We simply do not know where biology stops and culture starts, but it is clear that culture dramatizes, ritualizes, and extends whatever biological base there may be, creating myths.' The tone of that first half seems terribly dated now, patronizing and as 'purposely dreary and discouraging and filled with foreboding' (p. 37) as its authors maintain novels about lesbians are. It is difficult to see it as 'a liberated view of lesbianism' and there is no evidence that the authors are presenting their portrait of 'the lesbian' tongue-in-cheek.

The second half of the text is quite different; there the fight for survival is transported onto the open platforms of feminist activism because, as the authors write:

> We were Feminist before we were Lesbian activists, and we know that both Feminists and Lesbian activists fight to become self-reliant; both find

> dependence on men unnatural. The common political goals of the two
> groups make sexual preference seem an unimportant difference. (p. 16)

Some lesbians might well wish to contest this last point,[14] but the
importance of the debate among women about the relationship
between their politics and their sexuality in the 1960s and early
1970s should not be underestimated, for it was in part in this context
that lesbians acquired a public forum.

The section in *Sappho* entitled 'Mirage' offers a documentary
account of lesbians' struggle in the United States to gain acceptance
within the all-female, nationwide organization, the National Organization for Women (NOW). This was a three-year struggle (1969–71)
which is all the more interesting because it involved people like Rita
Mae Brown, Kate Millett, Susan Brownmiller and Betty Friedan, all of
whom have become household names among lesbians and feminists
since. According to Abbott and Love, when lesbianism as an issue
and as a lived reality first emerged in NOW, women like Betty Friedan
saw it as the 'lavender menace' which threatened the women's
movement by sidetracking women from their alleged main concern,
gaining equality with men. Abbott and Love document the extent to
which the term 'lesbian' was seen as a threat to the fight for women's
rights and to women's identity. 'Lesbian' was a term of abuse, feared
by women who felt they had a particular heteropatriarchally oriented
role in society to maintain. The sexism guiding this view was not
immediately obvious to all but was highlighted by the article 'The
Woman identified woman' published by the Radicalesbians in 1970.
(See Hoagland and Penelope's *For lesbians only*.)

The struggle for the acceptance of lesbians within the women's
movement meant a reviewing of what that movement was supposed
to be about and of what fuelled women's oppression in society. It was
recognized that 'the women's movement has to be about sexuality.
Otherwise, it's just another civil rights movement and that's not
dealing with the problem women have to face. If sexuality is at the
base, then Lesbianism is totally relevant' (*Sappho*, pp. 128–9). At a
press conference on 17 December 1971 Kate Millett read out a
statement which maintained:

> 'Lesbian' is used as a psychic weapon to keep women locked into their
> male-defined 'feminine role.' The essence of that role is that a woman is
> defined in terms of her relationship to a man. A woman is called a Lesbian

when she functions autonomously. Women's autonomy is what Women's Liberation is all about. (*Sappho*, p. 124)

The same point had already been made by the Radicalesbians in 'The Woman identified woman' who wrote that 'in this sexist society, for a woman to be independent means she can't be a woman – she must be a dyke' (*For lesbians only*, p.18). Autonomy, often conceived of as economic autonomy, was regarded as a central concern for women's liberation. As *Sappho* states:

For Lesbians, independence and responsibility for self are lifelong realities and not merely interim needs between support by father and support by husband. (p. 135)

While one needs to consider to what extent this statement reflects the middle-class bias for which Rita Mae Brown attacked NOW (*Sappho*, pp. 111–12), it is worth emphasizing that as recently as the early 1970s, the assumption was that women work only while unsupported by males, and that for a woman to work suggested precisely the absence of a supporting male. Importantly too, women's liberation was framed as an economic liberation and a striving towards autonomy *from men*. Autonomy as a concept has been rethought since[15] but it was the implication of such an autonomy which contributed to the debate about the relationship between women, politics and sexuality which eventually led to women turning away from the consideration of relations between the sexes to exploring relations between women.

Within this debate, the slogan 'the personal is the political' became increasingly prominent as women realized that the desire for control over their bodies and over their lifestyles signalled politically significant positions. At the same time, the construction of women's forums and women-only spaces, sought by women wishing to voice their dissent from patriarchy, their anger at how they had been treated by men, and their frustration at their lives was, rightly, perceived as threatening by men as women were *choosing* to congregate. Historically, women-only contexts had frequently been a function of necessity (men being absent to fight wars) or of men choosing to police female sexuality by confining women to harems, kraals, nunneries (some women, of course, chose and/or welcomed such confinement) and similar all-female enclaves. In the 1960s and 1970s, however, it was all too evident that women were *voluntarily* constructing their own spaces and were demanding equal rights with men. This raised questions about the nature of women's allegiances with each other and moved the concept of lesbianism into a fluidity of definition it had not enjoyed hitherto. Until that time lesbianism had been associated with women's sexual preference for women; now the 'political lesbian' emerged who, according to *Sappho,* could be:

1) a woman who becomes a Lesbian as a result of Feminist theory [and who] sees Lesbianism as a separatist, alternative lifestyle, for her a revolutionary step;
2) women who live a total commitment to women, even though they have never had sexual relations with women;
3) a Lesbian who is politicized, that is, she has analysed her situation in society according to the theory of sexism and the nature of sex roles. (pp. 152–3)

In the late 1960s and early 1970s women's organizing themselves politically meant that they had to identify and define their (sexual) position, often in public contexts. Abbott and Love cite Wendy Wonderful, one woman activist who declared:

I'm bisexual but it is for my homosexuality that I'm oppressed. Therefore I say I'm a Lesbian as a political statement. (p. 120)

Understanding the specificities of women's oppression meant accepting that 'there ain't no distinction between personal and political' (*For lesbians only,* p. 181). At the same time, the issue of choice became important; women were increasingly aware of the fact that their lives, lifestyles and sexual allegiances, though frequently presented to them as a matter of inevitability, could be a matter of choice, *their* choice. Sylvia Plath's *The bell jar* is a text which details both the problems and the possibilities inherent in seeing life in terms of choices to be made.

Becoming woman-identified: re-focussing in Adrienne Rich's poetry

One writer, whose work – from a lesbian viewpoint – charts the changes which women have gone through since the 1960s, is Adrienne Rich. In contrast to *Sappho,* Rich in her introduction to *Blood, bread and poetry: selected prose 1979–1985* presents the emergence of the feminist movement as a struggle against the sexist male left but *not* as a struggle among women of diverse sexual orientation. She, like many other women, made the transition from heterosexuality to lesbianism during this period. She states:

> I identified myself as a radical feminist and soon after – not as a political act but out of powerful and unmistakable feelings – as a lesbian. (*Blood, bread and roses*, p. viii)

Rich's poetry of 1969 is concerned with the realization that '*The moment when a feeling enters the body*/is political. This touch is political.' (*The fact of a doorframe*, p. 123). Part of this realisation is the sense that sex is not enough to connect women and men:

> Plugged-in to her body
> he came the whole way
> but it makes no difference
>
> If not this then what
> would fuse a connection
> (*The fact*, p. 131)

Rich's poetry of 1969, 1970, and 1971, the same period covered in the 'Mirage' section of *Sappho*, charts the struggle of a woman who is dissociating herself from men 'because this world gives no room/to be what we dreamt of being' (p. 131). Significantly, the poetry of that period is collected in a volume entitled *The will to change*, thus highlighting the voluntaristic aspect of the transformation detailed in the poems, the deliberate and considered refusal of the woman to inhabit the role of victim. The assertiveness inherent in that stance finds expression in poems like 'I dream I'm the death of Orpheus' in which the persona, using the present tense and the indicative, makes statements about herself such as 'I am a woman in the prime of life, with certain powers' (*The fact*, p. 119) and 'a woman with the nerves of a panther/a woman with contacts among Hell's Angels/a woman feeling the fullness of her powers' (*The fact*, p. 120) which affirm her strength *despite* the fact that she sees her powers as 'severely limited' and not to be used yet.

This awareness of self as powerful translates itself in the first section of 'Shooting script' (1969–70) into the woman being constructed as actively seeking change in a context where woman and man no longer connect while still being bound 'on the wheel of endless conversation' which has, however, become 'the dialogue of the rock with the breaker'. Where 'once it would not have occurred to me to/put out in a boat, not on a night like this' (p. 145), the woman now finds herself 'driven to odd attempts' (p. 145) in which 'Trying to talk with a man' is akin to 'testing bombs' (p. 149).

It is precisely this sense of violence, a violence associated in Rich's poetry with men and with urban existence, which is increasingly exposed as one reason for women's dissociation from men. Thus 'Waking in the dark' proclaims:

> The tragedy of sex
> lies around us, a woodlot
> the axes are sharpened for.
> ...
> A man's world. But finished.
> They themselves have sold it to the machines.
> ...
> Nothing will save this. I am alone
> (*The fact*, p. 153)

Rich's poetry of 1969 and 1970 focusses predominantly on women's failing relationship with men. In her poetry of 1971 and 1972, this theme continues, emphasizing the connection between individual experience and a generalized political reality governed by the Vietnam war and the destruction of the environment by men. Heterosexual marriage is regarded as one of the 'failures of the race' (*The fact*, p. 176) and the sense that 'His mind is too simple, I cannot go on/ sharing his nightmares' (*The fact*, p. 178) leads both to the question, '*You have the power/in your hands, you control our lives-/why do you want our pity too?*' (*The fact*, p. 183) and to the assertion, '*The only real love I have ever felt/was for children and other women*' (*The fact*, p. 168).

Simultaneous with the presentation of a coming to terms with the impossibility of a continued heterosexual existence, expressed in poems such as 'Waking in the dark', 'Incipience', 'Dialogue', 'Diving into the wreck', 'The phenomenology of anger', 'Translations' and 'Meditations for a savage child',[16] Rich's poetry from 1971 onwards marks a turn towards an exploration of relations between women. This exploration is frequently readable as an exploration of self. Thus 'After twenty years' focusses on women together in one space: 'Two women sit together at a table by a window.' Their relationship is ambiguous. Being 'two women in the prime of life' they could be sisters, friends, lovers or various selves as the second half of the poem suggests, which maintains that 'It is strange to be so many women' and that she/they will 'flow into history now as the woman of their time' (*The fact*, p. 157). A similar ambiguity governs 'The mirror in which two are seen as one' (1971) which ends with an image of self-birthing.

It is noticeable in these poems that even where they can be read in terms of a woman's exploration of self, this exploration is conceived as a relational one, a dialogue between one female self and another. An attempt is invariably made to understand that other female self (whether it is conceived of as a split off part of one person or as another person); thus in 'Translations' the persona imagines a woman whose man is in another relationship as having a 'sister' turn 'enemy' through this act which the new female lover cannot see as a grief 'shared, unnecessary/and political' (*The fact*, p. 170).

The sense of an overarching sisterhood that transcends differences among women is pronouned in Rich's work. In *Blood, bread and poetry* she states that 'At no time have I ever defined myself as, or considered myself, a lesbian separatist' (p. viii).[17] At the same time she insists that 'The necessity for autonomous women's groups still seems obvious to me' (p. viii). In Rich's poetry of the early 1970s the dividing line is between women and men and not among women, with an emphasis on enabling women, *against* the violence and destructiveness of men, *for* the survival of humankind and the planet. For Rich the fact that the personal is the political implies the need for a bonding among women.

Although a universal bonding among women was not achieved through the women's liberation movement and is, without doubt, a utopian ideal, it did prompt women to congregate and establish female group identities, often for specific, practical purposes such as fighting for particular rights. The increasing visibility of women fuelled the creation of structures that would support a visible women's culture such as women-only spaces. (See *Call me lesbian*, pp. 52–9.) Women now demanded and were invited to consume cultural products expressive of their specific experiences. In the 1970s women's presses like Virago, The Women's Press, Daughters Inc. and Persephone were founded,[18] catering for a specifically female audience and privileging women authors, lesbian and heterosexual. Journals such as *Spare Rib*, *Emma* and *Artemis* emerged; eventually, bookshops like Sisterwrite (opened November 1978) and Silver Moon (opened May 1984) were set up, initially frequently with sections like

'Women's Writing' under which one might find lesbian texts. Increasingly these bookshops have replaced 'Women's Writing' by 'Lesbian' sections. Feminist scholarship in a variety of disciplines emerged and in the United States women's studies as an academic discipline gained ground.[19] Women's theatre groups were set up.[20] The 1970s were an era of expansion of a woman-centred culture and as part of that process women gained confidence, expressed in writing by and about lesbians in a new assertiveness which transported lesbians out of the twilight and the house of shades[21] where they had existed either in a defensive isolation or in a form of interior prison (together but separate) into a position of visibility. As Adrienne Rich, drawing on Plato's cave myth, says of lesbian existence in her poem 'Origins and history of consciousness':

I want to call this life.

But I can't call it life until we start to move
beyond this secret circle of fire
where our bodies are giant shadows flung on a wall
where the night becomes our inner darkness...
(*The dream of a common language*, p. 9)

In particular, and as part of this new assertiveness, there was a rejection of the stance of women defining themselves, culturally or otherwise, always and foremost in relation to men. The debate shifted from difference being located between genders to difference being investigated between women. Julia Penelope wrote in 1974: 'I'm no longer interested in being defined by comparison or contrast with men.' ('Lesbian separatism: the linguistic and social sources of separatist politics', p. 48) Her diagnosis was:

We are a long way from Lesbian Nation. We don't know *who* we are, and our culture has somehow neglected to provide lesbians with an identity, beyond the traditionally-imposed characteristics of sinfulness, sickness, and illegality. ('Lesbian separatism', p. 45)

The growth of lesbian culture(s) throughout the 1970s and 1980s changed this situation, and it is to these changes that I now turn.

Notes

1 *Women like us* indicates that women born in the first half of the twentieth century

often had little choice but to marry; many of the women portrayed in this volume married in their twenties even if they had had lesbian relationships during their teens. Statements such as 'I got married as part of my effort to conform,' (p. 24) or 'I realized I wasn't very turned on by men, but I did marry – there were all sorts of pressures, sort of running away from things – I don't know, it's very hard to be positive,' (p. 75) are common.

2 The phrase 'compulsory heterosexuality' was popularized by Adrienne Rich in her article 'Compulsory heterosexuality and lesbian existence' (1980), variously reprinted as, for instance, in her collection of essays *Blood, bread and poetry* and in *Desire: the politics of sexuality*, edited by Ann Snitow *et al.*

3 For a discussion of the lesbian *Bildungsroman* see Bonnie Zimmerman, 'Exiting from patriarchy: the lesbian novel of development' in *The voyage in: fictions of female development*; Nicki Hastie, 'Lesbian BiblioMythography'.

4 *In Women like us,* several older lesbians describe this situation as having pertained to themselves. Thus one of them states: 'I was constantly being attracted by women, I would have been awfully active if I'd allowed myself to be in my twenties. I'd never heard the word 'lesbian' and when I finally did hear it I couldn't say it for years.' (p. 71)

5 'Naming' as a male prerogative has been extensively discussed by feminist theorists and feminist linguists such as Hélène Cixous in 'Sorties' (*The newly born woman,* Manchester, 1986, pp. 63–132), Deborah Cameron in *Feminism and linguistic theory* (London, 1985), and Julia Penelope in *Speaking freely* (Oxford, 1990).

6 An analogous situation is depicted in Maureen Duffy's poem '*Women four*' (*Collected poems 1949–1984,* London, 1985), p. 14.

7 An interesting, though misogynistic, version of this problematic is offered in Brigid Brophy's *The finishing school* (London, 1963).

8 For another reading of Bannon's novels see Diane Hamer, '"I am a woman": Ann Bannon and the writing of lesbian identity in the 1950s' in *Lesbian and gay writing,* ed. Mark Lilly (London, 1990), pp. 47–75.

9 This visibility was enhanced by lesbians' political writings (e.g. Ti-Grace Atkinson's *Amazon odyssey* or some of the texts collected in Sarah Lucia Hoagland's and Julia Penelope's *For lesbians only*) in which strategies for change concerning women's oppression in society, women's relations with men and women's relation with women were debated and proclaimed.

10 See ch. 16, 'The gay liberation front, 1970–72' in Jeffrey Weeks' *Coming out* (pp. 185–206).

11 For accounts of the problematization of 'equality' as a desirable end, see 'The equality-difference debate in the Netherlands', pt. I of *Sharing the difference,* eds. Joke J. Hermsen and Alkeline van Lenning (London, 1991); also pt. III of *British feminist thought,* ed. Terry Lovell (Oxford, 1990).

12 Men's views of women as expressed in writings had been the focus of a sustained and passionate discussion in section two of Virginia Woolf's *A room of one's own* (1928) where she tried to analyse the misogyny inherent in many writings by men about women.

13 This is also evident in Marilyn Frye's discussion of what 'having sex' means; she indicates that in a heterosexual sense it appears to mean 'male-dominant-female-subordinate-copulation-whose-completion-and purpose-is-the male's-ejaculation' ('Lesbian "sex"', p. 7). Frye argues that heterosexual sex is understood as sex for men with women's sexuality and sensuality remaining uncharted and unexpressed.

14 For a recent brief discussion of the diversity of lesbian identities see 'Lesbian identities' in Celia Kitzinger's *The social construction of lesbianism,* pp. 90–124.

15 The appropriateness of 'autonomy' as a desirable position has been debated across a range of disciplines; Nancy Chodorow's *The reproduction of mothering* (Berkeley and London, 1978), Carol Gilligan's *In a different voice* (Cambridge, Mass., and London, 1982), and Patricia Waugh's *Feminine fictions: revisiting the postmodern* (London, 1989) all offer sustained comments on this issue.

16 I would like to stress that I am aware of the fact that these poems could be read in a number of ways (thus the analogy I propose of the 'savage child' and 'woman' might be contested for quite diverse reasons).

17 Rich, like Audre Lorde, has male children and one might argue that women with male offspring find it harder to make the decision to become separatist.

18 See Jackie Jones's unpublished M.Phil dissertation 'A comparative study of feminist publishing houses and "conventional" publishing houses with feminist lists based on the growth and changes in feminist book publishing in the last ten years' (University of Stirling, 1986).

19 See Ellen Carol DuBois *et al.*, *Feminist scholarship: kindling in the groves of academe* (University of Illinois, 1985); and Catharine R. Stimpson's 'What matter mind: a theory about the practice of women's studies' (1973); Margaret Cruikshank, *Lesbian studies: present and future* (1982); Gloria T. Hull *et al.*, eds, *But some of us are brave: black women's studies* (1982).

20 In *Carry on, understudies* (1981), Michelene Wandor offers a brief survey of women's theatre (groups) in the wake of the women's liberation movement. So does Sue-Ellen Case in *Feminism and theatre* (1988).

21 Many novels from the first half of the century and through the 1950s and 1960s had titles which had 'twilight' or 'house of shades' connotations, e.g. Lois Lodge, *Love like a shadow* (New York, 1935); Merle Miller, *A day in late September* (New York, 1963); Winifred Lear-Heap's *Shady cloister* (New York, 1950); Monica Roberts, *Woman of darkness* (New York, 1966).

Chapter 3

Claiming our space: lesbian texts in the 1970s and 1980s

The defiant lesbian hero: Rubyfruit jungle *and* Oranges are not the only fruit

Lesbians claimed cultural space in tandem with and in the wake of the women's and the gay liberation movements. This resulted in the construction of lesbian culture(s) which, while still acknowledging the heterosexist legacy of lesbians as deviant in various ways, increasingly moved towards a position that was assertive, affirmative and celebratory of lesbians. Rather than fighting negative stereotypes, lesbians began to explore the opportunities inherent in their historically-conditioned situation. As Julia Penelope maintained in 1974:

> Because our culture has ignored us, we have the unique opportunity few people have: we can set about constructing our lives and deciding who we are. ('Lesbian separatism', p. 46)

According to her afterword to the recent *Naiad Press* edition of *Riverfinger women*, Elana Nachman/Dykewomon wrote this novel in 1971 because of her 'stubborn wilfulness not to be a tragic queer' (p. 185). The refusal of negative stereotypes of lesbians increasingly informed work on/by lesbians. 'Deviant' gave way to 'defiant' and one of the new images of the lesbian in literature to emerge in the early 1970s was that of the defiant lesbian hero.[1]

One of the first and perhaps best-known versions of this image is the protagonist of Rita Mae Brown's *Rubyfruit jungle* (1973), Molly Bolt, who has much in common with the first-person narrator of Jeanette Winterson's *Oranges are not the only fruit* (1985). Both novels portray a lesbian coming of age, literally and metaphorically, charting her progress from childhood to young adulthood which involves the affirmation of the protagonist's lesbian identity and her rejection and move away from the community in which she grew up. In parallel to the uncertainty concerning the origins of lesbianism *per se* – are you born one or do you become one – the origins of the protagonists of *Rubyfruit jungle* and of *Oranges* are to some extent uncertain. Both girls are adopted.

Interestingly, when their sexuality becomes an issue, a 'foreign' element in relation to their background emerges: Molly's father was a Frenchman and some of her traits supposedly index this (pp. 235–6); Jean's mother had an affair with a Frenchman which taught her to resist sexuality (pp. 86–8). Sexuality and 'foreignness' thus conjoin in both texts to highlight issues of difference. Uncertainty of origin leads to Molly being cast in the role of 'bastard' (p. 3), while the protagonist of *Oranges* says, 'I cannot recall a time when I did not know that I was special' (p. 3). Despite eliciting very different value-judgements, being a bastard and being special have the same function of setting the individual apart from the community. Molly, antagonizing everybody, appears at first destined to be a loner, Jean in *Oranges*, initially fully integrated into her community, is cast as a potential leader. Both make their mark on their respective communities from an early age.

One of the most striking aspects of both texts is that, as in Victorian novels, the identity of the individual is constructed as being established through her relation to the community of which she is a part. Being adopted, the precise nature of the protagonists' place in their community is under question from the outset. Molly grows up in the poor, rural south of the United States – she is, as another lesbian character in the novel puts it, a 'member of the proletariat' (p. 161), with an adoptive mother 'whose politics are to the right of Genghis Khan' (p. 242). Jean in *Oranges* grows up in the small-town north of England, in an evangelical community knit together by their subscription to a heteropatriarchal religious faith which provides them with a sense of identity. Both Molly's and Jean's contexts are constructed as provincial, conservative and bigotted. In the case of *Rubyfruit jungle*, this characterization of Molly's originary community is extended to cover all subsequent environments in which she finds herself: as she makes her way through a variety of educational establishments moving from junior school to high school to college and finally film school (with one section of the book dedicated to each), she leaves behind these establishments not only because she has passed through a particular educational stage but also because she comes to realize that these communities are all in their various ways as provincial, conservative, narrow-minded and heterosexist as her home-environment.

In contrast to previous lesbian novels, such as Ann Bannon's, where heterosexist society functions as a backdrop intervening in the lesbian protagonist's life by stigmatizing her, in the novels of the 1970s and 1980s this situation is reversed, with the lesbian protagonists serving to highlight the inadequacies and intolerance of the communities from which they seek to escape.

In both novels, the relationships between lesbian hero and adoptive mother is foregrounded. The mothers function as gatekeepers of heteropatriarchal values, while the fathers remain in the background, being either supportive or ineffectual. Molly's adoptive father Carl, cast in a similar vein to Sir Stephen in *The well of loneliness*, supports his daughter against her mother; Jean's father in *Oranges* fades completely into the background. Molly's mother's greatest desire is that her daughter grow up a lady, knowing how to catch a man who will provide for her, and Molly's resistance to this moulding in her mother's ideal image of hetero-womanhood is the source of constant strife between them. Jean's mother, too, wants her daughter to grow up living out the ideal life she would have liked to have had herself, being a celibate missionary in Africa. In both texts, resistance to the mother who endorses and defends her community's values equals resisting that community, and as Molly's surname 'Bolt' indicates, she (like Jean in *Oranges*) ultimately needs to escape from the community she grew up in to live her life as a lesbian.

Throughout *Rubyfruit jungle* Molly defies conventions concerning, for example, attitudes towards authority figures, gender role expectations, and social interaction. She shows courage, independence of mind and spirit, and resourcefulness. She knows how to 'play the system' and acts according to the rules in order to protect

LESBIAN TEXTS IN THE 1970S AND 1980S

herself, as is the case when she is sent to a psychiatrist for her lesbianism[2] by her Dean at college, or where she feels she can benefit. While laying herself open to a variety of (sexual) experiences, she never diverts from her path of wanting an education which will give her the possibility of earning an independent income and standing up for her values, rather than becoming – like Holly, one of the other lesbian characters in the novel – the kept mistress of an older rich lesbian. Her desire is to make an impact on the community at large: early dreams of becoming the president of the United States give way to wanting to be a filmmaker in order to make 'real movies about real people and about the way the shit comes down' (p. 174). In many respects Molly epitomizes an all-American person and all-American ideals. Jean in *Oranges* does not defy her community from the outset but is forced to review her relationship with that community when its leading figures, including her mother, turn against her on finding out that she is having a lesbian relationship.

To both protagonists their sexual orientation seems perfectly 'natural'. When Jean asks her first lover Melanie 'Do you think this is Unnatural Passion?' Melanie responds, 'Doesn't feel like it. According to Pastor Finch, that's awful', which leads Jean to conclude, 'She must be right', (p. 89). The protagonists' refusal to regard their sexuality as 'unnatural' has the effect – from the point of view of the lesbian reader – of creating positive role models through 'normalizing' lesbianism. As Molly says at one point, 'most lesbians I know look like any other woman' (p. 194). There is, however, a discrepancy between how Molly and Jean feel about their lesbianism and how their communities view it, as manifest in the communities' outrage and attempts at expulsion of the protagonists. But neither Molly nor Jean are cowed into giving up their sexuality. Instead they leave these communities behind to venture towards a context which may be more supportive of their life-choices. This is one of the reasons why they are defiant rather than deviant: no longer internalizing others' views of their sexuality or remaining in a context which castigates them, they reject those that reject them. Both texts suggest that their protagonists do not need the communities they grew up in in order to survive, a representation quite unlike the turn of events detailed in Radclyffe Hall's novels.

However, there is another crucial difference from Hall's novels in the construction of *Rubyfruit jungle* and *Oranges*: in both these texts, the protagonists are defying a community whose ideological bases are presented intratextually as intensely problematic. The negative light in which these communities are cast in terms of their bigotry and conservatism is such as to be likely to make *any* reader, irrespective of her sexual orientation, feel that one would want to leave this setting behind. Identification with the protagonists is thus made very easy and depends to quite a significant extent on the particularities of the communities depicted. The novels aid this identification between central character and reader by the use of humour which operates at the expense of these communities. Molly decides to use humour as a strategy at school to render herself acceptable to her fellow pupils who do not necessarily share her stance, and both authors utilize humour in the construction of their texts to the same end. Molly states:

> I decided to become the funniest person in the whole school. If someone makes you laugh you have to like her. I even made my teachers laugh. It worked. (p. 62)

Similarly, Brown's and Winterson's novels make their readers laugh – one cannot help but like them. At the same time, and on a more general level, it is typical for novels offering a defiant lesbian hero that the protagonist is put in a context which is likely to be considered so awful by *any* reader that she will be able to identify with the lesbian hero's rebellion against this background without having to engage with the protagonist's lesbianism. This, I think, is one reason why the BBC production of *Oranges* was so successful (see Hilary Hinds). I suspect that the depiction of a community which the average reader would be more likely to be able to identify with would make it harder to achieve the success *Rubyfruit Jungle* and *Oranges* enjoy(ed).

For all their similarities, the differences between the two texts indicate their historical specificity. Molly's pronounced drive towards autonomy and self-reliance ('listen to nobody but your own self', p. 92) connects her with the desires of women expressed in the period of the women's liberation movement. Repeated discussions about lesbian role-play[3] highlight an aspect of lesbian culture which in the course of the 1970s 'went underground'. In *Rubyfruit jungle*, it is older lesbians who are cast as living butch-femme roles,[4] and one of them ruefully remarks to Molly: 'What's this world coming to when you can't tell the butches from the femmes.' (p. 147) Molly herself rejects such role play, saying,

What's the point of being a lesbian if a woman is going to look and act like an imitation man?[5] (p. 147)

Molly represents a new generation of lesbian who does not wish to engage in role-play. Role-play does not arise for the hero in *Oranges* except as an accusation levelled at her by her mother who says she is 'aping men' (p. 127). But Jean's response to this reflects the fact that in the mid-1980s, when *Oranges* was written, role-play was considered inappropriate in a large section of the lesbian community. Jean counters, 'Now if I was aping men she'd have every reason to be disgusted ... At that time I had no notion of sexual politics, but I knew that a homosexual is further from a woman than a rhinoceros. Now that I do have a number of notions about sexual politics, this early observation holds good. There are shades of meaning, but a man is a man wherever you find it' (pp. 127-8). Even the older lesbian characters in *Oranges* are not represented as inhabiting the butch-femme world which the older lesbians in *Rubyfruit jungle* seem to dominate. Perhaps because of this difference, *Oranges* is in many respects a less problematic read than *Rubyfruit jungle* has become over the years. *Rubyfruit jungle* is, for example, terribly ageist.[6] It is very difficult to judge to what extent Molly's pejorative attitude towards older lesbians (e.g. pp. 157, 160, 212) is constructed to indicate 'the prejudices of youth' or is unwittingly endorsed by the writer. Similarly, comments made about coloured people [I use 'coloured' as this is used in the text] and about Jews[7] are highly problematic and unlikely to occur in a text written a decade later. Molly's go-getting manner which operates on a 'vengeance is mine' basis also seems alienating at times.

Two further points mark *Rubyfruit's* difference from *Oranges*: its representation of sexuality and its engagement in what I call the labelling debate. In her afterword to *Riverfinger women*,[8] Nachman writes:

> I thought I had to include at least some hetero- and bi-sexual scenes. There was (and is) an enormous pressure on lesbians not to be "exclusive," and many quasi-anthropological arguments about how, in a different world, we'd all be bi-sexual. (pp. 188–9)[9]

The same stance seems to inform *Rubyfruit jungle*, where Molly at one point decides that she will sleep with 'around twenty or thirty men and twenty or thirty women and then I'll decide' (p. 70). From the viewpoint of a lesbian reader, one of the 'advantages' of this position is that when Molly repeatedly compares sleeping with women with sleeping with men, her assertion that making love with women is much better than making love with men (e.g. pp. 69, 159) is based on 'experience', thus offering reinforcement – if such is desired – to all those lesbian readers who may not feel the urge to try the comparison for themselves. Molly's commitment to lesbianism is thus constructed as being underwritten by 'informed choice' (see Julia Penelope's *Call me lesbian*, p. 42). In *Oranges* the situation concerning sexuality is quite different since the protagonist lives in a community in which men, except at the level of fantasy and spirit, are marginalized and ridiculed, 'not particularly interesting, but quite harmless' (p. 127). For Jean the question of choice does not arise as she is constructed as lesbian from the outset and is not socialized into heterosexuality. Furthermore, her mother has destined her to live a celibate life, dedicated to 'the Lord'.

Jean is also not presented as concerned with the 'appropriate' label for herself,[10] whereas the issue of how to label yourself repeatedly emerges in *Rubyfruit jungle*, indicating the extent to which these labels are freighted with negative meanings and tend to be used pejoratively. When Leroy, for example, tells Molly he thinks she is 'queer' he explains it to her as meaning 'unnatural' (p. 63). Carolyn, one of Molly's lovers, points out to Molly that they will be labelled as 'lesbian'. Molly initially rejects this description with 'No, we just love each other, that's all. Lesbians look like men and are ugly. We're not like that' (p. 104). A discrepancy emerges here between how the lesbian protagonists think of themselves and how they think of other lesbians. Carolyn, for instance, exclaims, 'I'm very feminine, how can you call me a queer?' (p. 106) and Connie says, 'I don't remember that I ever cooed and giggled in true female fashion, so why don't you come right out and call me a dyke too ...?' (p. 106). Molly finally explodes:

> I don't know what I am – polymorphous and perverse. Shit. I don't even know if I'm white. I'm me. That's all I am and all I want to be. (p. 107)

All the labels on offer, – 'queer', 'lesbian', 'dyke' – seem in this text to be understood by the protagonists as denoting women who are masculinized either physically and/or behaviourally, reflecting the difficulties lesbians in the 1950s and 1960s had in finding a language to describe themselves (see Faderman's *Odd girls*, pp. 168–9). Given the absence of a sustained public discussion about lesbians during this period, it is also the case that many lesbians either had not come across the terminology used for describing gay women or did not, like Molly and co., connect it with themselves.[11] Resistance to labels is, of course, one way of registering defiance.

From country to town: Adrienne Rich's 'Twenty-one love poems'

Where *Rubyfruit jungle* and *Oranges* show the lesbian hero moving out from an inadequate heterosexist small-town community, Adrienne Rich's most sustained early affirmation of lesbianism in *The dream of a common language,* her sequence 'Twenty-one love poems', is firmly located in an urban environment. Rather than advocating splitting or 'bolting', it urges, 'We need to grasp our lives inseparable/from those rancid dreams' (I, p. 25). Expressing 'the desire to show you to everyone I love,/to move openly together' (II, p. 25), this sequence offers a *femmage* to a lesbian love relationship while acknowledging its setting in a contemporary urban world, full of violence against women,[12] and its embeddedness in the lesbian lovers' different pasts. Against that past, 'freighted with different language, different meanings' (XII, p. 31) the persona asserts, 'The woman who cherished/her suffering is dead. I am her descendant./I love the scar tissue she handed on to me,/but I want to go on from here with you' (VIII, p. 29). This constitutes a refusal to be cast in the role of victim; it is an act of defiance further expressed in the statement that 'Only she who says/she did not choose, is the loser in the end' (XV, p. 33). Affirmation in this sequence of poems comes in the guise of voluntarism, the insistence upon the possibility of control: 'No one's fated or doomed to love anyone./The accidents happen, we're not heroines,/they happen in our lives like car crashes' (XVII, p. 33), culminating in the final poem in which versions of the word 'choose' appear three times. This determination (*'I mean to go on living'*, XIX, p. 34) is affirmed in the full realization that 'two women together is a work/nothing in civilization has made simple' (XIX, p. 35) because 'we're out in a country that has no language/no laws' and 'whatever we do together is pure invention' (XIII, p. 31). This reflects the sense expressed by many lesbians in the 1970s that they had no sustained history of their own constructed by themselves

– the terms used to describe lesbians were those discussed and rejected in *Rubyfruit jungle* because of their heterosexist negative connotations.

One result of this was the use of a nature based vocabulary in the context of lesbian sexuality. Where many of the titles of lesbian texts in the 1950s and 1960s stressed the marginalized position of lesbians and projected an internalization of heterosexist negative views of lesbians,[13] in the 1970s and 1980s the affirmation of lesbian existence resulted in their 'naturalization'. The titles of three of the texts referred to in this chapter highlight this: *Rubyfruit jungle, Oranges are not the only fruit* and *Riverfinger women* all invoke nature. In Rich's 'Twenty-one love poems', too, nature signals sexuality. '(The floating poem, unnumbered)' which most directly pays tribute to lesbian lovemaking talks of 'half-curled frond/of the fiddlehead fern in forests/just washed by the sun' and of 'my rose-wet cave' (p. 32). In one of the earlier poems, XI, there is a description of the scaling of a 'sacred mountain', a volcano, which could easily be read as a metaphor for the female body, with 'the small, jewel-like flower' – 'that detail outside ourselves that brings us to ourselves' (XI, p. 30) a reference to the clitoris.

In Rich's poetry, this vocabulary is particularly noticeable because of its juxtaposition with a set of phrases and terms reserved to describe the brutality and violence of city- and male-oriented life. Thus 'Twenty-one love poems' begins with 'Wherever in this city, screens flicker/with pornography, with science-fiction vampires,/victimized hirelings, bending to the lash,/we also have to walk' (I, p. 25). A subsequent collection, *A wild patience has taken me this far*, begins in a similar manner, 'Close to your body, in the/pain of the city/I turn' ('The Images', p. 3) and ends with 'We are the thorn-leaf guarding the purple-tongued flower/each to each' (p. 5).[14] In the same poem the persona asserts 'I can never romanticize language again' (p. 4). Rich's poetry manages to avoid being sentimental about lesbian relationships by using nature imagery in a very contained, intermittent way, and pleading, as part of her integrative approach, for ordinariness: '(I told you from the first I wanted daily life,/this island of Manhattan was island enough for me)' and 'two people together is a work/heroic in its ordinariness' ('Twenty-one love poems', XIX, pp. 34, 35). Defiance, in Rich's poetry, does not come through the extraordinary but through understanding the relativity of one's position in time and space. This leads to the search for what is shared and for sharing rather than to distancing oneself.

In 'Transit' there is the sentence, 'When sisters separate they haunt each other' (*A wild patience has taken me this far*, p. 19). Written in 1979, this line predates one of Rich's most famous pieces of writing, the essay 'Compulsory heterosexuality and lesbian existence', by one year. 'Compulsory heterosexuality' fell into disrepute in the late 1980s because its concept of the 'lesbian continuum' which was intended to encompass all women denied, from some lesbians' viewpoint, the specifically sexual nature of lesbians' relationships with each other.[15] The debate about the 'lesbian continuum' has obscured the historical specificity of this idea which is part of a lesbian idealism found in other writings too, trying to preserve a sense of bonding among women in the face of an increasing awareness of fragmentation.

A language of our own: Lesbian Peoples

The fragmentedness of Rich's verse on the page, her use of gaps, reflects the history of silence around women she is attempting to transcend. The same project informs Monique Wittig and Sande Zeig's *Lesbian peoples: materials for a dictionary*, first published in French in 1976, in English in 1979. As *Lesbian peoples* states under the entry 'dictionary':

> The arrangement of the dictionary allows us to eliminate those elements which have distorted our history during the dark ages ... This arrangement could be called lacunary. The assemblage of words, what dictated their choice, the fiction of the fables also constitute lacunae and therefore are acting upon reality. The dictionary is, however, only a rough draft. (p. 43)

Wittig and Zeig share with Rich a preoccupation with language, an understanding that language shapes reality. They also share 'the dream of a common language', an expressed sense of lesbian existence having remained undocumented and a sense that lesbians need to develop a language of their own to describe themselves. Wittig and Zeig develop this into a dictionary in which old myths and words are given new, entirely female-centred meanings. Lesbians are described as 'companion lovers', thus drawing together the romantic ('companion') and the erotic ('lover') so that the various positions on

Rich's 'lesbian continuum' are, in some respects, concentrated into one point. Like Rich in 'Compulsory heterosexuality' (p. 229), Wittig and Zeig make cross-cultural and transhistorical references to establish a sense of continuity, a lesbian tradition. This is linguistically encoded in the repetition of certain formulations which appear each time a lesbian tribe is described.[16] But as the text comments:

> [Companion lovers] incorporate hallucinations into tales which are long, repetitive, monotonous for those who lack the patience to remain attentive to the distortions introduced each time into the repetition. (p. 69)

Paying attention to detail in this text pays off because the text offers some hilarious and imaginative re-visionings of the meaning of commonly-used words and, more to the point here, offers intermittent comments on its own rather ambiguous status as text. This self-reflexivity, as well as the play with language and experimentation with form, are typical of some of the celebratory writing of the 1970s and 1980s, when lesbian writers like Rich, Wittig and Mary Daly began to experiment with style and form. It is this which also distinguishes *Oranges* from *Rubyfruit jungle:* the latter presents itself as a realist narrative, but the former weaves together various narrative traditions and styles and several tales, retelling its central story in a number of ways. *Lesbian peoples* is, in some respects, similarly organized. Asserting that

> One cannot imagine that [the old amazon] language was composed of 'sentences' with a construction and a syntax as rigid, rigorous, repressive as those we know. (p. 94)

Lesbian peoples seeks to intervene in language as it is commonly used, though most sustainedly at the level of etymology, rewriting the 'origin' of words so that 'heroine', for example, is derived from 'heraine', meaning a follower of the goddess Hera. This inscribing through reformulation of the lesbian self into cultural history is just one affirmative aspect of *Lesbian peoples*. It is taken further with the suggestion that its companion lovers live in the 'Glorious Age' when, with the help of 'vanishing powder', men have disappeared and companion lovers only exist. Additionally, the entries for most of the supposedly historical companion lovers indexed in the book begin with 'Celebrated as ...' All companion lovers speak a single lesbian language and the overarching uniting force is the harmony in which the lesbian peoples coexist in the Glorious Age.

Diversifying lesbian cultural production: lesbian short stories and poetry

Wittig and Zeig's part invention, part recovery of a lesbian cultural tradition in *Lesbian peoples* was matched in the 1970s and 1980s by the rapid expansion of lesbian cultural production.[17] The founding of presses publishing women's work in general and lesbian work in particular encouraged that production and aided its distribution.[18] Lesbian work, hitherto mainly available in novel form, was now published in a variety of genres, in genre-specific as well as mixed-genre anthologies. This was directly related to the proliferation of lesbian and lesbian feminist magazines such as *Feminary, Sinister wisdom, Chrysalis, Onyx, Common lives/lesbian lives*, and others which published lesbian work such as short stories and poetry,[19] thus creating the forum for such writing which could then be anthologized.

One such relatively early anthology is Seymour Kleinberg's *The other persuasion,* an excellent collection of short fiction first published in 1977. This book can be distinguished from others I shall discuss for three reasons. First, because it was edited by a man and contains writing by lesbians as well as gay men (another, slightly later such anthology is Adam Mars-Jones's *Mae West is dead* published in 1983); second, because it includes several short stories by male writers such as Marcel Proust, William Carlos Williams, and Ernest Hemingway which centre on lesbian lives (I shall not discuss these texts here for reasons outlined in the preface), and finally because it is organized chronologically. The collection therefore offers in micro, a useful version of historical changes in the representation of lesbians. Starting with Gertrude Stein's 'Mabel Neathe' (1903) and Radclyffe Hall's 'Miss Ogilvy finds herself' (1926), then reading 'Johnnie' (1958) by Joan O'Donovan, 'A step towards Gomorrah' (1961) by Ingeborg Bachmann and ending with Jane Rule's 'Middle children' (1975) provides an enlightening trawl through lesbian images.

Kleinberg describes Hall as a 'sentimental writer ... whose central theme is the tragedy of lesbianism' (p. xiii) (see Chapter 2). This is not quite the case in the pieces of the 1950s and 1960s, which all seem to focus on the issue of uncertainty about sexual identity, to be full of characters who might be lesbian, but either do not know it, as is the case with the first-person narrator of 'Johnnie', or cannot decide as in 'A step towards Gomorrah', thus causing unthinking pain to the lesbian character who desires the central protagonist. All the stories from this period involve male characters, as in Ann Bannon's novels, who are foils and rivals to the (potential) lesbian lover. The possibility of lesbian existence is pitted against heterosexual life and the issue of choice[20] invariably arises. In Helen Essary Ansell's 'The threesome' (1961) making a choice is side-stepped when the desired female love object, Margaret, tries to kill herself as she realizes that sexual desire for her has come between the hitherto 'sexually innocent' adolescent playmates Clover (a girl) and Joey (a boy), described as looking identical. In 'A step towards Gomorrah', the married central character's ruminations about whether or not to engage in a lesbian relationship with Mara take on a complicated form of reported thoughts as Charlotte tries to work her way through what it would mean to live as a lesbian (which she equates with freedom and power, power over others, such as men have over women) and what it means to live as she has done until then (as a 'weak dependent creature' subservient to a man). Predictably, Charlotte is ultimately unable to move out of her heterosexual context, signified by the image of a room full of dead men. In 'Johnnie' the eighteen-year-old first-person narrator is constructed as not really understanding what choices are available to her and therefore moving easily from one person who is offering her attention and affection to another, irrespective of that person's sex.

'Middle children' is very different in this respect, exhibiting a trait typical of Jane Rule's fiction – and one reason why I like her work. In several of her novels, Rule presents lesbians as *ordinary* people living in an ordinary world in which their lives easily fit together and they act as other people do, moving along in the world in predictable and essentially unproblematic ways. The dominant pronoun in 'Middle children' is 'we', standing for 'Clare and I', with which the story opens. In contrast to the conventional short story, which moves towards a climactic turning point in its narrative, often a disastrous one or one with disastrous consequences, 'Middle children' moves on smoothly and without disaster from one stage of development to another, this development being mapped out in terms of the protagonists' gradual maturation from student days to middle age. Much of the equanimity of the protagonists is represented as the result of their being 'middle children' (as in: 'We are both very good with babies. It would be odd if we weren't. Any middle child knows as much about colic ... as there is to know', p. 343) The two lesbians live a fulfilling life integrated into their community, supporting each other and their (heterosexual) friends without any friction. This narrative offers a complete contrast to the conventional short story, a typical example of which is 'The threesome' in which Margaret attempts to kill herself after Clover has declared her love. In 'Middle children' everything remains balanced and that precisely constitutes the surprise effect of this text in which readers' expectations of impending disaster are repeatedly thwarted. It comes as a welcome relief from the desolate narratives of the 1950s and 1960s. One might argue that 'Middle children' offers an idealization of lesbian cohabitation, but the amiable mundanity of the characters' lives is part of the affirmative stance which informed some of the lesbian writing of the 1970s and 1980s.

More common than the publication of lesbian short stories in mixed gay anthologies are collections edited by women, either single-author ones such as Jane Rule's *Theme for diverse instruments* (1975) or *Outlander* (1981), and Ann Allen Shockley's *The black and white of it* (1980), or edited ones such as Elly Bulkin's *Lesbian fiction* (1981) or Margaret Cruikshank's *New lesbian writings* (1984). None of these present their content chronologically. Elly Bulkin's selection seems to be based on the desire to give diverse women's voices a hearing and to represent lesbian peoples in the plural (as the title of Wittig and Zeig's text suggests). But whereas *Lesbian peoples* emphasizes harmony and the similarities among lesbians by offering similar descriptions of various lesbian tribes, Bulkin highlights difference:

> Because so many lesbian writers have reached a stage at which we can *assume* the commonality that stems from our lesbianism, many of the stories are grounded in differences among us. (p. xxxiii)

These differences may be ones of class, race, creed, age, political persuasion but they also relate to form, with different pieces reflecting different oral and literary traditions of telling stories. Most importantly, perhaps, Bulkin explicitly engages with the issue of the readership of her collection, emphasizing the difference which the knowledge of a lesbian readership (assured through texts like this one going to lesbian and women's bookshops) has for the construction of this writing:

> Many of these stories seem to assume the lesbianism (or at least the woman-identification) of their readers: as a result, lesbianism is a given

and various sides of lesbian lives – sexual and otherwise – can be explored, not explained or justified. (p. xxxii)

Margaret Cruikshank, author of *Lesbian studies* and an academic, discusses her anthology in terms of its usefulness in an academic context, suggesting that continuing homophobia or anti-lesbian sentiments in the community at large mean that 'lesbian writing necessarily serves a political and educational purpose regardless of its content, its quality, or the intention of its creators' (p. ix). *New lesbian writing* was put together with a 'lesbian and gay literature classes' audience in mind, but according to Cruikshank,

As I began to gather material I saw a broader potential audience – students taking classes in women's studies, ethnic studies, or contemporary culture, and lesbians and gay men in general. (p. xi)

Thus the question of readership resurfaces – if the anthology is designed for instruction as much as for entertainment, who is being addressed? Who, from Cruikshank's perspective, attends lesbian studies, and will that audience be different from an ethnic studies group? Do lesbians need to be 'instructed' about lesbianism in the same way that non-lesbians might? If this anthology is intended to counter anti-lesbianism, is it for a lesbian audience? The issue of the expected readership gained increasing prominence in the 1970s and 1980s.

Cruikshank's anthology contains both poetry and short fiction, some by well-known writers such as Suniti Namjoshi, Paula Gunn Allen, Henry Handel Richardson and Jane Rule, and others by writers less established. In contrast to *Lesbian fiction*, which is comprised of a range of 'fictional' short stories, quite a few of the prose pieces in *New lesbian writing* are seemingly autobiographical texts, first-person narratives that focus on the narrators' lesbianism and how it affects their work and lives. Despite the fact that many of these pieces (for example Monika Kehoe's 'The making of a deviant' and SDiane Bogus's 'To my mother's vision') deal with lesbians' being refused the continuation of contracts in academe following their 'discovery' or being asked to leave town for wearing inappropriate clothing, they are all, in the end, survivalist and therefore affirmatory. The final lines of Jane Rule's piece, 'Lesbian and writer: making the real visible', are typical for the whole. As she puts it:

I regret the distorting prejudices that surround me... and I can't alone defeat them. They will not defeat me, either as a lesbian or a writer. (p. 99)

One of the most important aspects of *Lesbian fiction* and *New lesbian writing* from a British perspective is that they both register diversity, getting away from the image of the white middle-class lesbian which has tended to dominate the world of novel-writing in Britain (less so in the United States, which has tended to take its multi-culturalism more seriously). Both collections contain writing by lesbians of diverse racial backgrounds such as Audre Lorde, Kitty Tsui, Aleida Rodriguez, Jewelle Gomez to name but a few. The availability of this writing in a British context is very important, as the visibility of Black and Asian lesbian writing in Britain is still very limited indeed.[21] Lorde's 'The beginning' in *Lesbian fiction* focusses on Black lesbian working-class existence, offering a 'biomythography' of a working-class woman who, having lost a lover at sixteen, feels she can no longer afford to get too close to anyone. The piece is written in a realist mode, as is much of the writing in this collection, which offers a contrast to the experimental writing and playing with form which underlies texts such as *Riverfinger women*, *Lesbian peoples* and *Oranges are not the only fruit*, for example.

As suggested above, the 1970s and 1980s saw a growth in the publication of lesbian writing in a range of forms which included not only short fiction but also poetry, again aided by the setting up of lesbian (feminist) magazines. Sappho's poems were republished by Brilliance Books (1984). Josephine Balmer's intoduction makes clear the difficulties which haunt the reading of Sappho's poetry when, as has been the case until quite recently, it is subjected to the eyes of male scholars intent upon imposing value-judgments based on assumptions about Sappho as a woman, as a possible lesbian, as a female writer, as a member of a particular society living at a particular period in time.[22] Adjectives such as 'lesbian', 'Black' or 'Asian' are frequently used to specify the identity of a writer in an effort to vitalize what Foucault calls the 'author function'.[23] It is also important to recognize that these adjectives are often used with the intention of making explicit a socio-cultural relationship involving producer-product-consumer which carries a number of implications concerning power in a particular society, for instance, or issues of identification. Where, however, 'very little is known' (*Sappho*, p. 3) about a writer, as is the case with Sappho, and the writer is unavailable for

77

comment, the focus must surely be on the relationship between text and reader and the extent to which the text, on the basis of what information is available as opposed to what might be conjectured, facilitates certain readings. The critical response then becomes an expression of its period rather than a stab at 'truth'.

Sappho's poetry, much maligned as the introduction to the Brilliance Books collection indicates, for its woman-orientedness, might not have been in fashion in a neoclassical period but its publication by a lesbian and gay press in the mid-1980s reveals the interest in writing that could be read as lesbian and the existence of a relevant lesbian market which would receive this poetry. Its affirmatory stance, expressed in fragments such as 6 ('I tell you;/in time to come,/someone will remember us') and 11 ('Beautiful women,/my feelings for you/will never falter') spoke to the celebratory aspect of the lesbian culture of the 1970s and 1980s.

The use of nature imagery in Sappho's poetry, too, finds reflection in some lesbian writing of this period. Thus Marg Yeo's poem 'To say yes' in *Beautiful barbarians* (edited by Lilian Mohin) resonates with a vocabulary and fragmentation associated with Sappho's work. 'To say yes' opens with 'to say/yes/the explosion of/leaf into/light' (p. 13) – a poem which operates with short phrases, joined through rhythm rather than demarcated by punctuation, utilizing words which, in the main, are simple and monosyllabic when making statements, polysyllabic when moving into explanations.

Part of the assertiveness of this poetry is that it can 'afford' a diversity of voices, can encompass a variety of positions, from Marg Yeo's anxious 'we have to/trust each other we cannot afford to be/divided against/ourselves divided within/ourselves any/longer' ('another love poem', *Beautiful barbarians*, p. 32) to Jackie Kay's 'Yomi's poem' which pitches a past image of what lesbians are like and an incredulity at the possibilities of being a lesbian ('how could anyone be happy/that way touching the very core/of anti-creation how could/... /she feel hot/for she' (*Beautiful barbarians*, p. 45) against a present where the persona has to look at 'my old pictures' (p. 46) in the light of what her lesbian friends are like.

Beautiful barbarians in its title recalls the lesbian peoples Wittig and Zeig imagine, for the final poem of *Beautiful barbarians*, 'A Consummation ...' by Suniti Namjoshi, from which the phrase 'beautiful barbarians' is taken, conjures up a world in which 'the men got discouraged, died out, gave up' and 'the barbaric women' (akin to the amazonian companion lovers of *Lesbian peoples*) 'have taken over' and 'partner each other' (p. 191). The lesbian world presented by *Beautiful barbarians* is, by and large, less beset than its counterpart in *Naming the waves* (edited by Christian McEwen), published two years later, in 1988. The persistence of Thatcherism and the rise of AIDS was beginning to undercut the optimism that had informed some of the earlier lesbian work. In *Beautiful barbarians* only Anna Freud Loewenstein's poem 'Living in the war zone' (pp. 95–6) registers in a sustained manner abuse of lesbians, surrounding this abuse with (predominantly physical) abuse of non-lesbians. The poem culminates in the persona's statement that she 'cannot even be gentle with you/whom I love more than anyone/in the world.' – an expression of the effect that constant exposure to violence towards women has on her.

Naming the waves is a more extensive 'transatlantic' anthology than *Beautiful barbarians*. The editors of both anthologies acknowledge the importance of differences among lesbians having surfaced in the course of the 1980s. Lilian Mohin writes, 'the commonality of purpose (with concomitant fervour and enthusiasm) which characterised feminism in the 1970s isn't evident in Britain in the 1980s.' (p. 7) Christian McEwen is more insistent about this, speaking from the second half of the 1980s and using Judith Barrington's poem 'Naming the waves' in her introduction to underline 'this naming and claiming and celebrating of difference which has preoccupied feminists in recent years' (p. xiii). Describing the 'three most common kinds' of poem submitted for her anthology as 'the right-on-dyke oppression poem, the cunt glorification poem, and the weepy lyrics of abandonment' (p. xiv) which she sees herself as possibly unjustly denigrating, McEwen's final selection strikes me as having as its cental concern 'difference' and 'difficulty' with an emphasis, perhaps, on the latter.

Difficulty comes in many different guises. It can be, as 'Not Speaking, Screaming' (p. 2) suggests, that 'Silence is *the* problem' when, for example, lesbianism is understood rather than named. This is the case in Dorothy Allison's 'Little enough' (pp. 3–4) in which two lesbian lovers talk to an older woman selling her possessions and although the older woman is friendly it becomes clear that 'none of us would say the word, say *lesbian* or even *lovers*' (p. 4). The same theme informs the narrative of Judith Barrington's 'Lesbian' (pp. 7–8) where, again, 'Nobody said *the word*/when the school dismissed two girls' (p. 7) and the persona also 'did not think *the word*/as her hand moved mine to her breast' (p. 8).

Difficulty comes also in the context of definition, picking up on the negative heterosexist stereotypes about lesbians already exposed in Jackie Kay's 'Yomi's poem' and taken apart in *Naming the waves* in Maria Jastrzebska's 'Which of us wears the trousers' (p. 82) and in Caroline Caxton's 'Lesbian' (pp. 30-1) in which she juxtaposes 'YOUR IMAGE' with 'HOW IT IS', contrasting the former ('I open cans with my teeth./I have a domineering mother,/except when I have a domineering father') with the latter ('I am complicated but/ surprisingly average.'). Difficulty can come in the guise of being mother, daughter, lesbian as in Eva Featherstone's 'There were three in the bed' (pp. 42-3), or Marilyn Hacker's 'Mother II' (pp. 72–3). It can present itself in the form of men's abuse of women, as in poems like Pat Parker's 'Womanslaughter' (pp. 144–50) and Minnie Bruce Pratt's 'Walking song II' (pp. 158–63) and 'Not a gun, not a knife' (p. 164). But difficulty becomes a position from which to assert difference and the final poem in *Naming the waves*, 'She grew whole' by Marg Yeo, in its title and in its content suggests the possibility of woman not being the victim of difficulty but of mistressing it instead.

Jewish and lesbian?

This same position is adopted in Evelyn Torton Beck's *Nice Jewish girls: a lesbian anthology* (1982). *Nice Jewish girls* was one of the first anthologies that made explicit multiplicities of identity, including sexuality, race, creed, class, gender. In 'The fourth daughter's four hundred questions' Elana Dykewomon highlights this problematic in her enumeration of difference:

> Yet she does not want to say she is a jewish lesbian separatist because that means she will only be with other jewish lesbians, which is not what she means. She has spent many years listening, hearing, the stories of what it means, how it feels, to be italian catholic in boston, working class irish in new york, dirt poor protestant in maine, middle class chicana in new orleans, catholic puertoriquena ... she is glad to hear these stories, she wants more, she does not want to waste a single flavor, she wants to agree

together on what is bitter and imposed, on what is essential, and what is unique. (*Nice Jewish girls*, pp. 158–9)

Nice Jewish girls highlights the fact that intersecting aspects of self, understood by some as parts of a whole self and by others as self-contained bits struggling for prominence in fact have to be negotiated simultaneously; individuals want to be recognized as, for example, female *and* lesbian *and* Jewish at the same time. As Evelyn Torton Beck, writes:

> I began to understand the limits that the dominant culture places on 'otherness.' You could be a Jew and people would recognize that as a religious or ethnic affiliation or you could be a lesbian and some people would recognize that as an 'alternative lifestyle' or 'sexual preference,' but if you tried to claim both identities – publicly and politically – you were exceeding the limits of what was permitted to the marginal. (p. xiii)

Nice Jewish girls amply demonstrates that each of the two categories 'Jewish' and 'lesbian' needs further qualification, and does not mean the same for all women.[24]

Two prominent interlocking issues repeatedly raised by the various texts in *Nice Jewish girls* are Jewish lesbians' relationship to Jewish history – specifically the persecution of the Jews in fascist Europe of the 1930s and 1940s – and the issue of having children. Thus Dovida Ishatova in 'What may be tsores to you is naches to me' asks:

> But to be a Jew, the daughter of a survivor, and a lesbian? How can that be? With a background like mine, how could I have ever wandered so far from the 'chosen path'? How could I *not* be in a hurry to replace the family that was killed; give you, my parents, the joy of grandchildren, and myself the security of a nice Jewish boy as a mate for life? (p. 174)

Similarly, Susan B. Wolfe writes, 'In spending time with other Jews, I learned that immortality, such as it existed, lay in one's children or the children of one's people.' ('Jewish lesbian mothers', p. 169) The demand on Jewish women to perpetuate their family line (important too because Jewishness is matrilinear)[25] places a stress on Jewish lesbians not necessarily experienced by non-Jewish lesbians. Being lesbian for Jewish women thus involves not only negotiating heterosexism but also the patriarchy and matriarchy of Jewry as well as Jewish history. The result of an alignment to multiple identities is a constant conflict, a conflict illustrated in Irena Klepfisz's work, for example. Discussing 'Resisting and surviving America' (*Nice Jewish girls*, pp. 100–8), Klepfisz maintains that 'I write out of a Jewish consciousness as I do out of a lesbian/feminist consciousness. They are both always there, no matter what the topic I might be working on.' (p. 108) Her article is concerned with the co-opting and corrupting of the memory of the Holocaust through a Hollywood glamorization process which trivializes the actual suffering that went on, the continuity of that suffering beyond the actual phase of the Holocaust, and the fact that 'this hype of the media, of publishing houses, etc. has robbed me of the possibility of really mourning the losses of my life, of even defining them or articulating them properly' (p. 104). In the face of this horror, Klepfisz's question, finally asked three-quarters of the way into her essay, 'So when you ask me to say something about being a Jewish lesbian, what can I say?' (p. 106) seems almost impossible to answer. For her it is in a sense not possible to put the two together, and she has 'not publicized [her] lesbianism in Jewish circles.' (p. 106) Her identity remains split:

> Irena Klepfisz. Oh yes, she wrote those poems about the Holocaust. But you know she wrote those other poems too. Well, we can always pretend we didn't read them. No need to mention them. (*Nice Jewish girls*, p. 106)

And indeed, they exist, side by side, in *Different enclosures*, an appropriate title for her collection of poetry and prose, first published in 1974.

Jewish *and* lesbian, Klepfisz's particular circumstances have made her receptive to poetry which reflects the experiences of alienation and struggle that characterize her life. She writes:

> I still value most a poetry that deals with people, especially those alienated and out of the mainstream – the overworked, and dreamless, Third World, women, gay – a subdued, earnest poetry that expresses their feelings, their struggles, the conditions of their lives. (p. 101)

In the specificity of her identifications Klepfisz may not resemble all other lesbians, but her statement that we look for points of identification in cultural production is important both in terms of the production and reading of lesbian texts. Identification is the key to commonality and many of the texts in *Nice Jewish girls* begin with statements that address the desire for such commonality as reflected in a lesbian readership. Elana Dykewomon, for example, opens her piece with:

> This story is written for lesbians. It is a more or less chronological account of the questions being a jewish dyke has put me up against in life. (p. 148)

Dovida Ishatova begins:

> So what's a nice Jewish girl like me doing in a book like this? Why, flaunting it, of course, and hoping maybe to meet some other nice Jewish girls. (p. 174)

Identity is asserted in a context where that identity is anticipated as likely to be reflected in the readership. Irena Klepfisz writes to the editor, 'I trust you and trust the anthology.' (p. 102)

These expectations of a reciprocal dynamic between producers and consumers of texts illustrate authorial awareness of lesbian communities in the 1970s and 1980s. Out of these communities and responding to the texts that had been and were being produced by and for lesbians, a new body of lesbian criticism emerged with the twofold aim of uncovering a lesbian tradition and culture *and* of critically engaging with that tradition. Among the early works of this kind was Jane Rule's *Lesbian images* (1975) which offered short portraits of twelve lesbian writers of the early and mid-twentieth century and their work, among them Radclyffe Hall, Gertrude Stein, Vita Sackville-West, Elizabeth Bowen, Colette, May Sarton and Maureen Duffy as well as sections on the history of representations of lesbians, and on non-fiction. Rule described her book as 'a statement of my own attitudes towards lesbian experience as measured against the images made by other women writers in their work and/or lives' and as 'an exploration into variety' (preface). The term 'variety' warrants some comment as, looked at from a 1990s perspective, one is instantly aware of the biases of colour, class, and period which inform Rule's selection of authors. Rule maintains that 'the reality of lesbian experience transcends all theories about it' and her notion of 'variety' appears to relate predominantly to differences in attitude and depiction of lesbians among lesbians writers. But her choice of writers seems very narrow now. As she writes in the introduction, she was 'limited by lack of information' (p. 3); in 1975, available material on lesbian writers and their work was still scant. At the same time, 'the popular' had not yet become popular among academics (and Rule was one), so that one could not expect Rule to discuss Ann Bannon's novels, for example, and race and class awareness were in some respects not as pronounced as they are now.

If a bias towards white middle-class writers is a shortcoming of *Lesbian images*, one of the merits of the text is that in its biographical approach it attempts to provide a seriously critical perspective of their work, which offers the reader positions to agree with or dissent from. The language Rule uses is the one of judgement and evaluation typical for literary criticism of this period. Thus she says of Gertrude Stein that she 'wanted to be a middle-class, ordinary, honest genius' (p. 73) and of Radclyffe Hall and *The well of loneliness*, 'The "bible" she offered is really no better for women than the Bible she would not reject.' (p. 61)

The beginning of the establishment of a cultural history of lesbians, of which *Lesbian images* forms a part, was continued by articles such as Catharine R. Stimpson's 'Zero degree deviancy: the lesbian novel in English' (1982), Bonnie Zimmerman's 'What has never been: an overview of lesbian feminist criticism' (1985) and Lillian Faderman's *Surpassing the love of men* (1981) which I shall discuss in chapter 4. All of them in different ways echoed Stimpson's point that 'we have yet to survey fully ... the lesbian writers who worked under the double burden of a patriarchal culture and a strain in the female tradition that accepted and valued heterosexuality' (p. 243), and all of them contributed to the uncovering and reviewing of lesbian writers' work. The emergence of lesbians from the twilight into the limelight in the 1950s and 1960s, and the claiming of a public space in the 1970s and 1980s, led lesbians to develop a culture of their own, discover a cultural history of their own and engage in a criticism of their own. This process resulted, among other things, in the making visible of differences among lesbians. Rule, for instance, wrote:

> For me, the difficulty of being identified as a lesbian writer has not come in the forms one might expect: rejection by family, loss of job, ostracism from the community, or even discredit as a writer. It came from other homosexuals who, living frightened and self-protective lives, were threatened by the quiet but growing candor of our own. (*Lesbian images*, p. 9)

Whether one 'came out' or 'stayed in'[26] could be one source of difference, issues of race, class, and creed, as evidenced in *Nice Jewish girls*, could be others. One thing is clear: in the 1980s especially, lesbians were no longer considering themselves predominantly in their differences from men, as in the 1950s and 1960s, but in their differences from each other. I would suggest that being able to explore this difference was a sign of the growing confidence of lesbian communities, demonstrating a sense of the ability to survive and cope with intra-sexual diversity.

Notes

1 For a discussion of the 'lesbian hero' and use of the word 'hero' rather than 'heroine', see Nickie Hastie's chapter on 'Lesbian bibliomythography' in Griffin, G. ed., *Outwrite*.

2 This response to the 'discovery' of lesbianism in a young woman was famously satirised by Judy Grahn in 'The psychoanalysis of Edward the dyke'.

3 See Joan Nestle's *A restricted country* for a reviewing of the history of lesbian role-play, especially 'Butch-femme relationships: sexual courage in the 1950s' (pp. 100–9) and 'Voices from lesbian herstory' (pp. 110–9).

4 In *Odd girls and twilight lovers* Lillian Faderman offers an explanation of the importance of role-play in the formation of lesbian culture and community identity (esp. ch. 7).

5 The idea of lesbians being imitation males is vigorously contested by many lesbians.

6 Faderman highlights the mistrust younger lesbians felt towards older ones in the 1950s and 1960s (*Odd girls*, pp. 167-72), a feeling given vent to freely by Molly Bolt.

7 See Evelyn Torton Beck's horrified comments in *Nice Jewish girls* (pp. xxiv-xxv).

8 *Riverfinger women* was co-published with *Rubyfruit jungle* (see *Riverfinger women*, p. 191).

9 This argument continues an early-twentieth-century view espoused by Sigmund Freud, for example, that bisexuality is an innate sexual predisposition, displaced either through 'maturation' or social conditioning. (*Three essays on the theory of sexuality*, pp. 52, 57).

10 For a discussion of the issue of labelling of lesbians see Julia Penelope's 'Does it take one to know one?' in *Call me lesbian*, pp. 17–38.

11 Issues of labelling are consistently raised by older lesbians in Suzanne Neild and Rosalind Pearson's *Women like us* (e.g. pp. 25, 71, 88–9). To quote just one example: 'And "lesbian" in the fifties, as I understood it, was just a short back and sides woman, with a waistcoat and I never saw myself like that. And so I didn't identify as lesbian at all.' (p. 91)

12 Rich continues the theme of women in urban settings in *A wild patience has taken me this far*, where in a number of poems such as 'The images', 'Culture and anarchy' and 'For Ethel Rosenberg', she explores how women have suffered from violence.

13 One need only think of titles such as Rita Mae Brown's *Women of evil* (1963), Paula Christian's *Edge of twilight* (1959), Assia Djebar's *The mischief* (1959), Marguerite Duras's *Destroy, she said* (1970), Joan Ellis's *Forbidden sex* (1963) and *The strange compulsion of Laura M.* (1962) or Carol Emery's *Queer affair* (1957).

14 The 'purple-tongued flower' brings to mind Georgia O'Keefe's paintings some of which, such as 'Birch trees at dawn at Lake George', are very suggestive of female genitalia. In the context of *Rubyfruit jungle* and Rich's metaphor, 'Red Canna' and 'Pink Sweet Peas' are particularly relevant images (See Jan Garden Castro, *The art and life of Georgia O'Keefe*, New York and London, 1985).

15 For a recent discussion and re-valuation of 'Compulsory heterosexuality' which reviews these debates critically see Deborah Cameron's essay 'Old het?' in *Trouble & Strife*, 24 (Summer 1992), pp. 41–5.

16 The following sentences, for example, are repeated in a number of descriptions of lesbian tribes:

> Their infants never suckled at their mothers' one breast but drank milk from the mares. 'Milk, honey, blood, raw meat, marrow from reeds' such was the regimen of the ancient amazons who never ate bread, whether of barley, wheat, oat, or rye.
>
> It can be said of the Furies as of other amazons that their daughter empires had an amazonian structure without compromise in contrast to the mother empires. (*Lesbian peoples*, pp. 58–9)

17 Both Dell Richards in *Lesbian* lists (p. 14) and Bonnie Zimmerman in *The safe sea of women: lesbian fiction* 1969–1989 (pp. xiv, 2) comment on the expansion of lesbian cultural production in the last two decades.

18 An interesting account of the 'fate' of one publishing house, Daughters Inc., is provided by Elana Nachman/Dykewomon in her 'Afterword' to *Riverfinger women* (pp. 185–97).

19 Elly Bulkin provides a discussion of the relationship between lesbian magazines and the publication of lesbian short fiction and poetry in *Lesbian fiction* (pp. xix-xxvii)

20 This issue is taken up by Adrienne Rich in 'Compulsory heterosexuality' where she suggests that we live in a society where we are not socialized into making choices concerning sexual orientation but heterosexuality is simply and deliberately assumed to be the norm.

21 Very little lesbian writing by British Black or Asian writers is easily available. Some material by Indian writers like Ismat Chughtai's ('The Quilt') and Afro-American writer Audre Lorde (the 'biomythography' *Zami*) can be found more readily.

22 In his essay 'Believing in fairies: the author and the homosexual' Richard Dyer discusses the importance of identity in the context of gay writing (D. Fuss, ed., *Inside/Out*, pp. 185-201).

23 Foucault's analysis of the significance of the author's name extending beyond its denoting an individual can be found in his article 'What is an author?' in *The Foucault reader*, Paul Rabinow ed. (Harmondsworth, 1984), pp. 101–20.

24 This is highlighted in Josylyn C. Segal's 'Interracial plus' in which she details trying to negotiate her identity in a situation where her mother was 'American Negro/Native American', her father 'Russian/Roumanian Jewish' and she herself comes out as 'an interracial Jewish lesbian', all of which 'makes [her] a target for a wide range of bigotted attitudes' (*Nice Jewish girls*, p. 55).

25 Both Elana Dykewomon in 'The fourth daughter's ...' and Marcia Freedman in 'A lesbian in the promised land' discuss the difficulty of Jewish mother-daughter relationships when one or the other is lesbian; Dykewomon focusses on this dilemma from the point of view of the daughter, Freedman from that of the mother.

26 *Came out, it rained, went back in again* which features Clare Downie and was toured by the Sixth London Lesbian and Gay Film Festival in 1992 offers a humourous look at the whole issue of 'coming out'.

Chapter 4

Daring to dream
– imagining lesbian worlds

Lesbian versus female worlds

This chapter was initially going to be called 'Imagining female worlds' and it was going to focus on women's science fiction. Two things made me change my mind: one was an essay by Sonya Andermahr in which, discussing 'The worlds of lesbian/feminist science fiction', she argues that 'the politics of lesbian feminism and the stress on female community have been central to the development of the feminist SF genre as a whole and thus I have not distinguished rigidly between lesbian and non-lesbian works.' In thinking about Andermahr's decision, and while respecting the choices she made, I realized that for me there was a difference between lesbian and feminist science fiction.

For one thing, and very importantly, lesbian science fiction draws on specifically lesbian culture and tradition which the writers uncover, utilize and rework. Further, there is a difference between the nature and status of the all-female community envisaged in lesbian and in feminist texts respectively. In another essay, 'The politics of separatism and lesbian utopian fiction' (in Munt's *New Lesbian Criticism*), Andermahr distinguishes between 'political' separatism (i.e. strategic, temporary withdrawal from an androcentric world in order to effect change in the position of women) and 'utopian' separatism (i.e. permanent withdrawal from an androcentric world). This seems to me to express the difference between lesbian and feminist science fiction very well. Thus feminist science fiction, such as Zoë Fairbairns' *Benefits*, is based on 'political' separatism; lesbian science fiction, like Sally Miller Gearhart's *The wanderground*, on 'utopian' separatism. This chapter is therefore going to be about 'imagining lesbian worlds' rather than 'female' ones.

What is striking about women's sci fi is that it gained prominence in public consciousness in the context of developments in the field of reproductive technology and genetic engineering, which raised questions about 'the future of motherhood', given the possibilities of 'test-tube babies'. The mid-1980s saw a flood of publications on this issue[1] and it was in this context that the Women's Press decided to launch its women's science fiction series in the spring of 1985.

Since then, the issue of reproductive technology has gradually receded in public consciousness and other concerns such as the sexual abuse of children have come to the fore. In consequence, interest in the depiction of women has moved into other areas, too, such as the detective story or thriller (see Paulina Palmer),[2] and, most recently, the cultural representation of women as violent has been given much space (particularly in mainstream cinema such as *Fatal attraction* and *Basic instinct*). I picked up many of the women's sci fi books I now own in remainder or discount bookshops – an indicator of what has happened to the sales of these books.

On reflecting about the texts I wanted to discuss in this chapter I realized that I wanted to look at books that dealt not only with the future – which is what I tend to associate with sci fi[3] – but also at texts dealing with the past, the history of lesbian communities. Groups who do not control the dominant discourse in their culture always have to uncover and assert both their tradition and their continuity; lesbians are no exception in this respect.

Separatism and the nature of history in the presentation of lesbian communities

A consequence of the emergence of a lesbian nation (see Jill Johnston) and the growth of lesbian communities during the 1970s (see Faderman's *Odd girls*, chapter 9) was the publication of a range of texts looking at female communities constructed on the basis of separatism. On the surface, the idea of all-female communities might seem very daring or dangerous; indeed, Bev Jo has maintained:

> Separatism is a dirty word in the 'women's' and lesbian communities. In my experience, of all the groups of lesbians who exist, separatists are the safest to attack. ('Female only', p. 74)

However, separatism – here taken to mean segregation by sex – is and has been practised in most societies in some form. It certainly exists in contemporary British society in social and cultural formations such as public toilets, women's magazines, single sex schools, hen parties, and gynaecologists. As Marilyn Frye wrote in 1977:

> The theme of separation, in its multitudinous variations, is there in everything from divorce to exclusive lesbian separatist communities, from shelter for battered women to witch covens, from expansions of day-care to abortion on demand. ('Some reflections on separatism and power', p. 62)

Not only are some forms of separatism institutionalized in contemporary society; such separation is also inherent in lesbian existence, which is always at some remove from the dominant heterosexual culture. In so far as such separation is represented through spatial metaphors, there is a longstanding cultural tradition of locating lesbians as separate from others. In the early twentieth century spatial definitions occurred along the evolutionary scale through the designation 'the intermediate sex'; here the others were hetero-sexuals and 'the intermediate sex' was regarded as occupying a point of transition from whence a more advanced human race would emerge (see Edward Carpenter's *The intermediate sex*).

In the 1950s and 1960s spatial metaphors were increasingly registered in novel titles pointing to the twilight, the underworld, the house of shades. This differentiation seems closer to the Greek idea of a transitional space between the underworld and the world above. The underworld is the world of the dead, which in negative representations of lesbians found its socio-cultural counterparts in presentations of the lesbian as infertile, or as a vampire. (See the little-known 'The sisters', by Leonora Carrington.)

The 1970s and 1980s were more optimistic by comparison. Wittig and Zeig poked fun at the death and vampire associations (see BLOOD, CADAVERS and GHOUL – I use upper case as in the original – in *Lesbian peoples*). Separatism was, at least by some, regarded as a form of empowerment for women;[4] the actual living out of female communities[5] was a practical enactment of what such communities might be like. They constituted the development into a lived reality of a sense, illustrated particularly in Judy Grahn's *Another mother tongue*, that lesbians have a culture,[6] a tradition, a way of living and loving which is different from a heterosexual mode because 'heterosexual people have a different mindset from Gay people' (p. xiii). This difference was revalued, regarded as endowing lesbians with special abilities derived, in the case of Grahn's depiction, from the socio-cultural traditions of lesbian peoples.

Reviewing the difference between lesbian and heterosexual existence in texts depicting female communities can take two forms, both of which I shall discuss in this chapter: the re-visioning of the past, encoded in the rewriting of history to make it *her*story, and an envisioning of a future, presented in lesbian/feminist science fiction. Both kinds of texts are grounded in contemporary reality, (see Armitt and Lefanu), take that reality as their starting point from which to envisage difference, usually difference concerning women's situation and setting up a comparison between what it is like today with what it might have been like in the past or what it might be like in the future.

Through their explicit or implicit focus on the relationship of either present/past or present/future, both kinds of texts engage with the concept of history, of social and cultural change over time. Joanna Russ's collection of short stories *Extra(ordinary) people*, for example, has as a framing device an exchange between a tutor (who/which can be turned off!) and a schoolkid. This framing device comes into operation and acts as a bridging mechanism between the short stories. It explicitly begins with a reference to history as the basis for the stories:

> 'Today,' said the tutor, 'we study history.'
> The schoolkid listened.

Then the first story, which delves into the past starts. As Carol Ann Douglas suggests:

> Feminists [and, I would argue, lesbians] have a personal, collective, material, intellectual stake in fundamental change in all aspects of society – change in a feminist direction, of course. (*Love and politics*, p. 105)

According to Douglas, there are two basic ways in which history can be viewed, either as *cycle* or as *progress*, a difference which matters because 'the two historical strategies lead to a different analysis of the present or different strategies for the future' (*Love and politics*, p. 103).

I would suggest that another way of looking at history is in terms of continuity and discontinuity, and that part of the (self-)validation of a community is the sense of a continuity in its history, a continuity that may not necessarily either resemble progress or cycle but may have the function of signalling permanence. This function, I would further argue, is particularly important for those who have no control over dominant discourses and are therefore constantly threatened with impermanence within dominant discourses by being assigned the position of a passing or an intermittent phenomenon.

Another mother tongue: the continuity of lesbian worlds

Establishing permanence in history is, I would suggest, the function of the (re)construction of gay history in Grahn's *Another mother tongue*. This text offers a series of mirrors across time and space in which gay people are reflected and which serve to illustrate their permanent presence.

According to Grahn:

> What gives any group of people distinction and dignity is its culture. This includes a remembrance of the past and a setting of itself in a world context whereby the group can see *who it is* relative to everyone else. (pp. xiii–xiv)

In *Another mother tongue* the lesbian community is thus established through the ways in which it is unique and distinct from other groups.

Grahn sets out to delineate what the gay world is and was like, using three narrative strands: in italics she presents a direct intimate address to her first lover Von, the woman who initiated her into lesbian existence in the late 1950s and early 1960s ('She taught me the words of Gay life; she could not tell me what they meant.' p. 3); Grahn also discusses the history and lifestyles of gays from the 1950s to the early 1980s in part autobiographical, part socio-descriptive terms ('My own life story weaves in and out of other Gay stories' p. xv); and, finally, she uses her knowledge of contemporary gay culture as a springboard for exploring the forgotten or hidden origins of gay customs such as the wearing of rings on the little finger of the left hand and for uncovering a history of gay people, reaching back into pre-Christian times and mythological pasts. Grahn presents this history imaginatively and persuasively, as in her etymological enquiry into the term 'bulldike', a term often used abusively to deride lesbians but which she traces back to Boadicea or Queen Boudica of the Iceni (pp. 134–44) and thus reclaims and re-images in positive terms. Much of this historical presentation is conjectural[7] and thus a way of *imagining* female worlds. The necessity for such imagining is a function of the status of gay culture which is separate from heterosexual culture. Grahn writes: 'Underworlds of all kinds have long been a part of Gay life. Coming out from one world into another is a Gay cultural attribute' (p. 37). The underworld of gays is constructed as the other of the discourse of heterosexuality and therefore has to exist outside that dominant discourse. In consequence, it exists and has to be pieced together from cultural traditions that are 'off the record'.

Grahn attempts to show that contemporary gay culture has its origins in a specifically gay past: 'Gradually I formulated theories that Gay culture is ancient and has been suppressed into an underground state of being...' (p. xiii); therefore,

> Gay characteristics, as we have seen with the drag queen and the bulldike, are far more original to the Gay underground culture than they are imitative of the aboveground heterosexual culture. (p. 145)

Gay people, she argues, have a history of their own; it is the history of those gradually disenfranchised, of female power displaced and extinguished, sent underground by the rise of the Roman empire and Christian dogma, the shift from tribal nomadic existence to settled, landowning stasis and the construction of nation states:

> One Gay pattern common to all modern or 'emerging' nations is the closeting of Gays into an underground society. Apparently this shift from visibility to invisibility happens in the often centuries-long changeover from tribe to village to modern industrial state. (p. 23)

While the gay underground and the heterosexual overground coexist, they do not merely function in parallel:

> Homosexuals ... are not living on the 'fringe'. This is an inaccurate image. The universe, let us say instead, consists of interlocking worlds. Gay culture is always on the cusp of each intersecting world or way of life, on the path between one world and another. (p. 270)

From this position 'the function we so often choose, is that of mediator between worlds. We transfer power, information, and understandings from one "world" or sphere of being to another.' (p. 269). Specifically, 'the Gay function has been to make crossover journeys between gender-worlds, translating, identifying and bringing back the information that each sex has developed independently of the other' (p. 269).

This representation of what Grahn calls 'the Gay function' is very close to 'mission-based' versions of sci fi such as *Startrek Enterprise* or *Voyager*. Indeed, such programmes might have taken that notion from gay culture rather than the other way round, a point which could be extended by considering other attributes of sci fi which frequently involve precisely the issues highlighted by Grahn as important in the context of gay culture: the idea of a separate world, the idea of ritual and custom, the emphasis on different cultures signalled, among other things, through distinctive modes of dress. But where sci fi is, in the main, concerned with the future, Grahn's *Another mother tongue* focusses on the past and the establishment of a continuity between past and present. This continuity, according to Grahn, is maintained by the 'core members' of the gay community who 'keep to the older ways':

> These are its historians and 'true' practitioners, its fundamentalists, traditionalists, and old-timers, the orthodox who retain the dances, chants, laws, festivals, customs, clothing, sciences, meanings. They retain the culture in a continuous line from one century to another, one government to another, one economic state to another, one land to another, even one language to another. (p. 85)

Underlying this representation of 'core members' as guardians of gay culture across time and space is the notion that inherent in gay culture is a universality and transcendence of specific historical circumstances. More than simply testifying to the existence of gays across time and space, Grahn sees them as sharing certain characteristics independent of the specificity of the circumstances of their existence. Thus she writes: 'Gayness involves three levels: same-gender relationship, socially acknowledged function, and mythic/ceremonial dimension' (p. 107). Yet, once Grahn begins to investigate the detail of each of these levels, considerable differences among women emerge. When discussing 'same-gender relationships', for example, Grahn acknowledges that

Within any era, the external appearances of the bond between two women
vary according to what society expects, tolerates, and defines as a bond.
(p. 154)

Thus there is a considerable difference between Grahn's descriptions
of Western role-playing lesbians of the gay bar culture of the 1950s
who lived together as couples (e.g. p. 154–8), her account of a lesbian
friend having a relationship with an Indian woman, 'a member of the
Untouchable caste ... and citizen of a country whose Lesbians say they
are allowed no open expression' (p. 110), an Indian woman who called
her American lesbian lover 'sister' in ways suggestive of familial
bonds (what subtext here), and Grahn's presentation of spinsters
where she maintains, 'spinsterhood is a Lesbian domain, a Gay
office, whether Lesbian sex is acted out or not' (p. 112). All three
examples are freighted with associations of oppression and female
powerlessness as well as lives lived in secrecy. To that extent there are
clearly similarities among them. Indeed, Grahn insists that 'across
cultural lines the *bond* is essentially the same and for the same
purposes – to strengthen the position of women in society, for
instance, to model alternatives to existing forms, and to retain older
traditional forms in danger of being lost' (p. 155). This ignores,
however, that many spinsters, for example, function in isolation from
other women (like themselves) and live without the bond described
by Grahn, and further, perhaps more importantly, assumes too
readily a voluntaristic choice on the part of women concerning the
life they lead. The very real and important differences among
lesbians, among women in general, are eradicated in Grahn's
insistence on similarity which, I would like to add, is not ahistorical
in its impulse but all-inclusive, utilizing history to emphasize
continuity and permanence.

Intra-sexual difference: amazons versus mothers

A different kind of imagining of a female world occurs in Monique
Wittig's and Sande Zeig's *Lesbian peoples* which, like *Another mother
tongue* and as suggested in the last chapter, plays with textual conventions and boundaries – a feature typical of some lesbian writing of the
1970s and 1980s. Here, however, I want to home in on *Lesbian
peoples*'s envisaging of a female world; *Lesbian peoples* takes a sustainedly separatist view of the world, dividing it not between a gay and

a heterosexual culture, but establishing difference in terms of differences between women. Men or the male do not feature in *Lesbian peoples* in which even the sex of animals is specified, with lesbians riding mares and witches turning enemies into wolverines. *Lesbian peoples* thus presents an all-female world without compromise.

Like *Another mother tongue*, *Lesbian peoples* is concerned with the past and its relation to the present. Its dictionary-style, alphabetically organized and eclectic entries offer a narrative of the fall and rise of the lesbian peoples which, in direct analogy to the Edenic myth of the Bible, suggests a nostalgia for a paradisical past, the 'Golden Age' of *Lesbian peoples*. This 'Golden Age', however, is – in contrast to the biblical version – re-enacted in the present of *Lesbian peoples*, the so-called 'Glorious Age'. In the beginning, as the entry under HISTORY tells us

> They were called amazons and they created harmony on earth. This was easy because their world was gentle and good to live in. Work, suffering, death did not yet exist in the terrestial garden. (p. 74)

The destruction of this harmony comes about as a result of the conflict between two groups of women (pp. 35–6), the amazons who wish to continue their nomadic, hunting and gathering existence, and the mothers who decide to settle, discover agriculture, watch their abdomens grow, and develop a static lifestyle:

> The first generation of static mothers who refused to leave their cities, began. From then on, they called the others 'eternal, immature daughters, amazons'. (p. 109)

The conflict between these two groups of women led, according to *Lesbian peoples*, to different lifestyles which are the source of all subsequent ills until the arrival of the 'Glorious Age'. The mothers 'were no longer separate, free, complete individuals and they fused into an anonymous collective consciousness' (p. 76). 'Languages diversified' because 'The mothers modified the original tongue by introducing the sacred into the "meaning", confusing the basic literal sense with their symbols' (p. 78).[8] The division between amazons and mothers led to the amazonian wars:

> Amazons were banished from the cities of the mothers. At that time they became the violent ones and fought to defend harmony. For them the ancient name amazon had retained its full meaning. From now on it signified something more, she who guards the harmony. (p. 5)

In the 'history' entry, the amazons' guerilla warfare tactics are described (p. 77), their 'violence' defended by suggesting that the mothers' pacifist attitude brought about the mothers' enslavement:

> the mothers discussed violence as if one could choose time and necessity for violence. Therefore they were defeated and wore the slave attire for centuries. (p. 159)

It is worth noting that in *Lesbian peoples'* own terms, the amazons do not survive or come to dominate due to their violence but through magic. In 'Separatism and utopian fiction' Sonya Andermahr comments on the differences between 'political' and 'utopian' separatist fiction in terms of their relative stance to political action for which the latter proposes less of a recipe than does the former. This could be regarded as a criticism of utopian separatist fiction. Many of the entries about amazonian tribes detail their defeat in battle rather than their victory (for example entries under FURIES, pp. 58, MEDUSA. p. 106, OREITHYIA pp. 119–20).

Through 'lesbianhood ... the rebirth of amazonian love for one's companion, the last challenge to the destroyed culture of the mothers and its degenerate remnants' (p. 64), change is brought about. The Glorious Age is initiated by the Red Dykes of Gaul (France) inventing a vanishing powder which is taken by half the population (and it is unclear whether this half is men or mothers) at the end of the Concrete Age. This 'caused a double disappearance through which both parties forgot each other, did well and continue to do so' (p. 128). The suggestion seems to be that mothers or men and lesbian peoples still coexist (the former have not become extinct) but without reference to each other.

The Glorious Age is one in which lesbian peoples live in what in many respects seems to be a version of the flower-power era and hippiedom (Grahn suggests that hippiedom depended on gay culture), a return to a quasi-Edenic existence, living in warm climes on islands where they hunt and gather, and where idleness and altered states of consciousness are celebrated. This is a post-industrial, post-technological, post-capitalist utopia where a population balance is achieved through absence of death on the one hand (pp. 43–4) and absence of procreation on the other (p. 121). All lesbian peoples again speak one language (p. 17) and there are no nation states (pp. 36, 113), only tribal, nomadic peoples living in harmony with each other and nature. Words such as 'slave', 'wife' and 'woman' are declared obsolete because they register the servitude into which females fell in the past and to which, in the Glorious Age, they are no longer subject.

Wittig and Zeig's *Lesbian peoples* fits Andermahr's description of the 'utopian' model of separatism in many respects. The utopianism (the word playing both on 'good place' and 'no place') of *Lesbian peoples* is highlighted through its reliance on the magic of the vanishing powder to transport the lesbian peoples into the 'Glorious Age', thus avoiding an engagement with the political dynamics through which social change might be brought about. *Lesbian peoples* does not detail concrete steps towards the achievement of political transformation. Rather, it offers a fantasy of what it might be like to be able to return to or re-establish a mythic amazonian past.[9] Indeed, it is more typical of dystopias – such as in Zoe Fairbairns' *Benefits* or Margaret Atwood's *The handmaid's tale* or, indeed, Suzette Haden Elgin's *Native tongue* – to discuss in realistic terms the moves by means of which the political world is altered, usually to the detriment of women. This change tends to be effected through alterations in legislation, implemented by a largely male-centred government, which move a country from democracy to an authoritarian regime, disempowering women. The context is frequently one of the issue of feminism and reproduction; the occasional subtext, the possibility of (women's) political apathy or exclusion leading to their disenfranchisement. In *Lesbian peoples*, too, women are divided by the issue of reproduction (mothers versus amazons), and although the mothers' disempowerment is related to their pacifism, both amazons and mothers seem to become disempowered, whether they subscribe to violence or not.

Lesbian peoples proposes a cyclical view of history in which the 'Glorious Age' is a replica of the 'Golden Age'. Progress in the sense of 'improvement' does not occur, for the desired end-state is the beginning; however, being able to revert back to the beginning is no guarantee for the permanence of the recovery of the 'Glorious Age':

> [The] conflict [between amazons and mothers] has marked our past in such a definitive way that one could expect this history to repeat itself. The mothers would develop their dream of absolute and totalitarian engendering, give birth throughout the ages, while the amazons would desparately try to find a breach in this reality. (p. 36)

Maternity divides women and is thus the 'enemy'; Wittig and Zeig do not advocate a matriarchy so much as a feminary, a world of companion lovers who do not have to engage with the procreative function. I would suggest that *Lesbian peoples* has to be read as a lesbian fantasy, as the representation of a certain kind of lesbian wish-fulfilment. As such, it is both interesting and entertaining.

What I find disturbing about *Lesbian peoples* is its attitude towards the body and to violence. Violence is considered a necessary part of amazonian survival; its exercise is alluded to in unsentimental terms and the paradox of 'fighting to defend harmony' (p. 5) is accepted unproblematically. The colonizing and imperialist impulses[10] involved in the amazonian wars remain unexamined as does their cost in terms of lives.

Together with this violence against others goes a violence against self, most sustainedly encoded in the amazons' searing off of their right breast. I find uncomfortable associations with mastectomy in this image. The entry under SCAR is of particular concern in this context, as it describes scarring in aesthetic terms as

> Embellishment added to the skin and practiced on its surface or through several layers of flesh by cuttings, burnings, stitchings, puncturings... Many companion lovers have one or several motifs on the body. Some prefer geometrical ornaments... It is recorded that for the ancient amazons the most celebrated scar was the one they had in place of their right breast.[11] (p. 137)

No distinction is made here between the mutilation of the body for aesthetic purposes and the amazons' mutilation of their breasts which was supposedly done 'so that they were better able to use their right arms, especially to throw the spear' (Weideger, p. 244). Both kinds of mutilation seem to me highly problematic as they involve the unnecessary infliction of pain on an individual.

Gender-bending by Extra(ordinary) people

Joanna Russ's *Extra(ordinary) people*, which in its title echoes that of Wittig and Zeig's text, shares with the latter a fragmentation, not into entries but into short stories which together make up a kaleidoscopic view of herstory.

> The kaleidoscopes containing the most diverse materials permit the best compositions. (*Lesbian peoples*, p. 89)

Russ's composition is, indeed, wonder-ful in that she combines five stories, at least three of which were written for separate publication, through a framing device – an exchange between a tutor and a school-kid – which establishes a relationship between herstory, or 'hystery' as Susan Cavin writes it, its presentation in stories, and the saving of the world. This raises the question of what makes the world continue, and what is the function of storytelling in this process.

Russ's five stories, organized in something of a chronological order, each deal with a moment in history, reaching, like a rainbow, from the twelfth century, through the late-nineteenth century, up into the future and then back down again into the present. At the centre of each story is an extraordinary person who might be described as a 'gender-bender',[12] a person who is outside the category of 'woman' or 'man' – not invariably from a biological perspective but always through acting in ways which defy conventional heterosexist gender roles. Indeed, the central story, 'Bodies', focusses on a world, two thousand years on, a kind of post-gender haven, in which the categories 'female' and 'male' have become meaningless except at the level of perform-ance. Russ thus does not construct separatist worlds but presents unconventional women who defy gender roles within settings in which both female and male operate but the distinctions between the two, at least at surface level, are blurred. She shows how cultural and other conventions may be rewritten to highlight a lesbian tradition.

From the point of view of this chapter, *Extra(ordinary) people* is something of a threshold text because it operates a threeway time-scale, dealing with the past, the present and the future, rather than a twoway one which is more common in texts imagining other worlds.

All Russ's stories rely on lesbian culture and traditions. Her first story, 'Souls', presents a character based on the notion of a continuity between present-day lesbianism and myths of fairy-folk (to which Judy Grahn, too, devotes one chapter entitled 'Fairies and fairy queens' in *Another mother tongue* pp. 73–100). In Russ's 'Souls' the origin of the central female character is unknown – like other characters in lesbian texts such as Molly Bolt in *Rubyfruit jungle* she has been fostered. The Abbess Radegunde is described as having 'great gifts', especially powers of healing. She becomes the female ruler and wise woman of her community, 'in every way an unusual woman' (p. 1):

> She was kind to everyone. She knew all languages, not only ours, but the Irish too and the tongues folks speak to the north and south, and Latin

and Greek also, and all the other languages in the world, both to read and write. She knew how to cure sickness, both the old women's way with herbs and leeches and out of books also. (p. 3)[13]

Radegunde herself is not sure whether she is 'a witch or a demon' (p. 43)[14] but she is defeated in body by the invasion of the vikings and in spirit by what towards the end of the story is called 'the new priest' (p. 56). After Radegunde's mystifying disappearance, it is suggested that she belonged to 'the Sidhe, that is the Irish fairy people, who leave changelings in human cradles ... [who are] one of the fairy-folk themselves ... and the other fairy-folk always come back for their own in the end' (pp. 56–7). Radegunde is also associated with matriarchy which is defeated by men. She herself maintains to the Norsemen's leader

> we all want the mother ... You Norse have too much of the father in your country and not enough mother, with all your honoring of your women; that is why you die so well and kill other folk so well – and live so very, very badly. (p. 35)

Here we have the same association of men and violence which is present in Adrienne Rich's poetry, and also the praise of the mother, prominent too in *The wanderground* which I shall discuss below.

Where 'Souls' offers an image of the female protagonist as one of the mythical fairy-folk who are part of lesbian cultural history, 'The mystery of the young gentleman', the second story in Russ's collection, invents a late-nineteenth century 'knowing' invert, travelling on a steamer and making a living by being a professional poker-player. This invert who travels as a man is fully conversant not only with her (heterosexist) society's rules and conventions but also with late-nineteenth century attitudes towards lesbianism – her presentation of the lesbian echoes the somewhat gothic images of lesbians to be found in Krafft-Ebing and Ellis – which she again utilizes to her advantage. Having read Charcot,[15] an early French physician and psychologist, as well as medical journals, 'Joseph Smith', the first-person narrator offering her story in diary form, uses the terminology of nineteenth-century physicians and psychologists when a doctor on board first begins to suspect something:

> Having had, you understand, perhaps ninety seconds to get his first really good look at me, he has put two and two together and got five: *Uranian. Invert. Onanist.* (These are words they make up; you will find them in

medical texts.) It may surprise you that this kind of thing does not happen often, but the division is so strong, so elaborate, so much trained into them as habit, that within reasonable limits they see, generally, more or less what they expect to see, especially if one wears the mask of the proper behaviour. (p. 73)

This is a key passage for understanding the image of the lesbian portrayed by Russ. For one thing, a division is set up between 'them' (which I take to mean heterosexuals) and 'us' (which I take to mean lesbians, and which in the story refers to the directly addressed reader and to the implied reader) whereby the 'they' are cast as having only misguided knowledge which, due to their overdetermined socialization into heterosexuality they frequently cannot use. In addition, the lesbian herself is presented as knowledgeable about herself and others which constitutes a marked contrast to stories about lesbians written at the time this story is supposed to take place. Further on in the story (p. 78) this contrast is additionally highlighted by the lesbian's ironic comment on the notion of 'the "fate" of my "type"', thus indicating the discrepancy between public knowledge and assumptions about homosexuality, and the private reality of the lesbian. Gender is clearly shown as a form of role-play, and indeed, all of Russ's stories in this collection treat the issue of identity as a matter of roles. 'The mystery of the young gentleman' shows how the lesbian, in order to protect herself when in heterosexist society, can use heterosexist gender fixation and prejudice to her advantage by creating a confusion about her identity which allows her to call the shots. The ending, however, also highlights the difficulty of the lesbian living her life in peace: 'Joseph Smith' and his lover-to-be are destined to retire to a far-flung ranch, there to live in social isolation but *'happily ever after'* (p. 92).

The centrepiece of Russ's collection is 'Bodies', a short story set in a future in which biological sex has become irrelevant, though all the resident characters appear to be female. No code concerning sexual behaviour exists, and sexual identity is not immediately discernible from people's exterior as their attire and body traits fuse the conventionally feminine and masculine. Into this world comes a lower-middle-class gay man, James, made from DNA (p. 97) dating presumably from the late twentieth century, whose set to identity is as rigid as the doctor's is in 'The mystery of the young gentleman'. 'James wants to be adored by a real man' (p. 105) and has to come to terms with the first person narrator's explanations:

> "Well, you see, there aren't any men and women, James, not any more.
> No one thinks that way any more."
> I said, "James, it's all different now."
> And then, after a moment, I said:
> "It's been two thousand years." (p. 105)

Just as James has difficulties coming to terms with this post-binary
sexual division world,[16] so the first person narrator has problems –
her longing for James is based on having, through coming from
similar DNA structures, a shared history, however horrible:

> I need your memories and your faults; you'll need mine someday. Come
> back and tell me how rotten it was – but who here knows or cares about
> that? (p. 113)

This epistolary story indicates how a shared history forges a bond,
here between a gay woman and a gay man.

Russ's final two stories, 'What did you do during the revolution,
grandma?' and 'Everyday depressions' also have a first person
narrator and a direct addressee, thus offering intimacy to bridge the
alienness of the context depicted. Both stories are self-referential and
discuss writing as part of a strategy of debunking convention. Again,
both stories deal with gender as *role*. The eerie world of 'What did you
do during the revolution, grandma?', for example, a future earth
'totally consistent, totally determined, and (as it were) totally real' (p.
120), features:

> Fairy Marvin ... six feet four, almost egg-plant colored, with long mauve
> fingernails and silver eye paint... unofficially he uses his intimacy with the
> working of the computer ... to dress in flowered gauze shirts, painfully
> tight pants, and sequin-covered tights... One evening in the cafeteria ...
> he's supposed to have appeared with nothing on but a tiny pair of pink
> gauze wings sprouting from between his shoulder blades, hence the
> nickname. (p. 118)

Fairy Marvin acts as a sidekick to the central, female character who is
asked to 'go into Storybook Land and impersonate an ambassador to
King Shahriyar' (p. 122) which she duly does, having been subjected
to cosmetic surgery and other bodily manipulations to turn her into a
'Lord of the Flies' demon-style figure. In Storybook Land, the narrator
has a series of adventures including being pursued and successfully
seduced by or seducing, the Princess Charlene. To the narrator the

people of Storybook Land become real (p. 128), thus raising the question of precisely what is 'real' and what is 'fairyland'. The narrator also receives messages from Fairy Marvin such as 'we of the Lavender Left understand ...' (p. 128). References to gay culture keep occuring, mingled with references to other cultural forms and formations, both of the supposedly 'high' and 'low' variety. The effect is decidedly anti-deterministic, undercutting all ideas of binarisms and hierarchies of values or truth.

In 'Everyday depressions' a first-person woman writer invents, in a series of letters, a plot for a nineteenth-century-style Gothic novel[17] in which, rather like in Daphne Du Maurier's *Frenchman's creek*, a lady in her spare time pretends to be not a pirate but a highway robber, and is finally united with her faithful maidservant to live a life of retirement and romantic friendship in a remote cottage.

Clearly established as a fantasy, the story ends with the narrator pre-empting a critical response from her reader (see Lefanu, pp. 173–98 for more on this):

> You are right; the book should be full of real politics, – but Oh Susannah, what wishest thou? Marxism-Leninism? Too doctrinaire. Women's Studies? Too respectable. Lesbian separatism? Too unrealistic. The 'women's community'? Too incestuous. Anti-racism? Too narrow. Cultural anarchism? Too crazy. Gay liberation? Too many realtors. Doing nothing? Too bourgeois. Marxist-Leninist academic lesbian feminist socialist culturally anarchistic separatist anti-racist revolutionaries? Too few. (pp. 158–9)

Refusing all alternative clichés, the narrator maintains that 'Middle-aged tolerance is hardly the thing to come to after such technicolored expectations as you and I had!' (p. 160). Her final '&c.' (etc.) is the sign of her continued resistance to definition and categories. No longer sure what will save the world (according to her, none of the above possibilities from lesbian historical romance plots to separatism will), the thing is simply to go on.

Nature and nurture in The wanderground

Where *Extra(ordinary) people* joyfully and ludically debunks notions of categorisation as the answer to all ills, *The wanderground* by Sally Miller Gearhart takes a simpler and more severe as well as binary line on gender relations. The fundamental division in this text is between lesbians and men, with 'gentles' – men who '[touch] no women at all' (p. 3) and appear to be homosexual – featuring on the edges of text (quite literally, in that most references to them occur towards the beginning and the end of the novel), and heterosexual women being completely marginalized. The novel proposes a complete division of the sexes in a context where 'maleness touched women only with the accumulated hatred of centuries' (p. 2) and 'they are no longer of the same species' (p. 124), where men, suffering from the 'madness of power,' are 'driven ... to destroy themselves and [women] and any living thing' (p. 3) because they find it 'difficult or impossible really to share power' (p. 124). In this situation 'the outlaw women [are] the only hope for the earth's survival.' (p. 2)

The wanderground pieces together a present (some time in the indeterminate future) and a past (an exaggerated version of the latter quarter of the twentieth century) in which the outlaws of that past (lesbians and women's liberationists) have become the outlaws of the intratexual present (the hillwomen), gradually gathering strength to 'confront whatever murderous violence threatened the earth' (p. 133). The first part of this confrontation has already been effected through the 'Revolt of the Earth' (p. 140) or the 'Revolt of the Mother' (p. 151) as it is variously called, a phase when natural energies interfered with man-made energies to immobilize and render impotent men outside their own environment, the City. As an idea of how to confront androcentric power, this replicates the magic of Wittig and Zeig's 'vanishing powder':

> As a fantasy or mythic resolution, Gearhart's solution is a stroke of genius; as practical politics, with which the novel does engage, it is a nonstarter. (Sonya Andermahr, 'Separatism and utopian fiction', p. 144)

The dichotomies between the sexes which *The wanderground* sets up reflect the traditional gender divisions of western culture: women are constructed as sharing, nurturant, in tune with animals (especially cats),[18] nature and each other, capable of great psychic and sensory perceptiveness, protective towards each other and those in their care, maternal, emotional, sensitive and respectful of their environment. Male violence against women and a kind of backlash against the rise in women's power (pp. 164–5) eventually resulted in women moving away from men by escaping from the city into the country. The women's return to the country and thus nature signals also their return to life-forms which are tribal, nomadic (significantly their terrain is called the *wander*ground), gathering and nature-determined. In this respect *The wanderground* shares much in common with Wittig and Zeig's *Lesbian peoples* and the envisaging of the 'Golden' and 'Glorious' ages respectively which also celebrated such lifestyles.

Gearhart casts the persecution of women in the past in terms of the persecution of lesbian women and lesbian culture. One of her characters, Bev, recalls the history of that persecution, which is also the history of the development of women into a self-sufficient species. Beginning with 'stories of man-hating separatist women[19] who took off to the country with back-to-the-land-freaks and of vigilante women in the mountains who attacked and disarmed hunters' (p. 164), Bev moves on to recall the various aspects of lesbian culture and autonomy from men which emerged, such as the finding of 'a whole homoeopathic pharmacy', the 'tales of tribal gatherings of women, peyote circles, covens' which led to the 'reemergence of that word, *witch*' and 'the New Witch Trials' (p. 164). When women finally assert (as is, indeed, the case with the hillwomen) that they have children by virgin birth, full-scale persecutions by men ensue. It is worth comparing this history of how a separatist world came about with a similar historical description in Margaret Atwood's *The handmaid's tale*. In their difference lies precisely the difference between the imagining of a lesbian as opposed to a female world. In Atwood's novel, women liberationists, too, are persecuted, and the issue of procreation is a source of contention between women and men, but her characters are not cast as having been lesbians in the 'old world', nor are lesbian cultural traditions such as the links to witches and wisewomen invoked. Further, her central character is and remains a heterosexual female while the one lesbian figure is marginalized throughout. Additionally, when individuals are found out they are unmasked as politicos rather than, as happens to Ijeme in *The wanderground*, as 'dykes' (p. 70).

One of the major differences between *Lesbian peoples* and *The wanderground* is that the former rejects mothers as the 'enemies'; in the 'Glorious Age' procreation does not occur. The latter, by contrast, celebrates the mother, asserting that 'all roads lead to the mother' (p. 46), who is equated with the earth, and dying is represented as returning to the mother. One aspect of the reverence for the maternal is the veneration of older women who are presented as fully integrated into the hillwomen's communities. Older women do not appear to feature in *Lesbian peoples*, where 'age' is used only to denote a historical period.

I find *The wanderground* quite a difficult read. It seems to me to set up a contradiction between the idea of the 'freestanding' individual and commitment to the community. On the one hand, there are sayings like 'There are no words more obscene than "I can't live without"' (p. 4), and multiple mothers which are meant to free the individual from certain oppressive relational ties; on the other hand, there are constant communal events, like the gatherstretch, which involve the submerging of the individual in the community. From my point of view these latter events seem claustrophobic. This may be a function of the vocabulary employed – the prefix 'en-' is used a lot, as in 'enfolding', 'enwombing'. Such words may be intended to suggest loving care and convey a sense of security, but can seem oppressive.

More importantly, I find *The wanderground*'s recuperation of the women-equals-nature proposition problematic. There is an underlying insistence on gender fixity, reiterated later when the 'gentles' also begin to develop their 'non-violent psychic powers' which are however 'linear' rather than 'circular' (p. 193).[20] The implicit insistence on gender fixity in *The wanderground* has, perhaps, to be seen in the context of the period when *The wanderground* was first published (1979). The 1970s were very much a time of the assertion of gender difference along prescribed lines which – within feminism – were re-valued in positive terms. This is precisely what this book attempts to do.

What I find most difficult about this text is its sentimentality. It is, for example, very Victorian in its use of death as a springboard for (moral) pronouncements about the future of the world, and unashamedly tear-jerking. When a dying pony, which has been eyed up as dinner by a large wild cat for a considerable time, breathes its last and sends as its final message, 'I commend my body to my sister, the cat. May she feed well.' (p. 62), I, for one, don't know whether to laugh or cry. Indeed, some of the worst excesses of sentimentality occur in the context of the representation of the relationship between the hillwomen and animals as well as the rest of nature, all of whom commune in harmony. The fantasy of such beneficient anthropomorphism can be hard to swallow.

As, indeed, can be *The wanderground*'s suggestion that women have special psychic powers and sensory abilities. This notion, of course, relates back to evolutionary ideas about the perfectibility of humans, on the one hand, and the idea of gay people as inhabiting a more advanced point on the evolutionary scale, on the other. It also continues the tradition of considering people with special powers as being part of gay history (see Grahn's *Another mother tongue*, chapters 2 and 3). In that sense the book offers a view of lesbian history which is at once progressive and regressive, and thus circular: the hillwomen both advance and 'revert' back to nature, (re)developing their senses in ways that give them the sensory capacity which some animals have; at the same time, their move (back) into tribal, earth-bound existence is presented as progressive, intended to aid the survival of the species.

As in the framing structure of *Extra(ordinary) people*, the question of 'the dying of the earth, the dying of the race' (p. 207) is raised at the end of *The wanderground* and, as in *Extra(ordinary) people*, there is no answer. What the women are left with instead is 'the task':

> *To work as if the earth, the mother, can be saved.*
> *To work as if our healing care were not too late.* (p. 211)

This is at once more optimistic than Russ's 'etc.' which simply points to undefined undirectional continuity, less laconic, but also more sentimental.

Imagining lesbian worlds

The construction of lesbian worlds in women's sci fi and other writing during the late 1970s and the 1980s offered a revision of the genre of sci fi and of how lesbians' relation to the past and future might be textually encoded. In contrast to sci fi produced by/for men, the focus in these texts was on the restructuring of the inner world and on human relations rather than on the refashioning of the outer world through advanced technology. Where men's sci fi frequently sets up authoritarian, quasi-feudal, alien other worlds against which the central figures fight, lesbian sci fi world tends to offer a vision of a world which has recovered communal tribal structures, inhabits a pastoral idyll of sorts, and is concerned with establishing harmonious emotional and sexual ties between women. In her essay 'Is gender necessary? Redux' (1976), Ursula Le Guin offers an interesting discussion of how the feminist movement impacted on her writing by leading her, in *The left hand of darkness*, to envisage a world in which gender operated differently from how it operates in patriarchal society. In particular, and this is where her imaging bears close relation to constructions of lesbian utopias, she noted that the social structures she envisaged were tribal and that there was no war. She also re-imagined sexuality to stop it being 'a continuous social factor' (p. 142).

In the light of developments around reproductive technology, the issue of surrogate motherhood was discussed. This issue was particularly pertinent to lesbian women who had grown up in the 1960s and so were less likely to have children in marriage (as did Adrienne Rich, for example) than many of the lesbians of previous generations.[21]

This sci fi, whether it dealt with lesbian or with female worlds, and in contrast to science fiction by/for men, paid much more attention to female life-experiences, imagining worlds in terms of female rhythms. The chapter 'Diana and the moon' in *The wanderground* is a good example. Quite a few of the novels explicitly deal with the menstrual cycle which is re-valued and celebrated in various ways.

Most importantly in the texts envisaging lesbian worlds, the emphasis is on a revisioning of social relations based on lesbian history and culture. There are numerous references to that tradition in *The wanderground*, from one of the characters being called 'Amazon' by a 'gentle' (p. 195), to the retelling of the Demeter-Persephone myth[22] (pp. 80–1), the use of gay slang as when one character calls another 'baby butch' (p. 95), as well as the casting of women in terms of butch/femme appearances (pp. 66–8), to references to gay bars being closed[23] (p. 91) and to softball teams being discontinued[24] (p. 92) All this constitutes a retelling of lesbian history which records and continues it and this is, perhaps the most distinctive feature and significant function of the texts that project images of lesbian worlds.

Notes

1 The most prominent of these in Britain were, perhaps, the Warnock report on human fertilization and embryology, entitled *A question of life* (1984) and Rita Arditti *et al.*, eds, *Test-tube women: what future for motherhood* (1984). In the same

year Ann Oakley published *The captured womb* and Adrienne Rich's *Of woman born* was reprinted.

2 It might be worth investigating what the correlation between the increase in (reported) crimes against women (domestic and other violence) and child sexual abuse, and the emergence of women as investigators/detectives in popular culture is. The two very clearly come together in Katherine V. Forrest's *Murder at the nightwood bar* (1987), in which a lesbian detective investigates the murder of a young lesbian prostitute who turns out to have been the victim of child sexual abuse.

3 Typical examples, from my point of view, are Zoë Fairbairns's *Benefits*, Doris Lessing's *Memoirs of a survivor*, or Marge Piercy's *Memoirs of a spacewoman*.

4 See, for example, 'Freedom' by Redwomon and 'x-tra insight' by flyin thunda, cloud, rdoc. for statements of separatism as empowering. A wider discussion is offered by Carol Anne Douglas in her chapter on 'Separatism: when and how long?' in *Love and politics*.

5 For a discussion about literary representations of lesbian communities see Bonnie Zimmerman '"An island of women": the lesbian community' in *The safe sea of women*, pp. 119–54.

6 Grahn, like Russ in *Extra(ordinary) people*, and, more recently, Duberman, Vicinus *et al.* in *Hidden from history*, takes an integrative approach to lesbian and gay history, dealing with both; I shall focus on the lesbian aspects here.

7 Maureen Duffy's recent novel *Illuminations* bears a striking resemblance to aspects of this short story; half of Duffy's narrative is concerned with a past very similar to that of 'Souls'.

8 It has to be said that this presents a rather naïve view of language; a different yet dykish view is offered by Julia Penelope in *Speaking freely*.

9 Wittig and Zeig's version of the ancient amazons is very different from Judy Grahn's who, for example, repudiates the idea that the amazons seared off their right breasts (*Another mother tongue*, pp. 165–201).

10 How one interprets the amazonian wars depends, of course, on one's attitude towards war and the subjection of other peoples.

11 For an ethnographic account, see Paula Weideger's *History's mistress*, pp. 244–8; for a refutation of this practice, see Judy Grahn, *Another mother tongue*, p. 172.

12 There is an interesting play by Pam Gems, entitled *Aunt Mary*, which offers a not dissimilar 'gender-bender' scenario.

13 Being able to speak *all* languages is of course the reverse side of Wittig and Zeig's *Lesbian peoples'* speaking one language.

14 Judy Grahn explores the relationship between lesbians and witches in *Another mother tongue*, pp. 275–9. In Sally Miller Gearhart's *The wanderground*, the lesbian women finally decide to leave the city and men when new witch trials are conducted.

15 Elaine Showalter discusses the work of Jean-Martin Charcot in *The female malady*, pp. 147–55.

16 For a recent discussion of binarism in sexual identity and its discontents see Judith Butler's *Gender trouble*.

17 In 1991 The Women's Theatre Group toured with a play by Bryony Lavery, unpublished to date, entitled *Her aching heart* which was described as a 'lesbian historical romance' and played with conventions of the nineteenth-century romance plot in ways not unlike 'Everyday depressions' does.

18 Cats as important animals to lesbians – and one might consider the tradition of witches as having cats as familiars in this context, too – are also celebrated in *Lesbian peoples*, where they warrant a separate entry (p. 28).

19 Issues and expressions of man-hating are frequently raised/occur in the context of separatism in which women, for very good reasons, have decided to withdraw their energies from men and invest them in women only. See, for example, Hoagland and Penelope, pp. 227, 268–73. In *Between friends*, Gillian Hanscombe delineates a character, Jane, who starts with a man-hating position and then has to examine her separatist stance when she falls in love with a lesbian who has a son.

20 A theoretical framework for this differentiation between female/circular and male/linear in cultural production is offered by Julia Kristeva in her analysis of the genderization of language use (*Desire in language*, pp. 124–47).

21 Both in Suzanne Neild and Rosalind Pearson's *Women like us* and in Marcy Adelman's *Long time passing*, there are many examples of older lesbians who started their adult lives with marriage and children. Indeed, in their article 'Lesbian history and gay studies' Rosemary Auchmuty *et al.* report that in a mixed gay and lesbian studies class – in contrast to the men – 'most [lesbians] had experienced heterosexuality, many had been married and several had had children within marriages' (p. 94).

22 *Lesbian peoples* (pp. 41, 42) and *Another mother tongue* (pp. 33–5), too, reclaim this myth as a basis for considering the nature of mother-daughter relationships and their original love relation.

23 On gay bars in the 1950s, see Grahn, *Another mother tongue*, pp. 28–33, Faderman, *Odd Girls*, pp. 161–6, and Katie King's *'Audre Lorde's lacquered layerings: the lesbian bar as a site of literary production'* (in Munt, ed.).

24 In *Another mother tongue*, Grahn mentions the importance of softball teams as a meeting ground for lesbians (pp. 153–4).

Chapter 5

The new romanticism, or the celebration of friendship

The rise of feminism and gay liberation in the 1960s and early 1970s promoted the exploration of women's relationships with each other through highlighting the differences which exist among women. Issues of generation in the form of explorations of mother-daughter relationships,[1] of race,[2] of class[3] and of sexual orientation[4] all became subjects of vigorous discussions.

One of the effects of this growth of interest in women's relationships with each other was the reviewing of representations of friendships between women, both in terms of what they revealed about women's emotional bonding and their potential sexual bonding. As Liz Stanley describes it:

> Like other strands of feminist history, it involves partly the recovery of this 'lost' aspect of women's history and partly the reconceptualization of such friendships. ('Epistemological issues', p. 161)

The two books that were and still are sustainedly discussed in this context are Marilyn French's novel *The women's room* (1977) and Lillian Faderman's *Surpassing the love of men: romantic friendship and love between women from the Renaissance to the present* (1981). I shall not discuss the former which is a very interesting novel in its own right, because it forms part of a twentieth-century tradition of predominantly hetero-oriented fiction on female friendship which in-

cludes novels like Mary McCarthy's *The group* (1963) and Fay
Weldon's *Down among the women* (1971) as well as her *Female friends*
(1975). I would like to concentrate on Faderman's text, on which I
wish to take a slightly different angle from the one often taken.[5]

It seems to me that one of the elements that tends to be missing in
the discussions of *Surpassing* is the socio-political context in which
that book was written. One can, of course, argue that this text was in
one way or another a product of the women's and gay liberation
movements' impact on how women conceptualise themselves, an
argument which I would support. But that appears to me to be an
insufficient explanation for why from the second half of the 1970s
onwards and through most of the 1980s a number of books on
female friendship appeared. What I therefore propose to do here is to
discuss four non-fictional texts on female friendship to indicate the
different ways in which such friendship was written about, and to
show how ideas on female friendship changed over time and how
they related to the socio-political realities of the day. Juxtaposing
these texts with some of the lesbian fictional writing on female
friendship (which is distinct from the women's writing on this subject informed by hetero-bias as *The women's room*, for instance, is),
suggests that there is a dichotomy between how non-fictional and
fictional writings represent female friendships. This difference needs
to be accounted for.

Communities of women *according to Nina Auerbach*

One of the first non-fictional texts on female friendship in the post-
second-wave feminist era was Nina Auerbach's *Communities of
women* (1977) which focusses mainly on nineteenth-century writing
by women and men (Jane Austen to Henry James). Auerbach attempts to unravel a history of representation of female communities
from classic Greek mythology to the present. Her opening sentences
indicate the framework for her investigation:

> Initiation into a band of brothers is a traditional privilege symbolized by
> uniforms, rituals, and fiercely shared loyalties; but sisterhood, the subject
> of this book, looks often like a blank exclusion. A community of women
> may suggest less the honor of fellowship than an antisociety, an austere
> banishment from both social power and biological rewards. (p. 3)

Here 'brothers' take precedence over 'sisters'; female community is defined negatively against and in opposition to male fellowship. Men are at the centre, women on the margins. Auerbach begins as she means to go on. When discussing amazons, she states:

> In Greek folk etymology, the community's name immortalizes its defect, not its strength: with more meaning than accuracy, common tradition gives the derivation ά+μαζός, 'without a breast,' reminding us that these mythic warriors sliced off their right breasts in order to shoot more effectively. (p. 3)

Both amazons and the Graie, 'three mythical sisters who are isolated from time' (p. 3), are described as 'communities of women without men, and, as such, they are seen immediately as mutilated', as 'outcast', lacking, in the case of the amazons, 'womanly biology' (p. 4). Amazons and Graie are contrasted by Auerbach with the three Muses and the three Fates who she sees as symbolizing power over men. Auerbach sees a development in the representation of female communities from the former to the latter:

> A triad of sisters begins as an image of maimed and outcast pathos and ends as a unity of force neither god nor hero dare invade. (p. 5)

Auerbach maintains that 'This corporate and contradictory vision of a unit that is simultaneously defective and transcendent forms part of all the novels this study will examine' (p. 5). She cites Charlotte Wolff:[6]

> The effect produced by a group of women alone is different from that of a group of men alone. Women by themselves appear to be incomplete, as if a limb [or is it 'a member'?] is missing. They do not come into their proper place and function without the male. (p. 7)

Granting that 'mutilation may be in the eye of the beholder', Auerbach offers a critique of Wolff's claim that only lesbian communities have the integrity of 'a group of men alone' and that 'by herself, a heterosexual woman can constitute only a sexual plea'. At the same time, she denies the fictional construction of lesbian existence in the texts she analyses by asserting:

> Yet though lesbianism is a silent possibility in two or three of the novels discussed, in no case is it an accomplished fact bestowing on these communities extrinsic power. Their strength is inherent, though rarely initially apparent. (p. 7)

I quote these sections at length because they indicate the flavour of Auerbach's text. Auerbach's communities are constituted of hetero-sexual women. Her comparison is hetero-oriented, distinguishing between male and female community. This intersexual differentia-tion, as indicated in the previous chapter, formed a fairly common basis for analysis in the late 1960s and early 1970s. It is sustained throughout this text, which ends with a detailing of the ways in which the formation of fictional and actual female communities in the twentieth century has relied on and exploited (in Auerbach's view) war between men and male aggression, against which male and female writers have posited a female community-centred alternative. This alternative world, so Auerbach argues in her final chapter, is called into existence and sustained by masculine violence (pp. 162, 182). The implication appears to be that once such violence disap-pears so will female communities. When Auerbach quotes Elizabeth Janeway, she seems to me to offer a gloss on her own position:

> Locked out of the larger community of a man's world, women and homo-sexuals develop profoundly ambiguous feelings about any sort of commu-nity they may set up themselves. Both groups are notorious for tight but short-lived cliques and bitter personal rivalries. Cattiness and disloyalty are expected, and cattiness and disloyalty are found among all those who regard part of themselves as unacceptable. (p. 12)

For Auerbach, communities of women are and remain 'odd'. She suggests this is because 'we lack an agreed-upon common denomina-tor of womanhood' (p. 31); I would suggest it is because Auerbach is mourning what she regards as the proper sphere of women which, it predictably turns out, is the middle-class myth of the private sphere. Auerbach never questions conventional views of femininity. She of-fers the following dichotomies in her representation of 'women to-gether': are they 'a new woman's colony or a new wives' training school? The shrieking sisterhood or the holy sisters? A corrupt knot of inferior creatures or a charmed circle of selfless purity?' (p. 29) In nineteenth-century representations, says Auerbach, female commu-nities tend towards the latter, in twentieth-century ones they are (again) the former. Twentieth-century women's communities, with their incorporation of 'a dimension traditionally denied to women – the violence of history and religion', supposedly 'complete the de-struction of the woman's world as a haven of separate, cherished values' because

The autonomous and self-sustaining communities of nineteenth-century women, perforce cooperative because deprived of outside reality and power, lose focus and perfection with this acquisition of previously masculine territory. (p. 182)

Critiquing Ti-Grace Atkinson's *Amazon odyssey* (1974) Auerbach asserts:

Love, pregnancy, sex, and madness, those dear constituents of the private female world, are forcibly yoked to public, political life, leaving us stranded in the reality of our century, free from any womanliness into which to retreat. (p. 190)

The tenor of Auerbach's statement here as elsewhere is difficult to gauge; speaking of 'pregnancy' and 'madness' as the 'dear constituents of the private female world' seems hard to take as other than ironic commentary, yet the overall impression of this book is that it turns a nostalgic gaze upon a past where women knew their place which was private, outside history, selfless and serving. When Auerbach talks of Simone de Beauvoir's *The second sex* as offering 'a prescient warning against the lure of separatism' (p. 183), and speaks of 'conventional female duplicity' (p. 167), her writing becomes misogynistic. This misogyny is, I would suggest, the misogyny of a hetero-bias which uncritically assimilates and replicates stereotypes of femininity, translating these into statements such as '[women's] autonomy and their solitude are not institutionalized, but inward and unexpressed' (p. 32). Femininity and masculinity remain unexamined here. Auerbach's point that 'Since a community of women is a furtive, unofficial, often underground entity, it can be defined by the complex, shifting, often contradictory attitudes it evokes' (p. 11) might be describing her own response as evidenced in this book. Both the 'hope' and the 'horror' she ascribes to Victorian views of sisterhood (p. 14) shape her own text.

Communities of women is an interesting and complex text; it also needs to be seen as an expression of a particular historical period and ideological position: it looks backwards to the nineteenth century, when – it is assumed – heterosexuality and heterosexism were uncritically taken to be the norm,[7] thus allowing statements such as the amazonians being 'implacably remote from everything that normally constitutes the human condition' (p. 4), and it does so in a context when this gendered view of the world has begun to be questioned. This questioning finds its expression in the investigation of communities of women *as such*, the interpretation of their meaning and significance, however, resists a woman-centred view.

Female friendship in literature as read by Janet Todd

In Auerbach's text women come at least in threes (e.g. the Muses, the Fates) – as a threesome they seem to constitute a *community*. Janet Todd's *Female friendship in literature* (1980) focusses on twosomes, pairs of women forming friendships. Where Auerbach's work centred on the nineteenth century, Todd deals with writings of the eighteenth and early-nineteenth century. Like Auerbach's book, hers has the virtue of placing women centre-stage and of highlighting the different kinds of relations women may experience with each other. She distinguishes between five different kinds of friendship: the sentimental, the erotic, the manipulative, the political, and the social. Such categories can, of course, only be provisional and Todd herself suggests that they are constructed 'to order, not to cramp' and that the texts she discusses 'fail to fit neatly into any one of them' (p. 3). It is therefore interesting to consider which texts she analyses under what category and I shall confine myself to brief comments on two categories here, the 'erotic', which has obvious implications for representations of lesbians,[8] and the 'political', because of Todd's choice of placing Mary Wollstonecraft's *Mary, a fiction* in that category. While Todd recognizes 'erotic' friendship between women as a significant category, she writes about it from an androcentric, hetero-biased viewpoint.

Todd selects only male writers for her first three chapters, offering a discussion of John Cleland's *Fanny Hill* and Denis Diderot's *The nun* as representations of erotic friendships between women. Todd writes:

> Erotic friendship requires physical love. Cleland's *Fanny Hill* exemplifies it with Fanny and her sexual mentor Phoebe, although her other female relationships are simply social and supportive. (p. 4)

The point Todd makes here is significant: Fanny has only one erotic relationship with another woman, the purpose of which, as Todd indicates, is to initiate 'Fanny into sexuality and autoeroticism' (p. 81). In her examination of the text, Todd does not place it in its context, does not consider the issues either of author or readership, or indeed, as she promises in her introduction, the 'ideology' which informs Cleland's text. Her separation of the discussion of her chosen texts from 'the literary and biographical context' which forms part two of her book is, in this respect, unfortunate. As a consequence there is no critique of the patriarchal, heterosexist viewpoint which informs *Fanny Hill*. Todd is content to make statements such as 'Female intimacies are necessary for women who are learning success, but for women who have learned all and achieved success, they are detrimental' (p. 75). When she writes 'through Phoebe, Fanny comes to value herself as a sexual object' (p. 82) and 'Phoebe herself realizes that only men can give value and purpose to Fanny's beauty' (p. 83), Todd replicates without critical commentary those patriarchal attitudes towards women which deny women meaning except in (hierarchical) relation to men. She maintains that only *male* authors in the eighteenth century write about lesbianism and that:

> Lesbianism, erotic female friendship, enters the novel to shock, disgrace, or titillate, severed on the whole from any emotional concern. Women have seldom written erotically about women in any age before this one; conditioned as objects of love, they were ashamed to appear its subject, abashed by aggressive love itself, whether for man or woman. In addition, in the eighteenth century women authors must have recoiled from depicting a state that could so easily implicate themselves. A male author like Cleland might tease with lesbianism; a woman would be indicted. (pp. 412–13)

The comments at the beginning of this quotation suggest a rather narrow definition of 'the erotic', which is here – I think – taken to mean hetero-pornography, based precisely on the division of the emotional from the erotic Todd ascribes to Cleland's depiction of erotic female friendship.

From my perspective, a much more obvious and gynocentric textual candidate for the category of 'erotic friendship', in which the emotional and the erotic are conjoined, is Mary Wollstonecraft's *Mary, a fiction*, interestingly placed by Todd under 'political friendships'. Written by a woman and in overt refutation of conventional sentimental depictions of heroines in the fiction of Wollstonecraft's day, *Mary* delineates the relationship between two women, Mary and Ann, in terms which, from the 1990s, one might describe as lesbian. Todd characterizes the friendship as political because 'political friendship requires some action against the social system, its institutions or conventions' (p. 4). In her resistance to the cohabitation 'required' by her marriage as well as in her caring for Ann, Mary displays such action. This resistance is based on Mary's utter revulsion at male sexuality. The text suggests Mary's father's sexual abuse of both his female tenants and her mother as one reason for this revulsion. Seeking a love relationship that will not lead to her objectification and debasement, Mary fastens on Ann who becomes her emotional and physical focus. Their relationship is, in some respects, not unlike the lesbian relationship depicted in Radclyffe Hall's *The well*, with Mary acting as Stephen to Ann playing Stephen's feminine, dependent, ultimately heterosexually-oriented lover Mary.

Todd emphasizes Mary's resistance to marriage and conjugal sex at the expense of the emotional/erotic bond between the two women. She acknowledges this bond in her discussion of the text but nonetheless fails to see it as central. This seems to me to be an expression of the hetero-bias which informs her writing. The emotional/erotic bond between women constructed by a woman is, of course, much more threatening to patriarchy than Cleland's representation of lesbian relations in the context of pornography by/for men and its implicit assumption that lesbian relations set women up for their heterosexual destiny. In *Women's friendship in literature*, Todd confirms patriarchal views of women's friendship. I shall return to the reasons for this below.

Challenging patriarchy through surpassing the love of men?

While Todd considers erotic lesbian friendship as *one* type of relationship women might engage in, Lillian Faderman's focus in *Surpassing the love of men* (1981) is on lesbian relationships and how they were constructed and understood 'from the Renaissance to the present'. Faderman's work has been condemned for describing women's relationships with each other as 'romantic friendships' which were 'love relationships in every sense except perhaps the genital, since women in centuries other than ours often internalized the view of females as having little sexual passion'. (p. 16) *Surpassing* sets up the question:

> [U]nder what circumstances and using what kind of historical evidence is it possible to specify, one way or another, whether women's close and loving relationships of the past were romantic friendships or involved erotic/sexual behaviour? (Stanley, p. 162)

Indeed, it raises, more fundamentally perhaps, the question of how we define 'lesbian'. In terms of the definition of lesbian as signifying women's sexual commitment to each other, Faderman's writing has been criticized, as she includes under the term 'romantic' discuss-ions of relationships, the sexual component of which is difficult to assess.

In its title *Surpassing* offers a triple transcendence: the verb has Christian (and thus spiritual) connotations, associated with the 'love' – God's – which, so the saying goes, surpasses all understanding; 'men' can be regarded as referring either to 'males' or to 'human-kind'. What lies beyond the love of men and mankind is 'romantic friendship and love between women' with the second point here being of special importance since, contrary to Liz Stanley's critique of *Surpassing*, I would argue that Faderman is more tentative and subtle in her arguments than she has been credited with. Her point, for instance, that the major difference between romantic friendship and lesbian love has 'much less to do with overt sexual expression than with women's greater independence in the twentieth century' (p. 20)[9] strikes me as a valid one, and one that needs to be taken into consid-eration when discussing the depiction of relations between women. Faderman argues at various points in her text (e.g. pp. 48–9, 371) that friendship between women including sex is no source of threat to patriarchy *unless* it is accompanied by women making inroads into supposedly masculine spheres, that a reaction occurs where women seem to appropriate men's prerogatives. (This is, of course, what is argued in Faludi's *Backlash* and French's *The war against women*.)

Within a middle-class context such an appropriation is more sus-tained in the twentieth century than in the nineteenth, and in conse-quence the discrediting of female friendships by men through the imposition of medical and pathological frames does not seem illogi-cal. Faderman also does not seem to me to assume, as Stanley sug-gests, that 'women's relationships and behaviours have a meaning which has remained constant over the last 200 years or more' (p. 169). Rather, she attempts to document changes in how these rela-tionships were constructed and perceived over time. Stanley suggests that Faderman 'romanticizes the past by constructing a lost age of innocence, a time before patriarchal oppressiveness in the work of Victorian/Edwardian sexologists invented 'lesbianism' as a sexualized mannish stereotype and imposed it on passionate friendships between women in order to condemn them.' (p. 163) I would argue that Faderman highlights the 'ignorance' that existed in the nineteenth century and prior to that time about how women might engage erotically and genitally with each other to their satisfaction (e.g. ch. II/1, 'The asexual woman', pp. 147–56).

Gyn/affection and lesbian continuum

I want to look briefly at the perhaps most radical text on female friendship of the 1980s, Janice Raymond's *A passion for friends* (1986).

Raymond vigorously asserts that 'women together are not women alone' (p. 3); she re-visions women's relations with each other:

> It is not my intention to essentialize, romanticize, sentimentalize, or glorify female friendship. It *is* my intention, however, to represent part of the history and vitality of women's friendships and to speculate about the power of friendship in women's lives. (p. 20)

Implicit in the disawoval of 'romanticizing' female friendship is an acceptance of the critique levelled against texts like *Surpassing*. Nonetheless, there is a shared project of recovery and, more than that, a recognition, common to all the texts so far discussed, that female friendship can take a variety of forms and has a history which is recoverable. *A passion for friends* distinguishes between 'gyn/affection' and 'lesbian be-ing' in a pronounced fashion. Gyn/affection is defined as the 'personal and political movement of women toward each other' (p. 8), expressing, so Raymond states, 'a *continuum* of female friendship' (p. 15). The idea of such a continuum constitutes an analogy to Adrienne Rich's lesbian continuum. However, 'lesbian' for Raymond 'connotes a knowledge of and will to affirm Lesbian living' (p. 18). For Raymond there is no continuum between gyn/affective female friendship and lesbian existence. In her view there is a discontinuity or leap from gyn/affection to lesbian be-ing. Raymond writes that 'the content of this leap' is 'extremely difficult to characterize' (p. 17) but, from her point of view, it has to do with making a choice to live an existence which involves risks, due to the negative attitude towards lesbians in our society. (See S. Kitzinger's *Woman's experience of sex*, pp. 102–3.) Contrary to the early-twentieth-century sexologists' views (and to positions similar to theirs expressed in some lesbian writing that lesbianism is innate) she takes the line that 'women are not born Lesbians. Women become Lesbians out of choice.' (p. 14) In the essentialism versus relativism debate Raymond comes firmly down on the side of the relativists. In consequence, much of *A passion for friends* adopts a voluntaristic attitude towards the issue of female friendship. Raymond discusses women who appear to her to have made a deliberate choice to lead a gyn/affective existence – such as nuns, and marriage resisters in China.

Raymond also analyses at some length the obstacles to female friendship in what she terms *hetero-reality*. With reference to the psychoanalytical work of authors like Nancy Chodorow, Raymond suggests that it is not women's relations with each other that are transgressive, as is frequently asserted in hetero-reality, but women's relations with men. For, whereas female friendship provides a continuity to women's first relationship (with their mother), relations with men disrupt that primary bond and are established and maintained at a cost both to the female self who is subjugated and contained and to her relations with other women:

> As women regain our autonomous history with each other, we must also realize that hetero-reality is the real discontinuity and transgression in women's lives and friendships with each other. Male bonding and male bondage of women have disrupted the course and current of the history and culture of gyn/affection. (p. 47)

Raymond wishes to establish that 'the explanation for Gyn/affection is not hetero-relational deprivation, as the psychologists have theorized; it is the independent wealth and attractiveness of female friendship' (p. 47). She does so by considering a number of what she describes as 'loose women', women who are 'loose and free from bonds and bondage to men' (p. 64) and thus 'repudiate containment by men' and 'frustrate the traditional categories of hetero-reality (wife, mother, mistress, and so on)' (p. 65). Like Faderman, Raymond sees women's striving for independence from men as the reason for male desire to 'tame' women who are 'loose'. Women's (sexual) possession of the self, as manifested in the refusal to submit sexually to a man as well as all other forms of 'ownership' in women becomes a source of male antagonism. Raymond details how the contributions women have made to their society (nuns preserving culture; female silk-workers sustaining families) have frequently resulted in retributions from men who considered their roles to have been usurped by these independent women. Her ultimate plea is for the need to maintain a vision of female friendship which includes the unity between theory and practice, thoughtfulness, passion, worldliness and a promise of happiness in order to move towards a more sustainedly gyn/affective world.

Why celebrate female friendship in the late 1970s and 1980s?

The period in question is that of Thatcherism, with its concomitant rise of the New Right, the new Puritanism which reacted against the supposed sexual liberation of the early 1970s, and – most importantly here – a new pronounced investment in 'the family'. As Michéle Barrett and Mary McIntosh maintain in *The anti-social family*, first published in 1982:

> The early years of women's liberation saw a damning indictment of family life;[10] more recently the left has had to confront the equally militant pro-family stance of the new right. (p. 7)

Barrett and McIntosh argue that 'the continual evocation of the family in Thatcher's pronouncements does not mean that the government is pursuing a straightforward policy of "getting women back into the home"' (p. 12). This is supported by the emergence of the image of 'super-woman', the woman who manages both home and career. Significantly, she comes in the singular, not with female friends. Women's work, including middle-class women's work, once perceived as being '(in) the home', becomes increasingly necessary outside the home as well to maintain and advance standards of living in what initially appears to be a booming economy. The paradox of wanting women back in the home, and also needing them on the general labour market is resolved, I would suggest, by a process of familializing society, that is by endlessly reproducing an image of the family 'characteristic of the nineteenth-century bourgeoisie' (*The anti-social family*, p. 33). The stereotypes governing that family image recur in all political and economic spheres, ranging from projecting heads of state as family wo/men to the dominance of women in service industries. This familialization of society includes the regulation of sexuality; only certain kinds of sexual expression are considered permissible within the nineteenth-century bourgois family, here taken to be the transcendent model. If all of society is conceived of in terms of analogies to the bourgois family, then it is as if, even when the woman goes out to work, she never actually leaves the home and the role she inhabits within that home is 'simply' transferred onto all other situations.

I would argue that the familialization of society during the Thatcher years finds its expression in the writings on female friendship of the 1970s and 1980s. What is striking about these writings is that they focus on *friendship* rather than on sexual relations between women. Auerbach's *Communities of women* overtly recreates stereotypes of femininity associated with the family politics of heteropatriarchy through endorsements of notions such as 'the female world [being] a sheltered shared enclave whose values are private and unique' (p. 190) and 'women would be able to solve the problems of city government because the efficient management of urban affairs [involves] generalizing the skills of housekeeping which [are] exclusively feminine skills' (p. 27). Todd, too, invokes heterosexuality and the family when she writes:

> Because friendship is marked socially by the romantic plot and structured historically by the first female tie, I am also touching on the heterosexual and parental relationships. (p. 1)

When it comes to erotic friendships between women, the only texts she can find that fulfil her category are two pornographic and misogynistic texts, both by men.

Faderman moves away from the sexual in some of her work, considering 'romantic' friendships, the asexual woman and 'kindred spirits', but also 'Boston marriages' (and it's the term which is significant here). Starting from a sense that 'most of the female romantic friends that I was studying probably did not have sexual relationships' Faderman asks 'Was that then the primary difference between romantic friendship and love?' (p. 17) and seeks to discover 'why were [romantic friendships] so readily condoned in earlier eras and persecuted in ours?' (p. 19) Her answer is, in part, that romantic friendships in themselves were not perceived as threatening to and by men. Raymond, perhaps the most radical writer on female friendship discussed here, asserts the importance of women's friendships while at the same time pointing to the benefits heterosexist society derived from such bonds. Thus she describes how in China *pu lo-chia*, 'women who were forced to marry but who did not consummate the marriage or cohabit with their husbands ... often incurred long-term economic obligations to their extended conjugal families' (pp. 130-1).

The overall impression from these texts is that of a history of female friendships in which women's relationships with each other operated predominantly on an emotional rather than on a sexual level, where female friendship was considered non-threatening to patriarchy provided women did not seek to extend their powers beyond the conventional 'feminine private sphere' but where, if they did extend their powers beyond that frame, it could be 'justified' in terms of the utility value for hetero-society at large. In so far as these texts include discussions of lesbian relations (and this occurs on a sliding scale, with Auerbach's and Todd's works being the least and Faderman's and Raymond's being the most concerned with lesbian relations), it is as if these texts document a familialization of lesbian relationships in which the sexual element is played down (sex between women not being 'permissible' within the family) and the emotional and utilitarian aspects are emphasized. Women's striving towards autonomy (from men) which was one of the dominant concerns of late 1960s and early 1970s women's liberation is here reworked as an entry into a politically deflated sisterhood which works as a support unit for women while remaining firmly in its 'feminine' place and thus not offering much of a threat to either men or patriarchy. What Barrett and McIntosh maintain with reference to the family:

> Conservative thought is often said to focus on the idea of individualism: self-help, self-support, self-sufficiency, self-respect. It rejects dependence, 'scrounging', collectivism, the belief that 'the world owes you a living'. Yet in practice the unit of self-support is not the individual but the family. (p. 47)

could be translated into 'the unit of support is not the individual woman but the friendship'.

What is the relationship between this claim that the emergence of writing on female friendship coincides with and is expressive of the familialization of the family in the Thatcher era and lesbian fiction dealing with friendship from this period? I shall now turn to two texts, Joanna Russ's *On strike against god* (1980) and Gillian Hanscombe's *Between friends* (1982) to discuss how they represent lesbian relations.

Striking against god with female friends

Both *On strike against god* and *Between friends* were published in the early 1980s, and share a concern with lesbian be-coming and lesbian be-ing in the context of the normative force of heteropatriarchal relations and the bourgeois family structure. In both, women fall in love with each other, having been friends first. When, in *On strike against god*, Esther and Jean, who both have a heterosexual history, first become lovers their conversation about the progress towards their romance is constructed in the following terms:

> We talked about how everybody was bisexual, and how this was only the natural result of a friendship, and how we had better take our time, and then – like virgins – began to whisper, "When did you first – ?" and "When did you – ?" (p. 51)

Within the parameters of the narrative, regarding a sexual relationship as 'the natural result of a friendship' serves to reassure the protagonists who are trying to make sense of this experience in the light of their pasts as heterosexual women and as women involved with each other non-sexually. (See Joanna Ryan for an interesting discussion of women's moves from heterosexuality to homosexuality.) At the same time it offers a challenge to patriarchy by underwriting one of its fears, namely that close friendships between women can, indeed will (for, if it is 'natural', is it not also possibly 'inevitable'?) lead to sexual relations between women.[11]

The entire text of *On strike against god*, as the title already suggests, is presented as a challenge to patriarchy. The central protagonist Esther,[12] thirty-eight and divorced with a history of poor sexual relations with men and a bout of therapy behind her, falls in love with her friend Jean and finds that in trying to relate to Jean as a lover she needs to fight free from heteropatriarchy, in the image of which most of her ideas about relationships have been fashioned. Heteropatriarchy is described as a club:

> There's this club, you see. But they won't let you in. So you cry in a corner for the rest of your life or you change your ways and feel rotten because it isn't you, or you go looking for another club. But this club is the world. There's only one. (p. 84)

The centrality and dominance of the heteropatriarchal club is reinforced by Esther's friends (Ellen and Hugh Selby, for example, try to alleviate Esther's supposed singledom by pairing her off with a man ironically named Carl Muchomacho) and by the dominance of heteropatriarchal images in Esther's fantasies. Thus she thinks of Ellen and Hugh as 'my real momma and poppa' (p. 73). Most situations in which she is unsure of what to do evoke hetero-relational images in her. When Jean wants to leave after making love and Esther wants her to stay, the following image instantly surfaces in Esther's mind:

> She [Jean] began to put on her underwear. This is the part of the movie or TV special where he speaks authoritatively and she obeys, or he tells her how she's got to be honest, so she bursts into tears and reveals her problem, which he then solves. But you and I know better; I'm not going to give Jean an excuse to pick a quarrel with me. And I didn't even try to look forlorn and waif-like; I was much too happy. (pp. 61–2)

One of the most sustained heteropatriarchal images in the first half of the novel is that of the male psychoanalyst, here termed Count Draculule as he drains Esther of her sense of self. Like the analyst in Judy Grahn's 'The psychoanalysis of Edward the dyke', he attempts to convince Esther of her heterosexuality. In a series of hilarious internal dialogues, this figure encapsulates male resistance to female desire directed towards women, only to vanish out of Jean's imagination when she decides to go on strike against god and to strike against him, both by exorcizing her anger at men through shooting things in her backyard, and by embracing her love for women, regaining her sense of self against heteropatriarchal odds:

> What do you do when the club won't let you in, when there's no other, and when you won't (or can't) change? Simple.
> You blow the club up.
> (The mystery of courage. The mystery of enjoyment. One moves incurably into the future but there is no future; it has to be created ... I have a future because I willed it; I willed it because I'm strong. Unsupported... (p. 85)

Attempting to create a new relationship with Jean is not easy for Esther or for Jean; Jean runs away for a time and Esther has to defend her love for a woman against heteropatriarchal odds. Esther finally adopts a voluntaristic stance; she refuses to be victimzed by men and takes responsibility for assuming a lesbian lifestyle. On the final pages, Esther, as the first personal narrator, addresses successive 'you's', first male, then female. In line with her new lesbian assertiveness, her address to men takes a stance which, from a heteropatriarchal perspective, is threatening in that it insists that lesbians are here to stay and are part and parcel of 'the club' from which men think lesbians are excluded:

> You can't recognize us in a crowd. Don't try.
> You think Jean and I will go away like ladies and live in the country like Stupid Philpotts and the cats. We won't.
> You think we're not middle-aged. You think we're not old.
> You even think we're not married. (We might be, even to you.)
> Worst of all, you think we're still furiously angry at you, that we need you, that we hate you ... (p. 100)

On strike against god tells the story of how a woman with a heterosexual past becomes a lesbian. This does not (necessarily) involve a rejection of the physical specificity of men but of their way of thinking: 'my trouble with men did not come from what was between their legs but from what was between their ears' (p. 47). It involves making women the centre of one's existence:

> You see, we're real people. We're the best. I don't mean that we're "as good as men" or that "everybody is equal" or that "people should be judged as individuals." I'm not referring to those others out there at all. It's a question of what's put at the center. (p. 22)

For Jean what is put at the centre is her sexual love relationship with her friend. Friendship between women *can* lead to lesbian relationships. These threaten heteropatriarchy. That is the tenor of *On strike against god*.

> When I smile flatteringly at you, we're a liar.
> When we hate and need you, I'm dangerous.
> When they become indifferent, run for your life. (p. 101)

On strike against god threatens patriarchal assumptions about women as dependent on men by constructing a female character who turns from a heterosexual to a lesbian lifestyle. Many of this woman's negative and violent responses to chauvinistic men are played out at the level of fantasy. Here is one such example – Esther is being chatted up by a man:

> "You're strange animals, you women intellectuals," he said.
> "Tell me: what's it like to be a woman?"
> I took my rifle from behind my chair and shot him dead. "It's like that," I said. No, of course I didn't. (p. 6)

Throughout this novel Esther has fantasies of expressing her anger against men by shooting a man. But she never does. The issue of how to convert lesbian feminist convictions into action in hetero-patriarchal reality remains, and it is this which forms an important part of *Between friends* which offers its own threat to patriarchy, not by fantasy which is instantly identified as such, but by considerations of concrete political actions which will affect people's lives. As one woman, Meg, writes to another: 'Don't dream big dreams. See what is possible and support that' (p. 112).

Between friends brings together in epistolary form the views of four different women with diverse histories: Meg grew up as a lesbian in pre-feminist times, she has a son and lives in a non-separatist women's house; Amy lives with a man, Tim, to whom she is not married, and has a son whom they jointly parent though Tim is not the father; Frances is a heterosexual woman married to a sexist man who rapes Meg in the course of the novel, they have no children because he does not want any; Jane is a political lesbian and feminist activist, living in a separatist women's house. The letters these women write to each other detail the changing nature of their relationships with one another and serve as a vehicle for raising a plethora of issues debated within the feminist movement.

In terms of the diversity of viewpoints alone this book is extremely interesting; they concern, amongst other things, the relationship between feminism and lesbianism (with Frances taking the equivalent of the Betty Friedan line as indicated in the discussion of *Sappho was a right-on woman* in chapter 3), the role of sexuality in relationships between people and the issue of how far sexuality can be excluded from friendship, separatism versus non-separatism, the question of how you become a lesbian (with Amy expressing the view, already discussed elsewhere, that women are not *born* lesbians), the ideology of marriage and of heterosexual sexual practice in heteropatriarchal society, and many others. For the purposes of this chapter I want to deal only with issues of the nuclear family, marriage and lesbian relations.

The first thing to note is that at the start of *Between friends* none of the female protagonists lives in a supposedly conventional 'family'. Despite the persistent myth of the nuclear family, the novel's non-conformity to this image reflects contemporary social reality (see Barrett and McIntosh, p. 77). *Between friends*'s refusal to endorse the nuclear family, most forcefully embodied in the depiction of the relationship between Frances and her husband Jim, is aesthetically matched in the novel by giving space to *four* women's voices rather than just *two* or one person writing to another whose voice is never heard, both of which are common variations of the epistolary novel.[13] Further, to counter the notion of letter-writing as a private (and therefore supposedly depoliticized) event, the women circulate their letters among one another and describe discussing the letters with others outside the circle of four. Predictably, the woman who has the most problems with this is the married woman, Frances, who has a strong sense of 'the private' and finds it difficult to discuss her 'private sphere'.

All the female protagonists experience changes in the course of the novel. The three women who engage with feminism – Meg, Amy and Jane – register a politicization which is the consequence of this engagement. This alters their views both of themselves and of others as well as their lifestyles. Meg, the long-term lesbian, describes how she saw herself and marriage in the pre-feminist 1960s:

> [H]aving grown up lesbian in the days before feminism, when lesbianism was a sick and dirty word, I was convinced that (a) I knew nothing about heterosexual relationships which I assumed were totally and completely different from lesbian ones, and (b) I owed it to society and my friends to accept marriage as primary and inviolate. (p. 59)

At the beginning of the novel Meg has a lifestyle not dissimilar to a nuclear family, being in a one-to-one long-term, live-in relationship with her friend Jan with whom she is bringing up her son. Being raped by Jim leads her to understand that the penis still divides women from each other (her friend Frances, to whom supposedly she was the most important emotional anchor in the world, rejects her after the rape), and getting involved with the politically radical separatist lesbian Jane, also contributes to Meg finally changing her lifestyle. Jane, who has been living in a women's house and who does not want to engage with men, insists that she does not 'want to get involved in a lesbian copy of the nuclear family' (p. 159). Meg, very topically for the time in which *Between friends* was written, agrees that

> defusing all the Thatchers means dismantling their system. Guerilla tactics at the psychological level are fine, but they need to be counterpointed with weapons that the enemy uses and is vulnerable to – and that means

a solid phalanx of women and men who will burn marriage certificates and demand larger houses to live together, as well as carrying on the revolution in bed that is already taking place. (p. 166)

Between friends bases itself on the conviction that cultural conscious-ness has not caught up with the social reality of the day. While the nuclear family is (still) being propagated by Conservative politics, '*the revolution is already happening* ... No "moral majority" can halt the disintegration of the nuclear family.' (p. 139) The text sets out to show how such Conservative family politics and the consequent discrimi-nation against women in general and against lesbians specifically might be counteracted in political practice and action. This involves three concrete moves:

1) demonstrating for the abolition of marriage and for not allowing contracts between partners to have legal status;
2) refusing penetrative intercourse to change the nature of sexual exchange between women and men;
3) enacting the rejection of the concept of the nuclear family by living in alternative formations with larger numbers of people.

All these aims can be worked towards through bonding with friends who share the conviction that patriarchy, meaning men's power over women, ought to be obliterated.

Between friends celebrates friendship between women as a source of emotional strength and physical well-being. More importantly, it seeks to integrate the depiction of these benefits, which are evident in *On strike against god* also, with conveying the necessity for concrete political action and with the suggestion that with like-minded friends such actions can be translated into lived reality in which lesbians and women-identified women can work together towards the overthrow of patriarchy.

What are friends for?

Neither *On strike against god* nor *Between friends* is discussed in the other writings on female friendship considered earlier on in this chapter. Whatever the reasons for this (and it might be pure over-sight), I venture to suggest that there is a rift in the writings on female friendship during the late 1970s and early 1980s between texts that represent relations between women as essentially 'harm-less' to patriarchy, and texts which portray female friendship as a way of attacking patriarchy.

The subsuming of female friendship under a patriarchal umbrella is made possible by the multiple definitions of the term 'family', which include:

1. The body of persons who live in one house or under one head, including parents, children, servants, etc.
2. The group of persons consisting of the parents and their children, whether actually living together or not; in a wider sense, the unity formed by those who are nearly connected by blood or affinity.
3. Those descended from or claiming descent from a common ancestor; a house, kindred, lineage. (Barrett and McIntosh, p. 84)

Thus women who live under one roof together, whether biologically related or not, can be described as constituting a 'family'. In a conservative age which fosters an ideology of the nuclear family female friendship can thus be 'legitimated' by pointing to its 'family resemblance'. This does not radicalize society at large and it does not necessarily threaten patriarchy, particularly if female friendship is also desexualized so that male prerogatives of 'ownership' of the female body and sexuality remain preserved. One might want to ask oneself what is suggested by the fact that texts on female friendship which lack this radical element have been widely discussed whereas texts that argue in concrete terms for change[14] have fallen by the cultural wayside.

A final point: the 1980s saw various attempts to familialize homosexual relations. Campaigns aimed at gaining homosexual women and men equal rights with heterosexuals which focussed on issues of marriage[15] (the legal recognition of homosexual relations as equally valid with heterosexual ones) and parenthood[16] (issues of custody, adoption, artificial insemination, gay parenting)[17] were designed to 'normalize' homosexual relations in heterosexual terms. It is important to understand that the Conservative government recognised this phenomenon and finally sought to counteract it with the 1988 Local Government Act which 'prohibits local authorities from intentionally promoting homosexuality and the teaching in maintained schools of 'the acceptability of homosexuality as a pretended family relationship'. (Auchmuty *et al*, p. 90) This is important as it indicates that adopting heterosexual lifestyles as a model for homosexual relationships and political retrenchment are not necessarily the best strategy for fighting discrimination. This is *not* offered as a critique, nor do I wish to suggest that lesbians should not live in nuclear family formations. I am also not suggesting that individuals set out to imitate heterosexual relational structures. Rather, campaigning for certain rights which are, in this culture, associated with hetero-familial privilege, is likely to be interpreted as an attempt at appropriating some of that territory. This will occur *irrespective* of individuals' intentions in these matters.

I would argue that the celebration of female friendship in much writing from the early 1980s constitutes a form of retrenchment from the more radical stances of the early 1970s and is already part of the 'backlash' currently being debated in feminist circles. This makes it imperative that radical lesbian writings from any period are preserved and remembered and their suggestions for strategies for change engaged with seriously. It also foregrounds the necessity to examine carefully the meaning and significance of the adoption in lesbian representation of models taken from or associated with heterosexuality. What I have specifically in mind here are current recuperations of the 1950s-style butch-femme relationships (and I *am* aware of the fact that many women would argue that such role-play has nothing to do with heterosexist interactions). The final word in this chapter, however, I shall reserve for Hanscombe's character Meg, for both *On strike against god* and *Between friends* ultimately celebrate female friendship (here: lesbian relationships) as they optimistically maintain:

Your woman's power is like my own – we need not fail. (*Between friends*, p. 175)

Notes

1 Texts focussing on mother-daughter relationships include Adrienne Rich's *Of woman born* (New York, 1976); Nancy Chodorow's *The reproduction of mothering* (Berkeley and London, 1978); Tillie Olsen's *Mother to daughter, daughter to mother* (New York, 1984); Ann Oakley's *The captured womb* (Oxford, 1984).
2 One black woman who has sustainedly discussed the relationship between feminism and issues of race/colour is bell hooks whose *Ain't I a woman* (Boston, 1982) and *Feminist theory: from margin to center* (Boston, 1984) are pertinent here.
3 In anthologies such as Terry Lovell's *British feminist thought* (Oxford, 1990), or Robyn R. Warhol and Diane Price Herndl's *Feminisms* (New Brunswick, 1991) as well as in journals like *Feminist review* (e.g. vol. 23, Summer 1986) and Women's studies international forum, whole sections/issues are devoted to the feminism and class debate.
4 Sidney Abbott and Barbara Love's *Sappho was a right-on woman* (discussed in chapter 2) details debates around women's sexual orientation very clearly.

5 Liz Stanley's essay 'Epistemological issues in researching lesbian history' is the most recent example of a criticism of Faderman's work that raises the issue of whether or not Faderman's suggestion that romantic friendships between women in the nineteenth century had no sexual component is appropriate. See also Elizabeth Wilson's 'I'll climb the stairway to heaven: lesbianism in the seventies' in Cartledge and Ryan, pp. 188–9.

6 If I had had more space, I would have liked to discuss Charlotte Wolff's work in greater detail; she is one of the most interesting of older lesbians discussing lesbian issues from a psychological viewpoint. Among her works are two volumes of autobiography (*On the way to myself* and *Hindsight*) as well as studies on lesbianism and bisexuality (*Love between women* and *Bisexuality: a study*).

7 In the 1970s and 1980s, as part of the rise of feminist criticism in academe, there was a strong interest in the nineteenth century; many of the 'early' books on feminist criticism such as Sandra Gilbert and Susan Gubar's *The madwoman in the attic* were centrally concerned with writers from that period. An interesting reason for this is suggested by Cora Kaplan in her introduction to the Women's Press's reissue of Elizabeth Barratt Browning's *Aurora Leigh*: 'Our obsession is with the Victorian and Edwardian worlds themselves. They are our middle ages. There, in fancy dress, the still-present hierarchies of class and gender are displayed without shame, unsuppressed by the rhetoric of equality which glosses our own situation. Class conflict and the inequality between the sexes were the spoken subjects of much of that literature and sexual transactions across class lines the erotic subtext of many popular novels. In modern fiction sexuality is the spoken subject, power relations the subtext which must wear a fig leaf. Consequently our literary appetite for the Victorians is easily explained. They give us two kinds of coarseness: a coarse drama of class against class and men against women, picked out in strong colours, and even coarser interpretations of these conflicts.' (Introduction, p. 36)

8 As Celia Kitzinger states: 'A large part of the social definition of the lesbian is in terms of her sexuality. Very few women see their lesbianism primarily as a sexual preference, yet this is exactly how most people think of it.' (in Sheila Kitzinger, *Woman's experience of sex*, p. 108)

9 Faderman's insistence on women's greater independence (from men) in the twentieth century strikes me as applicable to only those women who are in a position to earn an income sufficiently large to sustain themselves independently from others' incomes. Welfare benefits are no alternative here as it is virtually impossible for people to live adequately on state support.

10 Marilyn French's depiction of the vicissitudes of bourgeois domestic life and marriage in *The women's room* provides a good example of this indictment.

11 This 'fear' has a long tradition in the writings of women as well as of men. Already in her *Vindication of the rights of woman* (1792), Mary Wollstonecraft had spoken out against too close a friendship between women, significantly in the context of discussing modesty: 'In nurseries and boarding-schools, I fear, girls are first spoiled, particularly in the latter. A number of girls sleep in the same room, and wash together. And though I should be sorry to contaminate an innocent creature's mind by instilling false delicacy, or those indecent prudish notions which early cautions respecting the other sex naturally engender, I should be very anxious to prevent their acquiring nasty or immodest habits; and as many girls have learned very nasty tricks from ignorant servants, the mixing them thus indiscriminately together, is very improper. To say the truth, women are in general too familiar with each other, which leads to that gross degree of familiarity that so frequently renders the marriage state unhappy. (p. 234)

'Besides, women from necessity, because their minds are not cultivated, have recourse very often to what I familiarly term bodily wit, and their intimacies are of the same kind. In short, with respect to both mind and body, they are too intimate.' (p. 236)

12 The protagonist of On strike against god shares with the protagonist of Sylvia Plath's The bell jar not only the first name, Esther, but also a number of other characteristics, such as having an identity crisis around what sexual identity to assume over the course of a summer, seeing an unhelpful male psychiatrist whom, in her fantasies, Esther addresses in terminology not dissimilar to the one used by Plath in relation to male authority figures (– 'Sir, sirrah, ober-leutnant, sturmbanns-feuhrer [sic], wherefore is it that you speak with a Viennese-Polish accent, whilst you are as Amurrican-born as you or I?' On strike, p. 43).

13 Compare this novel with, for instance, Mary Hays's The memoirs of Emma Courtney (London and New York, 1987), Mariama Bà's So long a letter (London, 1981) or Alice Walker's The color Purple (London, 1983).

14 Hanscombe's suggestions of strategies for change in Between friends are very similar to the ones advocated by Barrett and McIntosh in The anti-social family (pp. 131-59).

15 In Denmark marriage between homosexuals, so-called 'pink marriage', is accepted and legal practice.

16 This issue inspired a play by Sarah Daniels, Neaptide (London, 1986).

17 This resulted in various handbooks on the subject of lesbian parenting being published, two of which are Gillian Hanscombe and Jackie Foster's Rocking the cradle: lesbian mothers (London, 1982) and Rights of Women Lesbian Custody Group's Lesbian mothers' legal handbook (London, 1986).

Chapter 6

Wet caves and roses: representations of lesbian sexuality in women's writing

Lesbian sex and silence

In her essay 'Lesbian "sex"' Marilyn Frye maintains that in contrast to heterosexuals who 'do it' regularly (pp. 1-2) and to gay males' sex, which 'is articulate' (p. 5):

> Lesbian 'sex' as I have known it most of the time I have known it is utterly unarticulate. Most of my lifetime, most of my experience in the realms commonly designated as 'sexual' has been prelinguistic, noncognitive. I have, in effect, no linguistic community, no language, and therefore in one important sense, no knowledge. (p. 6)

Marilyn Frye's essay dates from 1988. The 'problem' of silence about lesbian sex, however, seems to go back much further than that.[1] One older black woman, writing about her experiences at boarding-school, states:

> You didn't give it a name, or at least I don't think I gave it a name. I felt it was just natural; just nice to be with women that you like and I think we saw it as fun, too. I mean, we knew there was some vigorous secrecy about not doing certain things – sort of kissing each other when other people were around, but I'm not even quite sure we did a lot of that. It was very much feelings and emotions that were important in those days. (Neild and Pearson, eds, p. 127)

Another woman writes that because 'all sexual activity is very private anyway … you can't envisage it' (Neild and Pearson, eds, p. 148) with the result that 'when it came to actually getting into bed, I got all sort of panicky. I didn't know what to do or what to expect or anything like that' (pp. 148-9). Pat Bond, a lesbian entertainer, describes this lack of knowledge more graphically:

> I have a spot in my show where I tell Bunny …, 'Bunny, if we're going to be real dykes, you gotta love 'em with your mouth.' And she said, 'Down there?' I said, 'That's right.' She said, 'No shit!' We were all terrified of that. (Adelman, ed., p. 170)

The issue here is one of information, and it raises the question of where one should or might get information about lesbian sexuality from. One source can be literature. However, in her recent article 'The naked majesty of god: contemporary lesbian erotic poetry', Caroline Halliday talks not only about 'the comparative *lack* of lesbian erotic poetry' (p. 77) but also says of her own work:

> For myself as a writer, erotic experience did not surface straightaway as a subject. There was a process of establishing the validity of poetry… Other issues – women's lives around me, coming out as a lesbian, being a mother, dealing with non-monogamy – all took precedence. (p. 78)[2]

These comments taken together raise a number of important issues: silence and articulacy in relation to lesbian sexuality, diversity in writings on lesbian sexuality over time and across different kinds of texts, the relationship between 'naming' and 'doing', the 'nature' of sexual activity as detailed in women's writings, the dearth or otherwise of lesbian erotic writing and the context(s) within which writings on lesbian sexuality are constructed.

One important point needs to be made immediately: I am not concerned with what lesbians 'actually' do sexually in this chapter but with *how lesbian sexuality is represented* in texts by women. This is not to suggest that the two are unrelated. But my starting point is texts. Marilyn Frye discusses both lesbians' supposed sexual inactivity and their supposed inarticulacy in order to question, with respect especially to the former, the appropriateness of comparing heterosexual and lesbian sexual activity. I want to begin by questioning Frye's assertion that lesbians are inarticulate about their sexuality, and I shall link that to a chronological review of lesbian writing in this century.

'... and that night they were not divided.'

This line from Radclyffe Hall's *The well* is frequently cited as an indication of the silence that surrounds lesbian sexuality and its expression. As Alison Hennegan wrote in her 1981 introduction to Virago's reissue of this novel:

> [Through *The well*] many people learned for the first time that sexual relations between women were possible. Those who turned to the book in prurient anticipation or even in a spirit of honest enquiry, however, often retired baffled: ' ... and that night they were not divided' is all Radclyffe Hall has to say about the actual consummation of her heroine's first affair. (p. viii)

Two issues come together here: that of who reads texts about/by lesbians [3] and for what purposes, *and* how lesbian sexuality is written about.

Texts about/by lesbians can be read by anyone,[4] whether they are lesbian or not, provided they can afford to buy them or have access to a library which holds them. With reference to a lesbian audience, it would appear that texts about/by lesbians are often both sources of entertainment and sources of information.[5] Regarding the latter, lesbian writing from the early twentieth century does not offer much insight into the practice of lesbian sex. Lesbian literature of this period is not constructed, by and large, to function as a sex manual. But then, and this is important to note, neither is heterosexist mainstream literature from this time. Literary texts that were to be sold in 'ordinary' bookshops during this era, whether their subject matter focussed on heterosexuals or homosexuals, did not discuss sex in graphic detail at great length. 'Common practice' in a given culture regarding the representation of sexuality is as much a determinant of how lesbian sexuality is represented as other factors such as the status of lesbians in that society. In western culture sexuality has been and still is, for the most part, a taboo topic.

Indeed, when looking at the representation of sexuality in writing, one needs to consider both the period in which such writing occurred and the kinds of texts in which writing on sexuality might be found: 'the notion that love and sex have been expressed in the same old ways since the mists of unrecorded time is pretence' (Harriet Gilbert and Christine Roche, *A women's history of sex*, p. 1). The representation of lesbian sexuality does not exist outside of or independent from the culture and period in which it occurs, and the structures and codes to which writing on sex is subject at any given time are reflected/expressed in texts on lesbian sexuality as much as in non-lesbian texts dealing with sexuality. In Sarah Lucia Hoagland's view, 'understanding sexuality is not just understanding a "drive" but understanding the context, indeed the institutions, that gives our urges and responses depth of meaning' ('Lesbian ethics', p. 167).

In general the representation of sexuality in our culture has become more widespread, more diverse, and more 'acceptable' in the course of this century. Further, one can distinguish between writing which contains some depiction of sex; erotic or pornographic writing the focus and purpose of which is sex (see Barbara Wilson) and which is intended for the entertainment of its reader; sex manuals which are intended to provide information for the edification of their readers; and theoretical texts about sexuality (in various kinds of writings). How readers actually use any or all of these texts is a separate matter.

To return to the lesbian literature of the early part of this century, the place it accords to representations of lesbian sexuality is, I would suggest, 'in tune with' the amount of focus and space occupied by depictions of sexuality in non-lesbian writing. (See Sheila Kitzinger's *Woman's experience of sex* pp. 17–26.) Sex is no more 'graphically' or otherwise represented in, for instance, novels by Virginia Woolf's or Dorothy Richardson than in writings overtly focussing on lesbians. It occupies a small and specifically coded space in each text.

It is not the case that lesbian sexuality is not represented at all but that it is represented in specific and indeed revealing ways.[6] Marilyn Frye's assertion of lesbians' inarticulacy regarding sex is based on what she regards as the absence of specificity in how lesbians talk about their sexuality. Gay men, by contrast, appear to have 'a huge lexicon of words' for 'acts and activities, their subacts, preludes and denouements, their stylistic variations, their sequences' (p. 5). Frye's assertion is dependent on her notion of what constitutes that specificity, which words she accepts as expressing lesbian sexuality and which ones not. As an article in the new, fairly silly magazine *Bitch* entitled 'What's yours called?' which discusses various names for 'vagina' or 'cunt' highlights, it is not the case that we have no words for our genitals; rather, these words are loaded in various and frequently heterosexist ways. Therefore I would support Anna Livia's statement:

I do not believe in an essential, purely sexual experience which it sufficeth to describe accurately and in detail, but rather that the words we choose create the experience; bestow context, metaphor, image, connotation; forge parallels with other, seemingly disparate, experiences: cunt as lotus blossom, pomegranate, dried apricot half, black hole, split beaver. ('Lesbian sexuality: joining the dots', p. 193)

Seen in this light, Hall's minimalism (' ... and that night they were not divided') indicates context and offers connotation: it highlights very clearly, for example, a division between private and public sphere with sexuality occupying the former and therefore not being available as a topic for sustained discussion. Some of the results of this attitude are clear from the comments cited in the introduction: the privatization of sexuality leads to ignorance about sex and constructs sexuality as a unique, personal, individual experience for which little publicly shared vocabulary is available, thus making it difficult to communicate about the variety of sexual experiences one can have.[7] Joanna Russ, for instance, writes in *On strike against god*:

The truth that's never told today about sex is that you aren't much good at it, that you don't like it, that you haven't got much. That you're at sea and unhappy. (p. 9)

Here she articulates an experience of heterosexuality – which can also apply to lesbian sexuality[8] – that remains frequently unencoded. She is *commenting* on sex as Hall does in her famous sentence rather than *describing* it which, beyond highlighting the supposedly 'private nature' of sexual experience, also gives us an indication as to what the experience is supposed to be like, namely a kind of merging, expressed as 'they were *not* divided'.

A similar view of sexual relations between women is suggested in H.D.'s *Her* (see p. 36). Both lesbian and heterosexual sexual encounters are recorded in this novel. In *Her*, the protagonist finds it impossible not to remain divided, outside the experience, watching both herself and her partner, while engaging in heterosex (see pp. 84–5, 172-3), and these scenes are marked by violence (the ripping of her clothes) and her sense of him being in some respects like an animal. This last point raises issues around the construction of male sexuality. In contrast to the heterosexual encounters, Hermione's sexual experiences with Fayne are described as mergers, in which Hermione and Fayne 'fuse':

> Her and Fayne Rabb were flung into a concentric intimacy, rings on rings that made a geometric circle toward a ceiling, that curved over them like ripples on a pond surface. Her and Fayne were flung, as it were, to the bottom of some strange element and looming up ... there were rings on rings of circles as if they had fallen into a deep well and were looking up ... 'long since half kissed away.' (p. 164)

H.D. names no genital parts in this novel; she describes sex in terms of the experience of it which her protagonist has, with a focus on shape and perspective, both of which act as dominant structurating devices. Sex is thus not represented as discrete from other experiences but informed by perspectives similar to the ones governing other situations. The novel portrays a character moving towards a state of 'at-oneness', a wholeness which that character first experiences in lesbian sex. *Her* also suggests that the fulfilment found through merging in sex can be found in other contexts, too, that the protagonist is able to survive her abortive lesbian relationship with a woman who then chooses a man because she can find satisfaction elsewhere. The analogies set up in *Her* between lesbian sex and other situations provide the basis for rendering sublimation of sexual desire possible.

A brief look at Djuna Barnes' *Nightwood* confirms the relativity of lesbian sex within the representation of lesbians in the early twentieth century. *Nightwood* is in many respects a much more experimental and transgressive text than either *The well* or *Her*. In its centralization of characters conventionally considered marginal to mainstream culture, in its depiction of 'gender-benders' and in its representation of history as psychological necessity and subjective construct, it questions the apparently fixed entities of its period much more thoroughly than the other two texts do. But, significantly, this questioning does not include either the representation of sexuality or its practice. Sexuality itself remains textually marginalized, discussed predominantly in terms of the emotions it arouses such as jealousy. Again, I should emphasize that this is not the same as saying that sexuality is not talked about. But the discussion centres on issues such as the transgressive nature of dreams which allow the sleeper to indulge in whatever (sexual) fantasy she wishes (pp. 126–9). In other words, here too sexuality is written about in particular ways which differ from how sexuality might be written about elsewhere. The effect in this instance is one of minimalizing the importance of *sexual activity* over states of mind.

Perhaps the writer who has produced the most complex representation of lesbian sexuality in the early twentieth century is Gertrude Stein. Halliday maintains that 'Stein created a style that circumnavigated the problems of explicit words, lesbian or otherwise' ("The naked majesty of god", p. 79). But what of the following passages:

> Now let us say pussy. When did I say pussy. You are so full of a cow factory. You manufacture cows by vows. The cows produce reduce reduce they reduce the produce. Cows are necessary after feeding. We are needing what we have after feeding. After feeding we find cows out. How are cows multiplied. By proper treatment. Thank you so much for being so explicit

> He ate she ate they ate there, she ate he ate and they are there. he ate she ate and do they care, they ate and we mate and we are there. ('A sonatina followed by another', p. 307)

How do we read words like 'pussy' (vagina?), the whole business about the cow factory (producing shit?), and the eating (oral sex?) here? 'Pussy' certainly seems a very explicit word.

Judy Grahn in *The highest apple* suggests that Stein 'collapsed into one the two supposedly oppositional extremes of perception – objective and subjective – collapsed them into one form, one technique, one mode of understanding' (p. 64). For 'objective' and 'subjective' we might read 'public' and 'private' here. Stein refuses the public conventions concerning language use in the realms of sentence structure and register. This enables her to violate the 'linguistic decorum' which dictates in what contexts it is appropriate to use what words. Once you can no longer specify along conventional lines what kind of a text you are dealing with, you can no longer assert the approriateness of a given style of language. The result of these transgressions is a heightened ambiguity regarding the meaning of Stein's texts which one could also describe as a privatization of meaning. How, for instance, do you read the following:

> The times, the times is a rose, the rose is a nose, in time the nose arose. To arise means to clean, to wash out. Thank you so much. ('A sonatina followed by another', p. 297)

Or:

> We know how to build a fire. Can tickle can tickle can tickle for sin is said by writing on the wall with lead with lead penciling. We have two pen

holders for which we have cared for which we have cared very much. We do not know this about these. ('A sonatina followed by another', p. 307)

By quoting these passages in the context of a chapter on representations of lesbian sexuality, I am, of course, suggesting that a lesbian sexual meaning attaches to them. But they could be interpreted differently. What I would argue is that Stein uses words that have specific sexual connotations (for example, rose connotes clitoris) but that the linguistic transgressions in her works bury and obscure these words. This has the effect of translating into public display the exchange around lesbian sexuality, through challenging linguistic conventions in so radical a fashion that ambiguities of meaning undermine possibilities of accusation of violation of both sexual and linguistic decorum. A separate issue, and one which I have no space to discuss here, is whether or not this writing is in any sense 'erotic'.[9] It certainly does not offer straightforward information about lesbian sex.

' ... the tingling and terrifying pleasure that spread in waves'

Where Stein refuses conventions and as a consequence carves out for herself a certain amount of freedom in her use of words with sexual meanings, much writing on lesbian sexuality in the 1950s and 1960s followed fairly restrictive narrative conventions, whether pulp fiction or 'serious' literature. I shall briefly discuss Patricia Highsmith's *Carol* (first published in 1952 as *The price of salt* under the name Claire Morgan) and Ann Bannon's *I am a woman*, which are very similar in terms of a plot structure based on sexuality:

> As frequently as the plot allowed (and sometimes the plot allowed for a great deal of frequency), the sexual tension would build up, description and dialogue tending toward a dual but united purpose (female abandon, [fe]male release). The hand on the thigh, the fingers on the breast, the unzipping, unbuttoning, moaning and groaning – whether or not the narrator/main character was a man or a woman you always saw the woman through the man's eyes. (Barbara Wilson, 'The erotic life of fictional characters', p. 199)

I am not going to dwell on this last very interesting point other than to point out that in both *Carol* and *I am a woman* males desiring the (lesbian) female protagonists hover on the edges and interfere with, even engineer the sexual action, a phenomenon not particularly evident in lesbian writings of the 1970s and 1980s when the focus had shifted towards centring the plot exclusively on women. Additionally, in these later texts there is greater evidence of women writers trying to establish conventions of their own when writing about lesbian sexuality so that, in some respects, they become more distinct from writings depicting heterosex.

I want to pick up the first point Wilson makes because it indicates one of the marks of difference between 'trashy novels' as Wilson describes them and to which the Bannon books supposedly belong and 'serious' literature which might include *Carol*. In 'trashy novels' sex is one of the mainstays and sexual encounters are recurrently detailed, often in virtually identical ways. In 'serious' literature, sex happens far less frequently; in the case of *Carol*, only one sexual encounter is described whereas in *I am a woman* there are several. 'The old question, *Is literature supposed to have sex in it or not?*' (Wilson, 'The erotic life', p. 202) can thus be answered with, 'On a sliding scale of frequency, depending on how "seriously" you want your literature to be taken.' Infrequent sex as a mark of literary respectability would, if Frye's assessment of lesbian inarticulacy is correct, instantly make much lesbian writing very respectable. Less frivolously put, the status of sexuality as a topic in literature contributes significantly to how (frequently) it is represented in any given text.

Though 'trashy' novels might describe sex more frequently than 'serious' ones, it cannot be said that the decorum governing how that sex is detailed varies tremendously between the two categories of texts. In the 1950s and 1960s certain bodily parts could be named, others not. Breasts are frequently mentioned, though nipples not nearly as much, the mouth (but not used, as is the case in the 1970s and 1980s, as a euphemism for the vagina), the tongue – occasionally, hands and head hair. No mention is made in either text of the vagina (words like 'pussy' and 'cunt', frequently found in later writing, do not feature at all), the clitoris (again, a staple of later writing on lesbian sexuality), or pubic hair. Concerning sexual activity, kissing is extensively referred to, as is touching (though caution is exercised concerning the parts that are touched), missionary-position type embraces are described, but no details are offered as to how lesbians stimulate each other towards the orgasm which they – in these texts at least – invariably reach. The sexual encounter in *Carol* is thus packaged as follows:

Her arms were tight around Carol, and she was conscious of Carol and nothing else, of Carol's hand that slid along her ribs, Carol's hair that brushed her bare breasts, and then her body too seemed to vanish in widening circles that leaped further and further, beyond where thought could follow ... And now it was pale blue distance and space, an expanding space in which she took flight suddenly like a long arrow. The arrow seemed to cross an impossibly wide abyss with ease, seemed to arc on and on in space, and not quite stop. Then she realized that she still clung to Carol, that she trembled violently, and the arrow was herself. She saw Carol's pale hair across her eyes, and now Carol's head was close against hers. And she did not have to ask if this was right, no one had to tell her, because this could not have been more right or perfect. (pp. 167–8)

This text marks sex as an exclusionary space in which 'nothing else' exists in the participant's consciousness, and physical experience transports into a heavenly space in which Therese herself becomes transformed into another object, an arrow. Relying on a vorticist image (the 'widening circles') already familiar from *Her*, lesbian sexual activity is here described as self-abandoned, disembodied (if we take 'body' to mean the literal body) movement through space in which Therese not so much merges with Carol as achieves a different sense of self which propels her out of 'reality' and out of thought into heavenly space. This widening sphere collapses at the point where Therese once again becomes aware of Carol and focusses in on the relationship between her two types of state. Her clinging to Carol, her trembling and her being the arrow are paratactically arranged, but their connection is not made explicit. Instead, the final sentence here quoted then fuses moral and sexual concerns. The first indirect question, 'if this was right', is ambiguous in terms of the meaning of 'right' – it seems to carry a moral weight (appropriate in this context due to the two women in a sense being on the run from Carol's husband who is intent upon proving Carol's 'immorality', i.e. her lesbianism). The second half of the sentence refuses a direct answer to the question. Its statement, 'this could not have been more right or perfect' because of the added 'perfect', seems to bring the issue back to one of sexual performance rather than to its moral implications. The question raised throughout *Carol* is, 'Lesbian relationships, including sex, are "perfect" but are they right?' The final reunion of Carol and Therese, of course, offers the answer, 'yes'. Although lesbian sexual activity is at the centre of the debate about the immorality or otherwise of Carol's desires, it is displaced in the plot into outer space with one sighting only.

More frequent representations of lesbian sexual encounters do not, however, guarantee a different approach. Here is an excerpt from one of Laura's encounters with Beebo from *I am a woman*:

> She only clung to Beebo, half tearing her pajamas off her back, groaning wordlessly, almost sobbing. Her hands explored, caressed, felt Beebo all over, while her own body responded with violent spasms – joyous, crazy, deep as her soul. She could no more have prevented her response than she could the tyrannic need that drove her to find it. She felt Beebo's tongue slip into her mouth and Beebo's arms squeezing her and she went half out of her mind with it. Her hands were in Beebo's hair, tickling her ears, slipping down her back, over her hips and thighs. Her body heaved against Beebo's in a lovely mad duet. She felt like a column of fire, all heat and light, impossibly sensual, impossibly sexual. She was all feeling, warm and melting, strong and sweet. It was a long time before either of them came to their senses. (pp. 93–4)

Like *Carol*, *I am a woman* celebrates a sense of loss of self which is not a merging with the other person but a being overwhelmed by sexual need which, in terms frequently used to describe males in hetero-romance, is represented as out of the individual's rational control. Sexual desire here transports the protagonist out of her mind just as is the case in *Carol* but it results in something akin to madness rather than in an experience of another celestial space. Either way, sexual experience is dissociated from rationally controlled reality. Again, as in *Carol*, there is no specifying of the actual sexual process beyond what one might describe as 'foreplay' of a very preliminary kind. The veil is drawn very quickly about what actually happens or is done; instead, the idea of sensations is evoked through words such as 'heat' and 'light', giving the experience by association elemental qualities, this being underwritten by the supposed unstoppability of the process. 'Irrationality' and 'nature' dominate in this description, seemingly accounting for the 'wordlessness' of the occasion.

I am a woman is slightly more graphic than *Carol* in its depiction of lesbian sex(uality), not in terms of being more explicit about the process of lesbian sexual loving, but as regards the representation of interactional dynamic between two people. The protagonists *do* more; there is more sustained assertion of desire, more use of active verbs, more general use of a vocabulary that suggests activity rather than passivity, and indeed more violence in the exchanges between two women (tearing of clothes, etc.):

> They sank to the floor, wracked with passion, kissing each other raven-
> ously, tearing each other's clothes. (*I am a woman*, p. 138)

This activity does not extend below the waist; after the tearing of the
clothes the rest is unspecified sensation. In effect, the reader is
offered a Hollywood-style fade-out, satisfaction guaranteed, with
simile taking over: 'All the lonely months of denial burst like fire-
crackers between her legs.' (*I am a woman*, p. 98)

'a woman's body must be taught to speak'

Concomitant with the 'sexual revolution' which began towards the
end of the 1960s, women's writing on lesbian sexuality grew more
open and diversified. In lesbian poetry, women 'starving for images'[10]
tried to find a language to express lesbian sexual experience. The
result is a poetry which veers between the prosaic and the lyrical.
Marilyn Hacker's sonnet cycle *Love, death and the changing of the
seasons* (1986) is a typical example of this phenomenon. In this
sequence Hacker uses 'everyday' language to record the female persona's fantasies about a woman to whom she is attracted but from
whom she is separated geographically and with whom she has not
had a relationship. Lines such as 'Tonight, you will or won't get in my
pants./Tomorrow night, fair stands the wind for France.' (p. 30) are
common; they conjoin literary allusion with colloquialisms, thus
undercutting the conventional cultural assumption that 'high culture' and 'base desire' expressed in slang are discrete entities. At the
same time, Hacker's poems are more graphic in their depiction of
lesbian sex than the texts from the 1950s and 1960s were. Specifically, they do not stop at the waist. Thus she makes jokes ('If you eat
pussy, why won't you eat rabbit?', p. 44), describes masturbating
('Which didn't deter me then from lying down/ ... / to let my hands
and mind go back a ways,/ and forward, in, against, above, around,/
until I said your name (what corn) and came./ (I didn't muck up the
upholstery,/', p. 44), and anticipates making love:

> I taste the morning light with such desire
> as I will (say I will) take from the flower
> of you, touch as I will learn your entire
> country, these tender hills seen from a tower. (p. 55)

146

The alignment of body with nature and landscape in Hacker's poetry is one very common strand in representations of lesbian sexuality.[11] In Suniti Namjoshi's poem (from *Naming the waves*, McEwen) 'I give her the rose', the clitoris is described as 'the rose with unfurled petals' and the female sex as 'the shell with swollen lips'. The request for love-making is expressed as 'Feed me on flowers/with wide open mouths.' Judy Grahn in *Another mother tongue* uses a similar vocabulary. She records in one of her journal entries an exchange between herself and Paula Gunn Allen in which, while making love, they share the vision of a rose:

> 'I know that rose. When you made love to me, there was a pink rose. And Guadalupe was there. She was holding it,' [Paula] said. 'she was showing me how to stroke the rose. She was using her first two fingers inside the petals and holding the flower in her other hand, her left hand, saying, 'This is how to stroke the rose.' She laughed. 'You've learned very well,' I said.' (pp. 254-5)

The specificity of this sexual instruction is not repeated in Judith Kazantzis's poem 'The bath' (*Hard feelings*, p. 47) which describes a menstruating woman masturbating while having a bath. Here the 'canoe finger explores' the vagina which is 'this cavemouth of water and blood' from which 'drifted anemones' emerge 'from my womb to sea/the lost fronds of a cradle unwound'.

Innovation of plants and the sea or a seascape, as happens in this poem, is frequent in poems on lesbian sexuality. This, in my view, does not testify to the paucity of representations of lesbian sexuality, rather, it highlights one important analogy in lesbian understanding of women's sexuality. Using nature imagery, describing, as Caroline Halliday does, 'the opening of your body/ a leaf/ plane trees stretching, expanding/like a belly' (*Some truth – some change*, p. 25) is one way of suggesting that lesbian sexuality is natural because of its affinities with nature. In a culture, in which the normality or otherwise of lesbian sexuality is perpetually under scrutiny, women's writing on lesbian sexuality can celebrate and affirm that sexuality by maintaining, through nature imagery, that lesbian sexuality is natural.

There are, of course, drawbacks in the use of such imagery. For one thing, one could argue that, fig-leaf like, it hides rather than reveals lesbian sexuality by using florid/floral language. But then not all writing is conceived as a sex manual. More to the point, perhaps, is the issue of the extent to which such imagery suggests a 'naturalness' and therefore 'instinctiveness' of lesbian sexuality which not only denies the cultural constructedness of our sexual behaviour, but can also prevent people from articulating their sexuality, leaving them to assume that either you know how to do it or you do not. It may be that many lesbians wish, as the persona does in Rich's 'The images', 'to cry loose my soul/ into her, to become/ free of speech at last.' (*A wild patience*, p. 5) But for others, the silence of 'nature' described by Rich ('I was mute/ innocent of grammar as the waves/ irrhythmically washing I felt washed clean/ of the guilt of words there was no word to read/ in the book of this earth', *A wild patience*, pp. 4–5), is a burden which mars their sexual existence.

Lesbian erotic writing

In the 1980s lesbian erotic writing, labelled as such and often in the form of anthologies, began to emerge. This writing created some controversy and continues to do so because some argue it objectifies women, an objectification which should be resisted by their female peers. Writer Judith Barrington maintains that writing on lesbian sexuality serves a particular need: 'What I needed was to see my own reality, my own feelings, and my own sexual behaviour – or, even better, a less guilt-ridden, more open lesbian reality than my own – reflected in the culture around me.' (*Lesbian writers on sexuality*, p. i) Sheba Collective simply insist on desire in explaining why they published *Serious pleasure*: 'We decided to publish a book of lesbian erotica because, quite simply, we wanted to read it and we knew that we were not the only ones, a huge number of lesbians 'out there' wanted to read it too.' (p. 8) Pointing out that the stories in their collection are fantasy, 'representing the diversity ... of our desires and sexual practices' they argue that what they regard as the two aims of erotic writing, 'to explore a crucial dimension of lesbian identity in a revealing, yet sensitive way' and 'to titillate, turn on, lead to masturbation or making love with someone' are legitimate ones which can coexist and which are not 'wrong' (p. 9).

    Serious pleasure is interesting because, unlike the erotic/pornographic writings of Joan Nestle and Pat Califia, for example, many of the texts in *Serious pleasure* register a self-consciousness about the construction of erotica which undercuts the texts' potential power as source of arousal. In other words, some of these texts might be very revealing but not necessarily stimulating (though enjoyable to read). This self-consciousness takes the form of producing erotic writing and commenting on it within one piece of work, frequently through highlighting the conventions and clichés which govern erotic representations. Maria Jastrzebska's 'Some orgasms I'd like to mention', for example, begins by debunking the idea of perfect (lesbian) sex by first decribing, in staccato mechanistic fashion, how sex is frequently depicted:

[Women's] slender (what else) fingers hold the stems of wine glasses/ before moving/left, right, up around nipple, thigh, breast, back/left shoulder again/by which time I'm lost/while they reach (what else) one perfect orgasm/after another (all at first try) moaning. (*Serious pleasure*, p. 14)

This is contrasted further on in the poem with the everyday interruptions that prevent 'the ordinary person' from having a similar experience such as 'having to go and pee', 'your mother calling', 'the cat trying to join in' or 'farting at the worst moment' (p. 14). The poem ends on a positive note, asserting that there are orgasms 'which make you feel ... all the worrying/then suddenly not worrying/anymore at all/what the neighbours can hear/what will happen/the nothing can stop us now' (p. 15). Jastrzebska here enacts the complaint voiced earlier in her poem that 'Even there/in lesbian books I've read, they didn't describe that much' (p. 15). The reason she offers for this absence, 'Perhaps they don't want to kiss and tell, after all. I don't really blame them./These things are personal' (p. 15) re-affirms the notion of the sexual as private already discussed and suggests why Jastrzebska, too, does not 'describe that much' beyond the clichés commonly used in erotica.

A rejection of this position is offered by Mandy Dee in 'Shy – fragments' (*Serious pleasure*, pp. 37–8) where, with reference to Radclyffe Hall's (in)famous line, the persona states: 'I want no more old coy quotes/about undivided nights.' Trying to avoid such coyness, 'The art of poise' (*Serious pleasure*, pp. 63–5) attempts to achieve a balance between the depiction of an engagement in sexual activity and commentary on it which indicates an awareness of conventions: 'I want you to undo me, re-create me, open me up and out like the cliché rose.' (p. 64) Thus sections such as:

I feel cold breath upon my cunt, making the wetness wetter. A finger probes me, dips in and takes a surreptitious mouthful, like a naughty child with frosted icing. Lick, suck, smack, smile – lips and tongue orchestrate the slippery dance. (pp. 64–5)

alternate with lines which raise questions about the nature of the sexual interaction: 'Slowly I realize that I am objectifying your face. I ask myself: who is fucking whom? Who is object of the gaze? Who is leader in the dance?' (p. 65) and one or two line statements to the effect that, '(*Later, we will discuss the politics of looking*.)' (p. 64) Barbara Smith here opens up issues around the politics of sexuality which, however, are treated as asides, to be picked up later, beyond the encounter and, indeed, text which never answers the questions it raises. Instead, it serves to problematize lesbian sexuality and to open it up for debate.

Many of the contributions in *Serious pleasure* are overtly described as fantasies, as narratives of desire which remain unenacted so that the texts seem to bespeak what lesbians would like to do rather than what they actually do. One example is Berta Freistadt's 'tennis skirt fantasy' in which the first person narrator imagines making love to a fellow (games) teacher, eventually 'making such a lot of noise that we are disturbing an important discussion on staffing levels' (p. 18). Before getting more explicit, however, 'I would take pity on us and transport us both to my bedroom with closed door and curtain.' Freistadt employs both humour and the fade-out technique to avoid becoming too graphic in what is clearly marked as 'only' a fantasy anyway. Eroticism is, at times, understood as what is suggested rather than what is explicitly described. Other writers in this collection such as Bernadette Halpin, also use humour. This has the effect of discharging erotic potential through invoking laughter.

Not all contributors, however, insist on coyness. When they do not, they display a number of characteristics which seem to me to distinguish lesbian erotic writing from other kinds of erotic writing and I want, very briefly, to point to one common feature in these texts, exemplified in the following sections from Caroline Halliday's 'Trapeze': ' ... and I tie myself to your lipped varied bushy tasting cunt not caring where the land is' (*Serious pleasure*, p. 30), and, 'Yr hair is beautifully lively dark and crisp it hides and covers glistens the edges of yr labia dark and velvet edged' (p. 32). The focus here is on the vagina, for which, in lesbian erotic writing, a number of words but most frequently 'cunt' or 'mouth' are used. Pubic hair, too, is referred to, and it tends to be done in terms of its being 'crisp' or 'springy' or 'wiry'. Many texts refer to the taste or the smell of the cunt which is described as desirable and as creating desire:

> She ran her hands up the inside of Lou's thigh, she played with Lou's pubic hair, circled her cunt, looking for the opening, waiting for the wet welcome to happen between her fingers. She breathed in the scent of Lou's sex and was excited again. (*Serious pleasure*, p. 97)

This offers a direct opposition to heterosex which does not engage positively with smell, unless it is artificial (i.e. perfume), indeed rejects it, especially the smell of a woman's vagina. I would argue very strongly that one of the positive aspects of lesbian erotic writing is that it celebrates the female body *as it is* rather than *as image*.

Importantly, too, the clitoris as a major source of sexual pleasure for women is foregrounded in lesbian erotic writing, which gives much space to describing the stimulation of that organ:

> She opened the lips of Annie's cunt gently before pulling the swollen clit into her mouth. Annie's gasp was sharp and Louise backed away, licking Annie's thighs and the small space between thigh and cunt lip ... Then she moved back ... Her tongue whipped over Annie's clit, hungrily. (*Serious pleasure*, p. 57)

Part of this engagement with the cunt in lesbian erotic writing is the emphasis on wetness and moistness, the vagina producing secretions during sexual arousal which is an indicator of desire. The focus on all aspects of the vagina, pubic hair, the clitoris, wetness during sexual arousal is part of the more explicit writing on lesbian sexuality which has been created during the 1980s and early 1990s. Lesbian sex no longer stops at the waist and with foreplay. Despite such overtness, two paradoxes appear to have arisen, both associated with articulating sexuality. One of these is that in erotic stories, texts which articulate sexuality, the protagonists are frequently depicted as either silent or monosyllabic. They *do* rather than *say*. Sentences such as, 'She seemed to know instinctively the things I liked. I stood in silent ecstasy as she sought out the places where I love to be touched.' (*Serious pleasure*, p. 42) or, 'I was just about to speak when the older woman put her finger to my lips and silenced me, as the younger slithered down my body, kissing me' (*Serious pleasure*, p. 127), as well as pure action sequences occur. If speaking it is important (see Betsy Warland in Barrington), why not construct speaking subjects? Does this replicate silence around lesbian sexuality? Or does it encode 'that ambivalent desire to have no choice but to be overcome, not in control' (*Serious pleasure*, p. 45), to suggest a fantasy scenario, everybody's dream, where one's desires will be met without having to be articulated, where one can trust that the other will do as one wishes, and where one is (sexually) known to the extent that speech becomes redundant?

The other paradox is that writers of lesbian erotica sometimes assert that lesbian erotica don't 'describe that much' while actually engaged in producing it. This, it seems to me, marks an ambivalence about the issue of what actually is erotic, about what readers want from erotic texts, and what kinds of erotic texts one should (and I use that word advisedly) construct.

Politicizing and policing lesbian sex, or what do you make of macho sluts?

Lesbian sex, as all other forms of sex, is political. When a writer like Caroline Halliday professes:

> Erotic loving is dangerous for lesbians in several ways. It is personally dangerous to write erotic lesbian poetry in a British society turning away from liberal personal politics to the legalising of homophobic attitudes shown in the British Section 28. ('The naked majesty', p. 79)

she is pointing to the political dimension of sex, the fact that it is subject to intervention from the state and is policed by the state through legislation, is therefore both a private and a public concern. Whether or not this is desirable is beside the point; it is the reality we face. When Joan Nestle invokes the McCarthy era in America as a period of persecution of lesbians (*A restricted country*, p. 144) in her defence of her erotic writing, she is pointing out the political dimension of sexuality. The rise of AIDS during the 1980s has heightened this political dimension, furthered the basis for state intervention in individuals' sexual lives, and intensified debates about how sex should be represented.

One consequence of this has been the registering of an increasing AIDS awareness in erotic writing. The editors of *Serious pleasure*, insisting that their texts are fantasies and not necessarily what their authors do, state:

Safer sex is a case in point. Interestingly none of the stories submitted to us included safer sex as an issue either to be addressed in the context of the story or built into a sexual encounter. (pp. 11–12)

The editors appear torn between feeling that 'it is important that the issue of safer sex is always acknowledged in some way' and not believing 'that all fictional writing or visual representation of lesbian sex should immediately incorporate safer sex guide lines' (p. 12). In consequence, they append 'Notes on AIDS and safer sex' at the end of *Serious pleasure*.

In this publication, 'safer sex' is constructed as an optional extra on the basis that the stories represent fantasy not reality. Pat Califia had no such option regarding *Macho sluts*, because her publishers Alyson had a 'policy against eroticising high-risk sex' (*Macho sluts*, p. 17). Califia, who had to rewrite some of her texts to conform to Alyson's standards, offers several explanations for her resistance to writing from a safer sex base as a matter of course:

> I hope I managed to retain the highly charged emotional content of these stories without cum touching taste buds or mucous membranes. Porn can be a valuable way to teach people how to have hot and satisfying 'safer sex.' But I don't believe 'unsafe' porn causes AIDS any more than I think 'violent' porn causes rape. Nobody ever caught a disease from or got assaulted by a book. Images and descriptions are forever getting confused with live acts. (p. 17)

One of Califia's explanations here is that safe sex is not sexy, loses 'highly charged emotional content'. This suggests the importance of the notion of risk that can be involved in sexuality as a significant aspect of 'the sexy' but it also highlights how difficult it is to re-vision sexual practice and cultural attitudes towards the erotic. The second reason given by Califia is similar to the one offered by the Sheba Collective, namely that descriptions and images are not 'live acts', in other words, that one ought to distinguish between 'fantasy' and 'reality'. But the last sentence of Califia's here quoted indicates exactly why her position is a 'cop-out'. It is precisely because 'images and descriptions are forever getting confused with live acts' that publications on sexuality have to address safer sex. It is because some readers do read lesbian erotica and porn for information that safer sex has to be an overt issue in these writings. Pretending otherwise is irresponsible *vis-à-vis* the lesbian community.

Which leads me on to the second point I wish to raise here, that of censorship in relation to lesbian porn and lesbian sado-masochistic writing. Censorship is a difficult and emotive area. It seems to me that many people recognize the infringement of personal liberty involved in censorship, yet are left with the question, should the individual and her desires be more important than the community? Given that we live as social beings, what should the negotiation between individual and community be? Further, if there is no censorship, does that amount to saying, 'Anything goes'? And, if everything does not go, what should the bottom line(s) be and how should it/they be decided on? Many people's 'gut reaction', myself included, appears to be that they want censored what they disapprove of and endorsed what they themselves find unproblematic. It is impossible, of course, to arrive at a solution to the issue of censorship on such an individualistic basis.

Joan Nestle and Pat Califia, both of whom write lesbian porn, are, of course, against censorship. In her essay 'My history with censorship' Nestle argues that the 'lesbian-feminist antipornography movement' and the 'homophobia and antisex mentality' (p. 148) conspire to

> create a new McCarthy period in the Lesbian community. Some Lesbians are more acceptable than others. Leather and butch and femme Lesbians, transsexuals, Lesbian prostitutes and sex workers, writers of explicit sexual stories – little by little we are being rounded up. (p. 149)

Nestle constructs the position of being anti lesbian-porn as a continuation of the persecution of homosexuals during the McCarthy era, thus suggesting that in being anti lesbian-porn one is anti-lesbian or indeed anti-sex. Her 'history with censorship' does little to analyse the reasons for censorship; instead she generalizes from the particular (lesbian porn) to the general (lesbians), insisting that *any* rejection of a specific lesbian practice or articulation is a rejection of lesbians in general. There is a good deal of emotional blackmail in Nestle's stance who, redirecting her guns, makes lesbians who do not support lesbian porn into the new 'enemy' intent upon excommunicating her: 'I have been homeless before and I can be homeless again, but I almost think I have lived too long when I see Lesbians become members of the new vice squad' (*A restricted country*, p. 150)

Pat Califia describes women's situation in not dissimilar terms:

> Women – especially lesbians – exist under conditions that make us

frightened to step out of line, frightened to challenge the status quo, almost unable to imagine what bold and brassy, peacock creatures we could be if we were free. (p. 14)

She considers her writing transgressive, striking against 'the self-image of the so-called majority' whose 'range of acceptable sexual behaviour' is 'narrow' (p. 16). She implies that most people act and fantasize about sex in a way that cannot be described as normal (p. 16) which suggests that she assumes that if people felt able to take the license, they would act/fantasize as transgressively as is imaginable. She also maintains that

'Feminist erotica' that presents a simplistic view of lesbian sex as two women in love in a bed who embody all the good things the patriarchy is trying to destroy isn't very sexy. (p. 13)

Clearly, what we find sexy is not easy to generalise. Califia's writing is certainly transgressive, in a variety of ways which include sado-masochistic practices and mother-daughter incest, for example. Lisa Henderson celebrates Califia's *Macho sluts* as an example of 'cultural transgression and sexual demystification' ('Lesbian pornography', pp. 176–81). Henderson argues that Califia's writings and lesbian porn in general 'declare some resistance to heterosexist and patriarchal cultural scripts' (p. 187). This may well be but what does it do for women?

Here I want to address what I find difficult about *Macho sluts*. I can understand Gillian Hanscombe's reaction against lesbian porn in 'In among the market forces?' where she posits an emotionally based passion and 'decent lesbian sex' against 'the current lesbian sex industry hype' which she regards not as 'postfeminist' but as 'antifeminist, since its stated values do not attempt to challenge patriarchy and do not promote egalitarianism between women' (p. 217). But she couches some of her response in a terminology which is so freighted with negative and bourgeois connotations that it undermines her argument. 'Decent lesbian sex' – and I find the word *decent* particularly problematic here – for Hanscombe means, 'satisfying' and 'ethically defensible' (p. 218). I think Hanscombe is on stronger grounds with her second than with her first meaning of *decent*.

What, then, do I find difficult concerning *Macho sluts*? I object to the notion that wanting something is a sufficient reason for providing it. Supporting that notion also means supporting the idea that the

F

individual *chooses* what she wants 'freely', that however she handles what she chooses is her responsibility. In addition Califia's arguments about the 'fantasy' and 'reality' aspects of sado-masochism are muddled. Thus she maintains on the one hand that 'fantasy is a realm in which we can embrace pleasures that we may have very good reasons to deny ourselves in real life' and that 'many people do not fantasize about the kind of sex that they actually do have' (p. 16); on the other, she maintains that through porn people find out that there are others who do the same things as they do (p. 22). Califia keeps alternating between asserting that S/M is fantasy occurring only in the mind and that it is reality, enacted by a number of people. Both arguments are used to support her position. I am not sure that either argument makes it 'all right'. Why not? There are three things I particularly object to in S/M as presented in Califia's book:

1) the patriarchal power structures that are replicated in the submission-domination routines between participants, articulated in lines such as: "'I'm nothing,"[12] Clarissa cried in ecstacy. "I deserve nothing but the most brutal and rigorous punishment.'" (p. 71);

2) the systematic humiliation and degradation of individuals expressed in sentences such as the following which refers to a female servant who during an S/M party, 'had been relieved of her serving duties and used solely as an ashtray' (p. 76);

3) the infliction of pain of any kind.

All of these central aspects of S/M are not rendered acceptable to me by pointing to consent. Califia has sections such as the following which, as far as I understand Lisa Henderson's chapter, are supposed to 'make pointed distinctions between sadomasochism and sexual coercion' ('Lesbian pornography', p. 184):

> Even when correcting serious misdeeds, Berenice was not brutal. She loved helplessness, she craved the sight of a female body abandoning all decency and self-control.[13] These things are not granted save in loving trust. Dominance is not created without complicity. A well-trained slave is hopelessly in love with her mistress. (p. 67)

It is assumed here, as it is by Henderson, that 'sexual coercion' means actual rape and unsolicited sexual violence and that consent equals the absence of such coercion. The fact that 'training' is referred to in this context and that sexual behaviour is learnt is disregarded. If someone craves to be humiliated, should we humiliate that person? Are they not victims of a socialization that encouraged them to allow themselves to be degraded in order to be valued, even before they encounter the 'top'(dominant person)? And should the continuation and reinforcement of such conditioning be encouraged? Contrary to Califia I do not believe that individuals can choose 'freely' but that what they consent to is a function of their socialization and acculturation. Where such processes have encouraged an individual to believe that a (positive) sense of self can be attained through humiliation, degradation and pain, should this be encouraged further?

This, of course, leaves one with the uncomfortable issue of who makes the decisions about what is 'good' for a woman? If it is naive to assume that there is such a thing as an autonomous individual operating from a position of free will, therefore capable of consent, is it equally naive to assume that censorship can operate for the good of a community? I cannot answer these questions but it seems to me of paramount importance that we remain aware of the issues involved in making sexual choices.

Notes

1 For an extended discussion see Amber Hollibaugh and Cherríe Moraga, 'What we're rollin around in bed with: sexual silences in feminism' in Ann Snitow *et al.* eds, *Desire*, pp. 404–14.

2 In their essay '"Doing it": representations of lesbian sex' Jenny Kitzinger and Celia Kitzinger argue, among other things, that in the current political climate, representations of lesbian sex may not be the most important thing to worry about and campaign around (in Griffin, ed., *Outwrite*).

3 As Caroline Halliday in 'The naked majesty of god' maintains: 'I shall put writing and reading poetry, which is concerned with lesbian eroticism, in the context of lesbians' struggles in general to survive. In writing of the erotic, lesbian poets are describing intimacies for ourselves, and yet need to protect ourselves, if we can, from public danger.' (p. 76)
Sheba Collective, explaining their decision to publish lesbian erotic texts, write: 'We know also that there are men out there who will get off on our 'perversity'. In a male-dominated world, lesbian sex is both a serious and disgusting affront to men's indispensibility and a rivetting turn on to some of them ... At a certain point our confidence must override our fears. That is the risk we are willing to take as opposed to remaining silent. (*Serious pleasure*, p. 10)

4 Pat Califia says in this context: '[Gay men or straights] might not recognize themselves when they are dressed up for lesbian consumption any more than we recognize ourselves in the lesbian magazines produced for straight men. (Although I certainly have no objection to non-lesbian readers enjoying this book [*Macho sluts*]') (*Macho sluts*, p. 17).

5 The influence of lesbian writings on lesbians is made clear in many of the inter-

views with older lesbians found in Neild and Pearson; Radclyffe Hall's *The well* features prominently as a source of (mis)information (e.g. pp. 34, 91–2, 97–9, 119, 127).

6 In 'Sexuality and the historian' Jeffrey Weeks discusses the changes in depiction and perception of sexuality, including homosexuality, over time (see *Sex, politics and society*, pp. 1–18).

7 In an interviw with Sue O'Sullivan, Cindy Patton discusses the problematic of an absence of a 'map' of lesbian sexuality, maintaining: 'In a context where many lesbians haven't even tentatively mapped out collective sexual categories, it seems what you describe as the normalization process – the opening up of sexual discussion – still has to be the baseline from which we start.' ('Mapping: lesbians, AIDS and sexuality', p. 128).

8 The traumas of lesbian sexuality are discussed in some of the contributions to Neild and Pearson, eds (e.g. pp. 72, 113–4, 121–2).

9 That some of Stein's writings are considered erotic by some is indexed by the fact that sections from two of her texts are included in *Erotica: an anthology of women's writing*, ed. Margaret Reynolds (London, 1990).

10 This quotation is taken from Adrieene Rich's poem 'The images' in *A wild patience has taken me this far*, p. 5.

11 See also McEwen, ed., 'Naming the waves' pp. 6-7; 'One fool to another' pp. 27–8; 'You like me' pp. 79–80; 'From the monkey house and other cages' pp. 102–6. These are just *some* of the poems aligning body with nature/landscape from *one* anthology – there are many more.

12 Rosanna Hibbert's narrative tells the story of what it feels like to be nothing, to feel that she did not exist in ways that make one question the desirability of such a state of mind (Neild and Pearson, eds, pp. 113–7).

13 Such voyeuristic desire which constructs woman as spectacle is discussed by Hélène Cixous and Cathérine Clément in *The newly born woman* (Manchester, 1986), pp. 10–26.

Chapter 7

'… when I'm sixty-four': images of older lesbians

New frontiers

On 20 August 1992 Esmé Ross Langley died. Esmé Langley was very important for the lesbian community in Britain;[1] she was one of five founder members of the Minorities Research Group, which was set up in 1963 and went on to produce the lesbian newletter *Arena 3*, a lifeline for many isolated lesbians around the country, a source of information and a written space in which to meet other lesbians (as detailed in Neild and Pearson's *Women like us*, pp. 73, 84). Reading her obituary in *The Guardian* on 25 August 1992, I was struck by the fact that the representation of her life seemed to turn her into a sort of super-Radio-4-listener kind of person, with 'wide interests' and an all-British personality, full of 'courage' and 'humour'. I understand how difficult it is to sum up a woman's life in so many words, and it is not that I believe that the things said in the obituary are not true of her,[2] but it seems to me that in the course of the obituary Langley underwent a 'normatization' process by the end of which she was the kind of person whose death *The Guardian* might acknowledge – but without having to address her lesbianism.

Her death is important not only because a life that did much to support the lesbian community came to an end, but because it reminds us of the fact that lesbians grow old and that a large older

159

lesbian community exists. Once upon a time we might not have known of such women because they were closeted, and were without public meeting-places or public voices. This is no longer the case. These days lesbians who came out in the 1950s, 1960s and 1970s are getting middle-aged and beyond – there is a generation now of *out* older lesbians. In the past fifteen years lesbian nation has experienced the existence of enough 'out' members at either end of the age spectrum to represent a life-cycle. Yet the ageing of the population as a whole and the increase in numbers of older 'out' lesbians has not resulted in older lesbians gaining a greater voice in the community to the extent one might imagine. As Suzanne Neild and Rosalind Pearson state in the introduction to *Women like us*:

> That ageism is a strong force in modern society comes as no surprise to most of us. Young is the thing to be – it's where the ideas are, where the power lies and certainly where the style is. Consequently, the media is not interested in older women – they are not considered newsworthy, not 'attractive' and have only a past to offer! (p. 11)

It has to be said that much writing on lesbians confirms this stance. Recent critical texts on lesbian writing such as Sally Munt's *New lesbian criticism* or Karla Jay and Joanne Glasgow's *Lesbian texts and contexts*, both of which are excellent anthologies, do not consider representations of older lesbians. They focus, as indeed do other such texts,[3] on a youthful lesbian, somewhere between her twenties and forties (though you would not think the latter to look at her – the beauty myth has clearly been unquestioningly taken on board).

It is different when you start considering older lesbians. They represent one of the frontiers in contemporary lesbian writing because for the first time we have older lesbians who articulate ageing and what this means (I'm thinking particularly of writers like May Sarton here) and, contrary to the point made by Neild and Pearson, they not only have a past to offer but also a present. This present, and this is a second and major reason why representations of older lesbians constitute a new cultural frontier, is full of the taboos our culture has found most difficult to address. The present and presence of older lesbians reminds us of the changes that have occurred in lesbian history, but also of how little has changed in some respects, of the fact that the clichés we have come to accept so easily as lesbian history are indeed only clichés; it reminds us of independent women's ability to survive in a society that seeks to tie women down, of women's *choice* to move from heterosexuality to lesbianism, ageing itself, the relationship between the older individual and her community, sexuality, illness (specifically cancer) and death. The last four concerns are especially silenced in this culture which has sold out to youth at the expense of age and is now faced with having to reconsider the cultural, socio-economic and political meanings of age in a rapidly ageing society. In this context, writings on/by older lesbians open up new areas of enquiry, breaking taboos and silences surrounding older lesbians' lives. Their stories to some extent map our futures, indeed our present.

Life as struggle: changing roles in middle/old age

One of the earliest texts focussing on older women in the post-liberation-movements period of the 1970s was June Arnold's *Sister gin* (1975). The text centres entirely on older women: women of middle age and women who are in their seventies. It explores the relationships of these women, several of whom are mothers and daughters,[4] with each other. In so doing it deals with a series of taboo topics including alcoholism, the menopause, unemployment, weight problems, cross-generational sexual desire, ageing and lesbianism.

Su and Bettina are a lesbian couple in their late forties. Having lived 'in the closet' for virtually all of their twenty-year relationship their roles reverse in the course of the novel; in part one, Su is the efficient, controlled, working partner in a relationship, with Bettina spending her days in an alcoholic haze at home; in part two, Su has been fired from her job as book review editor, spends her time at home, drunk, trying to write a play while Bettina loses weight and works. Su is going through the menopause, the effects of which are described at length, culminating with the assertion:

> Women, someone had once said, are water-shedders. Women's bodies collect and dispense fluids. From tears over lost love to flashes from absenting hormones, we drip onto the ground, wet our surfaces, slip and slide, through our race to grab onto each other on a layer of fluid more alike than not. We fail more often than not. We sweat more than we drool, vomit more than we feed, let loose a greater volume of tears than birthwater, more waste urine from bar drinks than menstrual blood from refused pregnancies... Until the year when we see that we have dripped away our energy and we can only weep for the past and ask, is this all there ever was? (pp. 54–5)

The novel makes clear that individual women's experiences of the menopause differ. For Su's mother the menopause, due to its coincidence with the loss of her son through cot death, signified loss. Su wants hers to 'be the beginning of something' (p. 78).

And this is what happens, though by coincidence rather than by design. Su falls in love with Mamie Carter Wilkinson, a woman in her seventies. Mamie acts as a catalyst in Su's life, enabling her to accept her lesbianism and to come out of 'the closet'. As Su eulogizes:

> Change of life by definition refers to the future; one life is finishing therefore another life must be beginning. The menopausal armies mass on the brink of every city and suburb; everything that was is over and there is nothing left there to keep our sights lowered. See the rifles raised? This army doesn't travel on its uterus any more. Bettina, you must see that to stay back in that young [premenopausal] section with you when I can reach out to age itself, lust after a final different dry silken life ... There is no more beautiful word in the language than withered. (p. 133)

Su's new-found sense of self constitutes a radicalization which, in the first instance, has a number of negative consequences for her. Ready to affirm her lesbianism, Su is willing to be supportive of women and uses her work as book review editor for a non-feminist magazine, ironically entitled *Commercial-Appeal*, to express this position. She is fired because she decides to publish a damning piece on a novel by Joyce Carol Oates which she regards as non-feminist and because of a review of five lesbian texts. Her job loss results in depression, an inability to work on the play she was going to write and alienation from Bettina. Su finally moves beyond this negative phase when she decides to become a feminist activist.

Sister gin suggests that physical change in the form of the menopause can also produce psychological change, such as Su finally acknowledging her lesbianism and coming to terms with her ageing through embracing age in her affair with Mamie Carter. That relationship allows Su (and the reader) to view the aged body from the viewpoint of Su's sexual desire:

> Su saw in her mind [Mamie's] coveted breasts, ... hanging now from the base of the breastbone like soft toys, too small to rest a head upon, fit for a hand to cuddle very gently like the floppy ears of a puppy... memory dropped her hand to Mamie Carter's sparse hair curling like steel – there was enough strength between her legs and no dough there where the flesh was fluid enough to slip away from the bone and leave that tensed

grain hard as granite and her upright violent part like an animal nose against Su's palm. (pp. 129–30)

For Mamie Carter 'the delights of old age ... include the fact of endlessly drawn out orgasms' (p. 129); in her Su can see what may be her own future which includes sexual activity, being loved by someone younger than yourself, and taking an active part in the politics of the day.

The construction of Mamie Carter seems, in many respects, rather idealistic; apart from presenting her as a woman with money who in age has come into her own and looks beautiful, Mamie is also depicted as someone in control of her life who refuses to allow either herself or others to be victimized. Together with five other old women she creates the *Shirley Temple Emeritae*, a group of elderly women – brought up to be Southern belles – who dispense justice to rapists in the form of tying them up and leaving them with the lower halves of their bodies exposed at the site of their crimes. Through this activism the older women are celebrated as significant members of their community; when they decide to run for political office and one of them wins, the demand that older people have a voice in the community is finally realized. The political activism of the older women towards the end of the novel, and Su's enhanced political awareness, represent cultural encodings of one of the 'lessons' of the liberation movements, namely that political activism is a method for change (see chapter 2). Such politicization is found less frequently in novels of the second half of the 1980s, a period when women's political activism in Britain and elsewhere declined.[5]

One of the points made in *Sister gin* is that women can facilitate change in each other. In this novel, such change is, by and large, for the better. Most of the older women in this text, for example, have a moment of triumph when aspects of themselves that had become buried resurface. This is particularly prominent in the case of Su's downtrodden mother who has spent a lifetime being ruled by her husband. When Su tells her that she is a lesbian and that Bettina is not her roommate but her lover, it triggers in Su's mother memories of an old woman friend with whom she lost touch. Without telling her husband, Su's mother arranges to meet her friend again; they have a wonderful and very close time together which culminates in Su's mother having an orgasm while at the dentist where her memories of meeting up again with her friend, the doctor's stories, and a gentle female assistant (inadvertently) help her to a state of arousal she has not experienced for a long time. Through this touching and funny episode, as well as through the depiction of the sexual relationship between Su and Mamie Carter, the idea of older women being capable of having and enjoying sex is emphasized. Further, it is suggested that their sexual orientation is fluid and that indexes of heterosexuality such as marriage and children do not necessarily define sexual identity. Heterosexual older women are presented as blooming through (re)focussing their sexual interest on women.

Butch to femme

In a very different text, Joan Nestle's 'A change of life', the issue of sexual identity and age are raised, as the author, in her mid-forties, surveys her lesbian past and present. Coming out of a butch-femme role-playing tradition, her past is that of the femme, of the submissive, taking body.

> 'After forty, femmes turn butch,' we would repeat laughingly, young women in the bars. But the transformation seemed so far away, and we stood so hot in our pants, that this prediction was emptied of its cultural wisdom. (p. 131)

Finding that in middle age she wants to act the butch with a woman, Nestle sees herself as transformed in and through lesbian history: 'I have become our own mythology' (p. 132). Her behaviour replicates and expresses the stories she used to hear. In its mirroring of lesbian cultural traditions, it affirms her part in and her being part of the community of older lesbians:

> I hear old butches laughing. 'I was waiting for when you would become Poppa,' Mabel said. 'It's about time,' she chuckled. Then later in the day, for the first time in our thirty-five-year-old history, she called me Mr. Nestle. (p. 132)

Mabel expresses the notion of a lesbian sexual life-cycle in which at certain times one fulfils particular roles, thus confirming both the myth underlying this narrative of the sexual life-cycle and simultaneously confirming Nestle's belonging.

Nestle herself sees in the younger woman who is femme to her butchness someone who is both self and other:

> I know her fears, they have been mine. I know her hungers, they have
> been mine. I know her delights, they have been mine. Yet she is not me,
> not what I was or what I am. (p. 131)

The sexual identity of the self and sexual identity as culturally
constructed are presented as changing over time. The younger
woman's femininity is different, 'more audacious' (p. 131) than Joan's
was, and yet they enact a relationship similar to the ones in Joan's
past. Sameness and difference are here simultaneously experienced.
But their respective significances are obliterated in an overarching
sense of transcendent lesbian mythology which envisions both the
future, represented by the younger woman, and the past,
encapsulated in Joan's memories of women from the past 'who tried
to teach me the ways of our people' (p. 133). Within this chain Joan
finds her place, not through affirmation from the subsequent
generation but, as does Su in *Sister gin*, through support from the
previous one:[6]

> I hear my elders, scarred and knowing, laughing kindly, saying to me,
> Come on girl. We welcome you. (p. 133)

Cindy Patton, in the context of discussing s/m practices as 'a career'
where you learn to 'master' certain behaviours, interprets Nestle's
representation of changing from being femme to being butch as
follows:

> I think what she's talking about is not so much a career, as the acquisition
> of a set of competences. It may be that certain sexual practices in our
> culture require expertise, or knowledge of your own body that takes time...
> it may be that there are cultural structures in place that make it easier to
> navigate sexuality in predetermined ways than to choose a different
> trajectory. (O'Sullivan, 'Mapping: lesbians, AIDS and sexuality', pp. 131–2)

It does not seem to me that Nestle's text centres on describing the
acquisition of sexual practices to be handed down to the next
generation once you have mistressed them. Rather, 'A change of life'
is concerned with detailing how identity within the lesbian community is, in part, determined by sexual practice and that it is through
sexual practice that Nestle asserts her identity, her sharing of a
mythology into which, by virtue of living it, she integrates herself. I
maintain this to some extent because in the opening essay of *A
restricted country*, 'I am', Nestle focusses on the assertion of an
identity against a sense of coming from 'people who have no

mythologies, no goddesses powerful and hidden, to call on' (p. 13). Nestle, in 'A change of life' is answering the blank of one history – her personal one – with the mythologies of another – a communal one. Lesbian peoples are her people and through living out those myths, she can affirm her self, construct a home for herself. These myths are the lesbian cultural structures which, to use Patton's words, 'make it easier to navigate sexuality in predetermined ways than to choose a different trajectory'.

Senses of belonging

In adopting identities, individuals tend either to work within the cultural structures of the communities to which they belong, or they refuse these structures. It is in this sense that Nestle's construction of living-out lesbian mythologies can be understood. Her alignment with the lesbian community and her sense of enacting lesbian sexual mythology are interrelated. Starting from the view that 'we need to know that we are not accidental, that our culture has grown and changed with the currents of time, that we, like others, have a social history' ('Voices from lesbian herstory', p. 110), and understanding that 'I [am] part of a special tradition and culture' ('Voices', p. 114), Nestle maintains:

> As we explore women's culture and its connection to Lesbian culture, we must realize that we no longer have to say that being a Lesbian is more than a sexuality. Sexuality is not a limiting force but a whole world in itself that feeds the fires of all our other accomplishments. ('Voices', p. 119)

For the central characters of Jane Rule's *Memory board*, sexuality is the dividing line that separates non-identical twins Diana and David and their respective homosexual and heterosexual worlds until they reach old age. As David realizes:

> It was not until Diana came home with Constance that David understood she had not intended him to wait for her, keeping their androgynous, virginal life intact for her. What separated them was not the gulf between the sexes but sex itself. She had chosen her own. (p. 183)

There is a nice ambiguity in the last sentence here in that 'she had chosen her own' can refer both to choosing women and to choosing what kind of sexual activity she wanted. The two are, of course, linked. But there is also the use of the verb 'choose', suggesting voluntarism.

Throughout the novel Diana is cast as someone who 'had lived out her desires mostly on blind will. She did what she had to do without counting the cost' (p. 60). From David's viewpoint, she has been 'true to her own desire' (p. 150) while he lived out roles allocated to him through social convention. The explanation offered for their difference is genderized, as David ruefully reflects: 'If you were a girl, you didn't have to be somebody; you could be yourself, Nobody cared, or cared as much.' (p. 5). But the novel does not set up crude binarist oppositions between the twins. Rather, it offers a complex view of the issue of life-choices. Diana does not regard her love for Constance with whom she has lived for forty years as a matter of choice (p. 135) and the text indicates that their commitment to each other has not been unproblematic. Diana's exclusive focus on Constance[7] was not reciprocal. Constance had affairs with other women including a temporary live-in one. Against David's assertion that their relationship is 'no less a commitment than marriage' (p. 195), Constance, who has a great desire to be free, insists: 'We're not *married*... we're two very separate fleshes.' (p. 67).

Diana is constructed as an individualist in this novel; having moved away from her family, partly through desire and partly through David's wife's virulent rejection of her for being a lesbian, she refuses to align herself with any group or community. She and Constance live a life of relative social isolation from both a heterosexual and a lesbian community. As Diana says to David: 'I don't have a world, David, not in that sense' (p. 153). This means that Diana, unlike Nestle, for example, is not presented as living in accordance with the history of a particular community but rather, that she 'pleases herself' as, in David's view, only extraordinary people do (p. 13). She has not, from David's perspective, done as he did, that is – to use Patton's words again – 'navigate[d] sexuality in predetermined ways' but has '[chosen] a different trajectory'. David's perspective of Diana's behaviour is influenced by his acceptance of the norms of a heterosexist community against whose imperatives Diana appears to have rebelled. However, she is not unique in her lifestyle; Diana has, in fact, lived out a lesbian existence not atypical for a gay woman who is 65 in 1986. Living a socially contained life without commitment to the lesbian community is not uncommon for older lesbians (see for instance June Patterson's story (Adelman pp. 109-15)).

Diana's relationship to the gay rather than the lesbian community changes in the course of the novel. She does not discuss her sexual proclivities with anyone to the extent that her family reject her on a hunch rather than on certain knowledge. Throughout the text she refuses all labels. She does not want to be part of 'a meaningful minority' (p. 154). When David, trying to reconcile himself with his sister, starts to buy *The body politic*, Canada's gay paper, in order 'to learn something from it' which might help him in his relationship with Diana, she gets angry, saying: 'Reading about a homosexual subculture to understand me is insulting' (p. 153). Diana does not wish to be labelled because she does not wish to be 'judged' purely in terms of her sexuality. She does not regard homosexuals as 'a meaningful minority' (p. 154). But she has no alternative way of viewing the homosexual community either.

The catalysing event which precipitates her need to engage with the gay community occurs when a young man who has been diagnosed as suffering from AIDS comes to seek her advice as a doctor and a lesbian. Even then, 'from behind that deep barrier, the real person of Diana was silent' (p. 219). She tells David:

> I wouldn't say, even to that dying boy, ... that, yes, I am gay or queer or homosexual or lesbian. I am Diana Crown, a proud woman nearly turned to stone, but for Constance. (p. 230)

Despite her unwillingness to identify with this any of the various labels denoting lesbianism, Diana attempts to help Richard come to terms with the fact that he will die of AIDS. She makes enquiries for him and finds that

> she was encouraged by how adequate a support system had been set up, not at the level of her profession, though there were responsible doctors involved, but by the volunteers who referred to themselves as members of the gay community or friends of the gay community, knowledgeable and personally concerned. These were the people whose existence she had always denied, who believed, as she never had, that they were members of a real minority and responsible to it. (p. 215)

Diana is not capable of taking on a community orientation but she is willing to help on an individual basis. The novel suggests an indirect reconciliation between her and that community.

Memory board is a novel about reconciliations, of trying to understand and come to terms with differences. Diana, who has lived her life in a lesbian relationship, and her twin David, who gave himself up to heterosexuality in a marriage to a woman 'as heterosexual as Eve' (p. 28) – what choice did *she* have? – are finally reunited under one roof in their old age. Diana is reconciled with a significant section of the rest of her family. Diana and Constance achieve an equilibrium through mutual need and support.

In these reconciliations and acceptances *Memory board* occasionally tends towards the mawkish. What saves it from being 'sugary' is that these moments of good will are embedded in a narrative which focusses to a large extent on the problems imposed on older people through the failing of their bodies and the changing of their roles in society. Constance's memory loss which 'secures' her to Diana by cutting her off from much of the rest of the world also ties Diana down. Diana's own declining constitution makes caring for Constance by herself increasingly difficult. This is complicated by the fact that they have a *lesbian* relationship, for at points of crisis the absence of a generally accepted, socio-legal framework for a lesbian relationship means that Diana has to invoke her profession:

> In all the complex dealings with authority Diana had had to do for Constance over the years, she was grateful to have had that key which unlocks all doors, her title; for as friend and lover Diana would have had a difficult time even reporting that Constance was missing. She certainly wouldn't get access to her in hospital or in jail. (pp. 95–6)

Implicit in this statement is a critique of a society which refuses to acknowledge the legitimacy of homosexual relationships, a fact that is highlighted in the context of crises when an individual needs support and when, as this novel suggests, those relationships which are legally sanctioned, can fail. The gay boy Richard, suffering from AIDS, is disowned by his parents who throw him out; he gets help from Diana's straight nephew and from Diana, a fellow gay person.

Memory board portrays individuals' need of support structures. However, it reverses the common representation of the supposed outsider, in this case the lesbian, as socially needy, by putting a heterosexual male in the role of outsider. What David finds is that

> [Diana and Constance] didn't, after all, view their life together as a banishment. They were not waiting to be forgiven and restored. David was the petitioner on behalf of himself and those members of his family who might be pleasing and even helpful to them. (p. 84)

It is the heterosexual, marginalized male who wants to be accepted by his lesbian sister and not the other way round. He has, in that sense, been defeated by her independence, by the fact that she and her lover do not feel guilty and have lived happily without him.

> When Una Troubridge was asked how she and Radclyffe Hall, as Catholics, managed confession, she said they had nothing to confess. (p. 161)

Constance, who is more willing than Diana to acknowledge publically her lesbianism and has in the past wanted to join gay pride marches, takes a slightly different view concerning lesbianism. Referring back to Troubridge and Hall she maintains: 'You want to be like them... You want to be innocent. I don't care about being guilty' (p. 161). Neither woman, however, manifests or lives a sense of guilt and the novel rejects that position, saying, 'Everyone has been taught to feel ashamed about sex. Most of us outgrow it' (p. 154). The novel makes clear that the meaning of sex varies from person to person but at the same time offers one specific distinction between heterosexual and lesbian women's experience of sex. Constance, who is described as having 'sexual vitality' (p. 147) considers 'linking sexuality with procreation ... as a misused piece of information' because what she and Diana are doing 'has nothing to do with making babies' (p. 68). Fear of pregnancy does not enter the lesbian sexual equation. In heterosex this is different. David recognizes that sex between him and his wife was tainted through its association with pregnancy: 'it was never a simple, joyful act as it had been before it was so clearly associated with birth and death. They were fallen creatures' (p. 147). Diana, who was an obstetrician, is aware that pregnancy and child-birth could result in women turning to other women and away from bad marriages whose badness was encapsulated in sexual problems related to issues of pregnancy, fertility and ownership of the woman's body. The fact that for lesbians sex is not associated with procreation is constructed as an asset which suggests that they never have to leave the garden of Eden, while heterosexuals fall and are banished.

In our own words: the narratives of older lesbians

One way in which gay people have attempted to (re)create their histories has been through the establishment of archives[8] which function as resource centres for the gay community and which collect material concerning gay history. This includes individual lesbians' life stories. Such narratives are of particular importance for people who are marginalized within a given culture, for marginalized people often have only limited access to recording their experiences and transmitting their histories. Oral histories and the life stories of older lesbians provide evidence of lesbian traditions and perceptions which may not have been recordable in the past.

Life stories are told retrospectively. They frequently unfold sequentially, starting in childhood and coming up to the present. The narratives I shall look at here are told with a particular objective in mind – to indicate what it was like to be a lesbian in the past and what it is like to be an older lesbian now. They are also told by women willing to tell their story, that means women who feel they can discuss their lesbian lives. In that respect they represent a particular group of lesbians who may not reflect the views or situations of other older lesbians. The narratives they offer are constructed from a contemporary perspective; they are therefore informed by the present from which the past is viewed. This enables comparisons and the detailing of differences between the 'then' and the 'now'. However, and this needs to be emphasized, for all these points of comparison and similarity across the various lesbians' narratives, what seems to me most striking is how diverse the life stories are, how different the trajectories from one woman to the next.

The two anthologies I shall discuss, Marcy Adelman's *Long time passing: lives of older lesbians* and Suzanne Neild and Rosalind Pearson's *Women like us*, both highlight the movement from ignorance about lesbianism to 'knowledge' and, relatedly, from being closeted to 'coming out'. The 'ignorance' I refer to here varies from one lesbian to another; many detail 'crushes' on schoolfriends during their adolescence (e.g. *Women like us*, pp. 33, 37, 57, 63) and for some this meant that they could say as does Eleanor in *Women like us*, 'I knew I was a lesbian when I was fourteen. I accepted it as natural. It was natural to me that I loved women' (p. 33). Others, however, 'went through a heterosexual phase' and 'didn't think about lesbianism until I had my first affair with a woman when I was 32 and married. I didn't consider myself a lesbian – just that I'd fallen in love for this first time' (p. 91). Several women refer to the fact that 'the only thing I'd ever read was *The well of loneliness*' (*Women like us*, p. 92); that 'there was no interference then from the media, nothing on radio, there wasn't even television then' (*Women like us*, p. 38; see also p. 70), and that 'I don't know in those days if I ever knew anything about the word homosexual or lesbian or anything like that' (*Women like us*, p. 113). This 'ignorance' had two negative effects: firstly, it left women open to being made to feel guilty either of their own accord or through 'well-meaning' others such as mothers (e.g. *Long time*, pp. 122–3) or psychiatrists (e.g. *Long time*, pp. 60–3). Secondly, it propelled women into marriage (e.g. *Women like us*, p. 24). In this context the need to live up to a heterosexist society's expectations becomes very apparent. The persecution of lesbians in the army, for example, is repeatedly discussed (e.g. Wilma and Roberta's narrative in *Long time*, pp. 131–43, and Pat Bond's story in the same text, pp. 164–76). The effect of such persecution was that many lesbians born in the first quarter of this century started life 'in the closet'. Rachel Pinney in *Women like us*, for example, describes how she denied her lesbianism until the mid-1970s:

> I had a series of girlfriends ... But no word would be spoken, and I denied it fiercely if anyone mentioned it. You've no idea how strong this thing was. Like if I'd committed murder, I wouldn't admit it, ever, to anybody. (p. 25)

Similar comments are made by a number of women (e.g. *Women like us*, pp. 78, 92), but not all lesbians had that experience. Some, like Sally Maxwell, made a positive decision not to live in the closet:

> Although I'm in my fifties, I haven't had this back history of things being bad. I think I acepted my lesbian position at a time when it was easier to do so and so I thought, well, blow that for a laugh, I don't want all this kind of closet business. You might as well say what you are. (*Women like us*, p. 150)

Some women were out all their lives. Dr Eileen in *Long time passing* interestingly comments on having lived in a gay community in the 1950s and 1960s, and on the differences between that community and how things are now:

> In those days the gay community was much different than it is today. It was a large community that was almost entirely closeted to the outside world. We were not openly gay – it didn't seem like an option to us. I think we all felt it would be a mistake to 'broadcast' that we were gay. (p. 117)

Nonetheless, within the community everyone knew of and supported one another. It may be that the closed-offness of the gay community made it difficult for some women to locate it; several report that they seemed to be the only lesbian across a range of circumstances, and/or that they found it difficult to make contact with other lesbian women (e.g. *Women like us*, pp. 71, 92, 122, 137).

Having found the lesbian community, many of the women stress how important that community was and is for them, especially at times of need such as when they or their partners are ill or dying. The support lesbians derive from their community is particularly noticeable in *Long time passing* which, more than *Women like us*, focusses on the current situation of older lesbians rather than on their past. This present features two recurrent concerns: the women themselves or their lesbian partners being ill – frequently suffering from cancer – and partners' deaths. One section of *Long time passing* presents, in diary form, the final months of a lesbian couple where one of the partners is dying from cancer.

Illness and death are a taboo topic in this culture, not only with regard to those suffering from a disease or dying, but also from the point of view of the carer or partner and their responses and needs. In comparing 'Healing group' (*Long time passing*, pp. 51–7) and 'A gift to share' (*Long time passing*, pp. 94–108), it is noticeable that both pieces, one written from the perspective of a breast cancer sufferer, the other from that of the partner of a woman dying from cancer, each present one side of the same coin which consists of the tissue of need. Reminiscent of *Memory board* one couple

worry about how we can be recognized as a 'couple'(!) if there should be hospital procedures. Red tape that may exclude all but 'immediate family' – one's *spouse*, but not one's lover (lesbian)... (?) There are Power-of-Attorney papers we will sign for each other... (*Long time passing*, p. 96)

As is demonstrated by the sorrow of one woman in *Long time passing* who was only informed of her long-term lover's death after her lover had died (p. 20), understanding the legalities of one's situation as a lesbian is vital. It is in this respect that oral histories can provide information and thus fulfil one of the functions/reader expectations of lesbian writing (discussed in the previous chapter in the context of lesbian sexuality).

They also provide a way of validating experiences and feelings other lesbians might go through. The breaking of taboo surrounding illness and death, for instance, is particularly useful here. The description of tensions arising in a relationship when one partner is ill ('She wants a lot *of* me, *from* me but can give little in return.' *Long time passing*, p. 100) undercuts the notion of the 'angelic female carer' and reinstates that carer's rights to have her needs recognized. This is where 'The healing group' provides an interesting example of how a group can offer support. In the healing group, 'almost as much attention was paid to Jill's needs as Alvah's lover, as was paid to Alvah' (p. 53). The community, functioning as an extended – but voluntary – family, takes on some of the roles the individual woman cannot cope with by herself or in the couple formation. The result is a bonding which can help deal with illness, separation and death.

Another issue raised by older lesbians is their sexuality. One woman writes:

> I don't know if I feel seventy-five. I don't know how seventy-five is supposed to feel. Maybe I don't get as many wide-ons as I used to. But I think about sex all the time. Sex really hasn't changed over time. I've kept up – I keep doing these things. (*Long time passing*, p. 32)

One reason why sexual activity may be more openly discussed by older lesbians is perhaps that many have spent their lives going through serial relationships and therefore frequently form new partnerships in older age. One woman enthuses: 'I met someone several months ago, and I had hopes that it was going to blossom – she's seventy-seven, and I fell for her like a ton of bricks' (*Women like us*, pp. 61-2). That relationship 'turned out to be a holiday romance' (p. 62) but many are longer lasting.

Cross-generational relations concern several of lesbians here; having lovers that are younger by ten, twenty or even more years makes some women self-conscious about their age. As a relational structure based on sexual choice, cross-generational love affairs involving an older woman, especially if she is in her sixties or seventies, tend to be regarded as taboo. In contrast to heterosexist writing which asserts that only older women who look like young women (*à la* Joan Collins) should have a sexual life, older lesbians' stories reveal the sexuality of those deemed to be beyond sex by heteropatriarchal society. Recognition of discrepancies can nonetheless lead to a resistance to live out the possibilities offered by having a younger lover. One older lesbian writes:

> Several affairs that I was really happy with I ended because I was over twenty years older. They seemed so stable, but I thought, 'Well, what's going to happen? When they're forty I shall be sixty, when they're fifty, still on the go, I shall be seventy-odd and somebody's going to get hurt, so

it's better that I hurt them now by breaking it off than hurting each other later on when I'm older.' (*Women like us*, p. 41)

Another older lesbian maintains that 'having an affair with a younger woman doesn't necessarily make you feel young' because, for one thing, it can force you 'into almost an ageing parent role, rather than a lover' (*Long time passing*, p. 23).

Not all older women draw this conclusion or feel worried about being involved with younger lovers; one disabled lesbian describes how at 62 she started a relationship with a woman aged 22, how she then made friends with an older lesbian in the same relational position as herself and finally engaged in mutual consolation when the younger women moved on (*Long time passing*, pp. 112–3). Another woman describes how having a younger lover makes her 'apprehensive about retiring' (*Long time passing*, p. 119) from her job.

One aspect of living in accordance with their desires is that all the narratives of older lesbians address the question of coming out to their own parents, to peers, and to their children. In detailing transitional stages in their lives, most people, and this includes younger lesbians, will report difficulties with parents. Many of the 'classic' lesbian narratives already discussed in this book, from Radclyffe Hall's *The well* to Rita Mae Brown's *Rubyfruit jungle* and Jeanette Winterson's *Oranges* centre on the conflict arising between the lesbian and her parents as the former moves to assume her lesbian identity. While parents can play quite a major role in older lesbians's lives (see Adelman, pp. 122–30), the issue of the children and their responses is of greater significance and pays tribute to the fact that many older lesbians married and had children before deciding to live as lesbians. For some this decision was traumatic as husbands responded badly, indeed as the husband of one of the protagonists of Patricia Highsmith's *Carol* does, namely by threatening to 'expose me as a lesbian and take the children away' (*Long time passing*, p. 61). If children were not taken away, life as a lesbian with children could be difficult: 'It was hard. We had to wait until the children were asleep... I don't think we ever had a comfortable time in our sexual relationship unless we went away from the children.' (*Long time passing*, p. 75). The same lesbian couple also report that the children, while respecting their mother, have a love-hate relationship with the mother's long-term lover who co-parented them (pp. 80–1). However, some older lesbians register very positive experiences with their or their lover's children. As one woman writes:

> Jane's wonderful daughter Penny lives out here and she's part of my family now. I used to come out to California and my daughter Alice was always living with a guy and never had room. Penny was always living with women and she always had a bed where I could stay. So I always stayed with Penny and I was just as close to her as I was to my own daughter. (*Long time passing*, p. 21)

One could argue that the crucial difference is that Alice seems to be heterosexual and Penny a lesbian who supports her mother's lover because their sexual identities are similar; however, later on in the text the same older lesbian reports that, encouraged by Penny, she told her own daughter about her lesbianism: 'And it was fine. Alice said, "That OK, Mom, it doesn't bother me"' (p. 21). Here a lesbian is coming out to an adult daughter at a time when the daughter has already established a life of her own and is not entirely dependent on her mother. For many older lesbians who married and have children this is the only point when they can start to lead a life of their own. As Paula Gunn Allen suggests: '... middle age frees a woman for making choices congenial to her experiences, circumstances, and nature' (*Long time passing*, p. 188). And Vick Robson, one of the women portrayed in *Women like us*, describes 'coming out again after forty years': 'I felt closed up and I'd locked it up for so long. It was tearing me apart' (p. 55).

Coming out in middle age or at a later stage in life can give the individual lesbian a sense of freedom. As one 'ageing lesbian athlete' puts it:

> Aging has produced freedom from those awful 'What if's?' of my years of stardom. What if my business manager learned the rumours about me were true? What if my fans found out? What if my respected coach learned the truth about my sexual preference? What if the parents of the junior athletes I coached knew? (*Long time passing*, p. 69)

The celebration of freedom which this particular lesbian engages in and which she links specifically to older age is in part what enables some of the older lesbians to be politically active, going on marches and campaigns, and helping in support networks for lesbians. Many of the lesbians in *Women like us*, for example, mention taking part in gay pride marches and campaigning in connection with Clause 28 (e.g. pp. 42, 55, 66, 81, 95). It is through such political activities that older lesbians can experience integration into the lesbian community.

Pleading with Venus

Come then Venus lay me back there
hang your heavy breasts above.
I am growing nightly older
give me one last taste of love.

Such is the plea of the persona in Maureen Duffy's sequence of poems entitled 'Carmine Veneriana' which invokes the desire for sexual love in old age. Maureen Duffy is one poet who has addressed the issue of lesbian love in her work and, in her more recent poems, that love is explored in the context of ageing.

In 'Carmine Veneriana' Venus embodies an idea of love against which the reality of the ageing person, still desirous of a sexual/ sensual existence but also fearful of it, is tested. In 'Song for an Irish Wolfhound' (p. 246) the persona 'Venus' lucky lapdog' asks of a 'passing stranger' whose lapdog that person is and, further, 'who will take your part?', thus offering a pun on 'part' to mean: who will defend you, who will succeed you, and who will make love to you. It has previously been made clear that the lapdog is the (sexual) servant of its mistress, sometimes 'called to see her right' in the form of laying 'your head between her soft thighs/lap and lap until she comes'. But who will pleasure the lapdog remains unclear.

'*In memoriam*' highlights the problem of being unheeded by a loved one who, with her view trained firmly into the past, walks 'with long gone lovers/through the landskip of her heart' (p. 248). This container of dereliction which fosters nostalgia and invokes autumn ('where leaves fall, hands lock, buns are buttered') prevents the other woman from actively and passionately engaging with the persona who wants 'her to pull down your zip'. This raises the question of how to attract a lover, expressed in the subsequent poem, where Thomas Mann's novella *Death in Venice* forms the basis for asking 'Should I die [her] hair/like Aschenbach/face powder?' Venus, in answer, rejects this; the signs of age are her 'accolades/got in my service'.

Coming to terms with one's age and ageing body is one concern in 'Carmine Veneriana'; the other is how to deal with a potential new lover. When, in 'Venus and the handmaid', the persona is faced with a 'handmaid' brought by Venus, in a sense her very own lapdog, the person to take her 'part', this does not result in unmitigated rejoicing. 'And what is this I'm to do' is the question raised by the persona who feels she has to decide between Venus and the handmaid or between death and love. Again, as in 'Song for an Irish wolfhound' the question remains unanswered. In 'All clear' (p. 250) the question reappears in the persona's momentary hesitation as 'in her hall I shake my grey locks/expecting her to start back' but the lover's own silver hairs undercut any anxiety about being too aged. Encoding the experience of insecurity about one's welcome by describing a mock-competition with other possible suitors, the poem ends with 'two middle-aged lovers' going to bed 'where silver may be still/prime ore'. The sparsity of punctuation here – as elsewhere – creates ambiguity, allowing 'still' to be read as either belonging to 'to be' or as an adverbial phrase referring to time, meaning 'yet'. Similarly, 'prime' could be a verb or an adjective. The multiple meanings constructed here suggest both the value of age and the fact that in bed the persona is still allowed to make love to (to 'prime') her lover.

In the final instance, the poems come down on the side of love and its enactment, even against the grain of ageing. In 'Firelight' (p. 251) Venus becomes the figure of an old woman whose words the persona repeats: 'you say you are old now/you want to say adieu to love' but whose position she resists. The persona who 'burn[s] still' decides that it is 'better to be daft and obscene/than to be ashamed of that once-has-been'. Implicit in these lines is an acceptance that there is something inappropriate in (sexual) desire in old age, that one becomes 'old and ridiculous' when 'panting after your favours' beyond a certain age. At the same time, the persona's persistence in the pursuit of sensual pleasures offers a countervision of need to this image, and not just of that need but of need being met as evidenced in the poem 'All clear'. The final line of the sequence is, after all, 'I burn still' and this insistence on sexual desire in an older woman is the parting image of the sequence.

Older lesbians' work expresses experiences and constructs images which resist the terms of heterosexist conventions, more so, in many respects, than the work of younger women who often engage either only with a limited number of issues that are taboo or not at all with some of the concerns which in our society are not allowed cultural space. Of these, illness, specifically cancer, death, and sexuality beyond fertility are perhaps the most important subjects raised by older lesbians. They represent one frontier in the cultural work and history of Lesbian Nation. Vick Robson's words, 'And you can't push us back in the closet, because we're coming out on our own anyway.' (*Women like us*, p. 55) have their echo in Adrienne Rich's lines:

What does it mean to say *I have survived*
until you take the mirrors and turn them outward
and read your own face in their outraged light?

That light of outrage is the light of history
springing upon us when we're least prepared

(*An atlas of the difficult world*, pp. 48-9)

Notes

1 In Neild and Pearson's *Women like us*, Diana Chapman describes first meeting Esmé Langley with whom she lived for eighteen months: 'It wasn't until Esmé that I met somebody who actually said that they were lesbian' (p. 100). Esmé Langley's setting up of *Arena 3* is commented on by several women in this text (e.g. pp. 20, 26, 93, 100–1).

2 It is worth noting that one of the leading contemporary women novelists, Iris Murdoch, who has occasionally portrayed lesbian and gay men's relationships in novels such as *Henry and Cato* (London, 1976), *An accidental man* (London, 1971), *The Italian girl* (London, 1964), *The time of the angels* (London, 1966) and *An unofficial rose* (London, 1962), and in 1964 wrote an article on 'The moral decision about homosexuality' (*Man and society* 7, pp. 3-6), added a brief note to Esmé Langley's orbituary, writing: 'I recall her very clearly from the days of *Arena Three*.'

3 See, for example, E. Hobby and C. White, eds, *What lesbians do in books*; D. Fuss, ed., *Inside/out*; M. Lilly, ed., *Lesbian and gay writing*.

4 Commonly, where mother-daughter relationships are addressed, they tend to focus on a teenage daughter, or a daughter who is a young woman and a middle-aged or slightly older mother. Typical examples are Sylvia Plath's *The bell jar*, Shelagh Delaney's play *A taste of honey*, or the collection of short stories *Close company: stories of mothers and daughters*, (eds C. Park and C. Heaton) which features some stories with lesbian daughters/mothers. In specifically lesbian terms one need only think of Radclyffe Hall's *The unlit lamp* or Jeanette Winterson's *Oranges are not the only fruit*. One recent example of a text which also explores the relationship between a middle-aged daughter and older mother is Vivian Gornick's *Fierce attachments: a memoir* (New York, 1987).

5 This decline is registered in a comment by Laura Jackson in *Inventing ourselves* where, as part of an interview given in 1988, she says: 'Most of my work now is in schools, partly because I don't know where the Women's Movement is anymore...' (p. 133)

6 It may seem almost profane to say so – *pace* Joan Nestle – but I was struck by the fact that her representation of her place in lesbian mythology and history is very close to T.S. Eliot's view of the relationship between 'Tradition and the individual talent' (*Selected essays*, London, 1932, pp. 13–22).

7 In 'Healing group', Elenore Pred discusses the problematic of lesbian couples living without a social support network; in *Memory board* Diana's twin David and his family take on the role that the 'healing group' does for Pred and her partner (Adelman, ed., pp. 51–7).

8 For details of such archives see Joan Nestle's 'The will to remember: the lesbian herstory archives of New York' (*Feminist review* 34, Spring 1990, pp. 86–94) and Alison Reed's 'International archives' (*Feminist review* 34, Spring 1990, pp. 94–99).

Conclusion

Culturally encoded images of lesbians have changed in the course of the twentieth century as, for instance, Elizabeth Wilson's 'Chic thrills' indicates at the level of dress. Similar changes have been registered in textual images of lesbians, which have expanded from a dominant focus of lesbians as isolated individuals 'warped' by nature rather than nurture in the early part of the century to a celebratory assertion of lesbian nation and lesbians as a diverse community of very different women. Whatever image of lesbians is presented, however, it is done in the name of 'difference'. Difference is perhaps the most crucial element in such representations, relying both on a presence and an absence, the other in relation to whom/which 'lesbian' is defined and identified. In looking at some recent lesbian writing, it strikes me that one of the points of comparison or reference for establishing difference for 'lesbian' has been masculinity. To illustrate what I mean I want to look briefly at two texts: Jane DeLynn's *Don Juan in the village* (1988) and Cherry Smyth's *Lesbians talk queer notions* (1992). My focus on these two texts, both of which I find depressing, is dictated by the fact that the former was given a particularly wide public forum through being chosen as a selected text for the 1991 'Feminist Book Fortnight' in Britain, and the latter addresses queer theory which has had considerable airing in the context of lesbian and gay studies in the last year or so.

The title of *Don Juan* highlights two issues which seem to me to be important aspects of current lesbian cultural considerations and which have repeatedly been a significant concern in representations of lesbians. One of these issues is lesbian sexuality and what it might (or might not) model itself on, a concern particularly pertinent in the age of AIDS. I shall return to this later. The second, related issue is that of lesbians' relationship to masculinity, its symbolizations and power.[1] Don Juan, after all, is a *male* figure in its original conception; as such that figure has come to represent an idea of male sexuality which denies all constraints imposed upon it by regulatory social and moral discourses.[2] Hence his name, as *Brewer's dictionary of phrase and fable* puts it, 'is synonymous with rake, roué and aristocratic libertine.' My concern here is, in the first instance, with the utilization of a symbol of masculinity to image a lesbian character's quest for an other, a quest which, as is the case for the male Don Juan figure, cannot ultimately be resolved and is only ever provisionally assuaged through a sexual conquest that is always temporary.

The issue of how lesbian culture relates to masculinity has formed a continuous thread in representations of lesbians, raising the notion of difference in terms of 'if not woman, then man?'[3] Within the dichotomous thinking which still dominates our culture, woman is defined as 'not man', man as 'not woman'. Women whose emotional and sexual focus is other women thus pose a problem. An awareness of this problem informs the frequent construction of the lesbian as having as her 'other' which needs to be opposed and subverted a heterosexual man symbolizing patriarchal power who seeks to police her sexuality.[4] Taking on that other, assuming his symbolization, is one means of destabilizing the groundedness of his position in a 'naturalized' association of 'man' with, for instance, certain items of dress.[5] One of the several functions which appropriating clothing culturally designated as 'male' therefore serves is to deplace that male by putting the lesbian self 'in disguise' in his place.

'Mascquerading'[6] as 'male' has been and still is one of the devices used by lesbians to interrogate positions of male power. Recent years have seen a shift in lesbian culture, resulting in a (re)new(ed) engagement with masculinity as it presents itself in gay male culture. The roving figure of Don Juan bears some resemblance to the notion of a gay male bar and club scene where men have successive brief encounters in which the sexual exchange is the only and primary motive. More importantly, the arrival of queer theory has helped to activate the interrogation of the relationship between lesbians and gay men.

One could argue that the destabilization of fixed categories and meanings in theoretical models provided by deconstruction and work on gender, in Judith Butler's *Gender trouble*, for instance, has exploded the boundaries which focussed women on women, with the result that the very instability of signs and categories has encouraged the reviewing of lesbians in images of masculinity. In other words, if masculinity is a role or a symbolization which is not attached to a biologically specifiable body, then it is open for women to adopt, and given accoutrements such as power may be even desirable to aspire to. Alternatively, one might suggest that few inroads appear to have been made in the revisioning of the gendered power structures which govern our culture and, as a consequence, some lesbians are modelling themselves on/in a male-centred culture in which women generally have little power because as women they still do not 'count'. In other words, to assert the self seems still to be synonymous with a masculine stance. Thus the protagonist of *Don Juan* who is prone to reading her self in terms of famous images of maculinity says of herself at one point:

I was Gatsby, Eugène Rastignac, Norman Mailer, Donald Trump. . . anyone who had ever conquered a city with the sheer force of longing and desire. (p. 187)

Except that in her case 'anyone' means men.

I found *Don Juan* a depressing read, and not just because the central character tends to construct sexual desire as 'masculine';[7] it reinforced, I thought, Bonnie Zimmerman's view that 'we appear to have replaced the naive but invigorating optimism and idealism of our recent past with an uneasiness and complacency, even a cynicism, that is new and disconcerting' (*The safe sea of women*, p. 208) *Don Juan* strikes me as a deeply pessimistic text and I wondered why of all the lesbian writing which is now published it in particular had been chosen for the Feminist Book Fortnight. It certainly cannot be said to promote homosexuality as a desirable identity or existence.

The central character and first-person narrator is constructed as trapped in the past, recounting her miscellaneous sexual adventures (fulfilled but not fulfilling, and otherwise), a sad figure who 'as the

song says. . . [does]n't get around much any more' (p. 237). That in
itself offers a rather depressing view of a lesbian present and future
for this character seems to have little sense of a present or a future.
Towards the end she maintains:

> I had come to the bar for knowledge, but it turned out that that knowledge
> was only about how to behave in bars such as this. Now that I had that
> knowledge I was too old to use it – or maybe it was only that I was too old
> to want to use it. (p. 239)

The home-town lesbian community which the central character roves
in is small, confined to two bars. Throughout the text she asserts how
bored she is with those places and despite a history of trips away,
encapsulated in the various chapters of the novel, the protagonist
projects a sense of circularity, of having been there before, of being
unable to break out into a more permanently fulfilling existence.

Don Juan could be an elegy for gay life before death appeared on
the scene in the form of AIDS. 'Who knew' the protagonist muses at
one point, 'that even then a virus was beginning to make its way
through the beautiful bodies, a virus that would eventually bring
seasons and death even to this place?' (p. 105) But it is not clear that
her lifestyle changes as a result of AIDS. Pointing to 'the virus' also
obliterates the fact that 'seasons and death' existed before AIDS, are
part of the natural ageing process of every individual. When the
protagonist towards the end of the novel visits a lesbian bar she is
acutely aware of her age:

> Although inside I was still sixteen, a bratty adolescent, the mirror over the
> bar told me that I was the age of the women I used to scorn, so perhaps it
> was only fitting that young girls raced their eyes past mine as I used to
> race mine past those of older women years ago. (p. 238)

Nostalgia for the past, nostalgia for youth, nostalgia for a lesbian
community that does not seem to exist for the protagonist anymore
contribute to this novel appearing to detail a lesbian history which
has somehow ceased. Against this pessimism, I would argue that
lesbian (cultural) history is only now in the process of being uncovered, charted, theorized. The gradual advent of lesbian studies[8] and
the proliferation of books on the subject suggest a growth which *Don
Juan* would deny.

Another point that *Don Juan* seems to make is that the assumption
of a lesbian subjectivity which simultaneously constructs itself as the

object of its scrutiny leads to a split which debilitates the lesbian subject. One of the problems which the protagonist of Don Juan experiences as preventing her from immersing herself in encounters with others is that she tends to be aware of herself as the object of her own self-depreciating scrutiny at the same time as being the subject of a particular experience. Thus she says at one point:

> I was so intent on finding the perfect moment, I was less able to be in the absolute present than the people around me, and my consciousness of this created a distance between me and those around me. . . I was caught in my self-consciousness . . . (p. 53)

Having internalized early on the notion that as a lesbian she has a 'condition, a sickness, an affliction that was not my fault but for which I was forever going to be blamed' (p. 38), the narrator has difficulty transcending the split between 'my self-love and self-hate' (p. 240) in the gap between which she negotiates her sense of self-worth or abjection. It seems that this split accounts for her inability to inhabit the present; always hyper-conscious of a (potential) audience, she tends to judge her behaviour in terms of others' possible perceptions of herself. Thus at one point she engages in sex with someone described as 'a fat woman'. Experiencing contradictions between wanting sex and not wanting to be seen to be dependent on an 'unattractive' person for sex, she spends much of the encounter rehearsing this conflict (p. 77–84). The effect is that a complex yet entirely solipsistic hall of mirrors of the protagonist's perceptions is created, constructing an image of a woman obsessed, and unhappily so, with self.

One might argue that the emergence of lesbian criticism and lesbian theory, the uncovering of a lesbian culture and history during the last twenty years or so constitutes an analogy to Don Juan's preoccupation with the lesbian as both subject and object. Yet the conclusion drawn in that text, that it is all an 'immense vanity' (p. 240), is only one way of interpreting this development and one that I would want to resist. It is equally possible to suggest that making oneself the object of one's own scrutiny is vital for the construction of one's identity, that only through such a process is a sense of one's history achieved, and that that can afford a change in the perception of lesbian culture and history which enables a more positive (re)reading of lesbian identity than the one offered in Don Juan. That text makes a case against such a possibility, maintaining:

> The person I was now could not remember the person I had been. I
> thought if I could remember the women I had been with then this might
> help me remember the woman who had been with them – the woman
> who was me – but I could not remember them. That is, even if I could
> picture their faces, they were no more familiar to me than if I had only
> seen them in a bar – or perhaps only imagined seeing them. (p. 238)

However, the fact that the text is written in the past tense as ulterior
narration, and that the first-person narrator (re)creates her various
sexual encounters as well as her responses to these, raises questions
about the narrator's asssertions concerning her memory and her
stance. It is clearly not the case that she does not remember. If,
alternatively, she is pointing to the quality of that memory, is she
suggesting that all recreation is, in fact, creation, that, in the end, it is
all in the (present) mind? The text itself offers no answer to this
question but implicitly poses the issue of the 'accuracy' or 'truth'
value of history, memory, ulterior narration. It is perhaps for this
reason that H.D. in a sequence of poems dedicated to her lover
Bryher set up as one position the refusal of history as illuminating:

> This search for historical parallels,
> research into psychic affinities,
>
> has been done to death before,
> will be done again;
>
> no comment can alter spiritual realities
> (you say) or again,
>
> what new light can you possibly
> throw upon them? (p. 539)

H.D. herself counters this stance in the poem by saying, 'We have
had too much consecration,/too little affirmation,' (*The walls do not
fall down*, p. 540).

Against the negative stance adopted in *Don Juan* towards the
possibilities that the knowledge of a lesbian culture and history can
offer I would set Joan Nestle's assertion that ' As a woman, as a
Lesbian, as a Jew, I know that much of what I call history others will
not. But answering this challenge of exclusion is the work of a lifetime' (*A restricted country*, p. 10). This work has begun to take shape.

One of its manifestations is the reclaiming of lesbian history and culture which has resulted in the re-evaluation of a terminology for lesbians that is associated with the lesbian culture of the 1950s. A discussion of the reclaiming of 'butch' and 'queer' is part of *Lesbians talk queer notions* which 'aims to document the emergence of queer politics and self-understanding in Britain' (p. 11). An immediately obvious aspect of the text is that it indicates fragmentation on the page: lots of short paragraphs in different type faces highlight different and often opposing viewpoints. In contrast to *Don Juan*, which looks nostalgically back at a past not fully realized, this text seems to me to embody an engagement with an embattled present where homophobia is finally met with a new lesbian aggression and assertion that seeks its allies among gay men. In a culture which has become increasingly violent and aggressive and in which wars are moving closer and closer to home, violence (sexual and otherwise) now appears to be firmly on the gay agenda too.

Queer politics raises issues about the relation between lesbians and gay men, lesbians' relation to the symbolization of masculinity and to power. Cherry Smyth writes:

> The new separation between sexual practice and sexual identity is allowing lesbians to expand our practice, to question the fixedness of our identities and to invent new metaphors for sexual pleasure that can embrace wider interpretations of sex and gender. But if lesbians can empathise with, imitate and reflect gay male culture, is there a similar appropriation of lesbian practices by gay men? . . . On the whole, there seems to be little reciprocity. . . (*Lesbians talk queer notions*, p. 44)

If, as Smyth appears to suggest, 'inventing new metaphors' for lesbians means 'empathising with, imitating and reflecting gay male culture', then not only does this not seem to offer anything new, it also does nothing to question conventional conceptions of masculinity and femininity. Why do gay men not imitate lesbians? The old power structures prevail – men set the agenda, women follow. Such seems to be the case in the context of queer theory which many lesbians, including ones cited in *Lesbians talk queer notions*, find problematic.

'Queer' in *Lesbians talk* is associated with a 'transgressive aesthetic' and 'transgressive sexual practices' as indexed in Della Grace's photography and in preoccupations with S/M, fetishism, leather, the new lesbian 'macho' stance. *Don Juan* belongs into this context as the narrator attempts to live a 'macho' lifestyle. While on the one hand this subverts a dominant culture which denies women power, it simultaneously affirms it through aligning power with masculinity. Old orthodoxies in new-ish guises.

Additionally, the question of the politics of this stance seems to me problematic. Smyth rightly points to the fact that 'there is also the suggestion that queer will simply engender a situation where people are being transgressive for transgression's sake' (p. 45). This mirrors the circularity of *Don Juan*'s protagonist's self-obsession and projects a conservative position. As Elizabeth Wilson is appropriately quoted as saying:

> An avant-garde and/or bohemian stance is no guarantee of 'progressive' politics, and both are are primarily rebellious reactions against bourgeois conformist notions. Nor is transgression per se radical. Historically it has been linked with fascism as well as left wing politics or is perhaps more likely to lead to an apolitical dandyism. (*Lesbians talk*, p. 46)

It seems to me not surprising that 'queer theory' and a lesbian engagement with masculinity have emerged in the conservative political climate of the last decade. But I doubt that either is particularly enabling to lesbians.

The general increase in lesbian visibility in this culture, on the other hand, has been very enabling to lesbians. Many bookstores now have lesbian sections. These testify to the diversity of lesbian cultural production and highlight the inroads into lesbian history which have been made. They also indicate that while 'Lesbian Nation' and *the* lesbian community may be mythical concepts, lesbian *communities* do exist and have a place in this culture. The question continually to be asked is what is this place, what is its relation to the culture in which it exists, how does it influence that culture?

Notes

1 As the protagonist of *Don Juan* puzzles: 'I would wonder if I were really not something else entirely, a man in a woman's body, perhaps, a redneck man in a woman's body, or may be something even worse – a man who liked to fuck men in a woman's body; that is, a man in a woman's body who fucked women because this was the closest a man who was a woman could come to being a homosexual.' (p. 237)

2 *Don Juan*'s narrator, watching men, finds herself envying 'the careless insouciance of their lust and the easy accommodation of their desires' (p. 235).

3 In 'One is not born a woman' Monique Wittig makes explicit the problematic and oppression of which 'woman' is the mark. She rejects that label altogether.

4 Such male others inhabit the pages of *The well* as much as those of Ann Bannon's Beebo Brinker series and, indeed, *Don Juan*.

5 See Katrina Rolley's 'Cutting a dash: the dress of Radclyffe Hall and Una Troubridge', Elizabeth Wilson's 'Deviant dress' and Inge Blackman and Kathryn Perry's 'Skirting the issue: lesbian fashion for the 1990s'.

6 Joan Rivière's 'Womanliness as masquerade' is pertinent here.

7 The protagonist of *Don Juan* shows some recognition of this but little concern: 'It disturbed me a little to be thinking the way men do, but perhaps not enough' (p. 63).

8 See Rosemary Auchmuty *et al.*'s 'Lesbian and Gay Studies: keeping a feminist perspective'.

Bibliography

Autobiography, biography, fiction, poetry, drama:

Adelman, Marcy, ed., *Long time passing: lives of older lesbians* (Boston, 1986).
Ansell, Helen Essary, 'The threesome' in Kleinberg, ed., pp. 227–38.
Arnold, June, *Sister gin* (London, 1979).
Atwood, Margaret, *The handmaid's tale* (London, 1987).
Bachmann, Ingeborg, 'A step towards Gomorrah' in Kleinberg, ed., pp. 239–57.
Bannon, Ann, *Odd girl out* (Tallahassee, 1986).
———, *I am a woman* (Tallahassee, 1986).
———, *Women in the shadows* (Tallahassee, 1986).
———, *Journey to a woman* (Tallahassee, 1986).
———, *Beebo Brinker* (Tallahassee, 1986).
Barnes, Djuna, *Nightwood* (London and Boston, 1987).
Benmussa directs: 'Portrait of Dora' and 'The singular life of Albert Nobbs '(London and Dallas, 1979).
Bograd Weld, Jacqueline, *Peggy: the wayward Guggenheim* (London and New York, 1986).
Brophy, Brigid, *The finishing touch* (Guernsey, 1987).
Brown, Rita Mae, *Rubyfruit jungle* (London and New York, 1983).
Bulkin, Elly, ed., *Lesbian fiction: an anthology* (Watertown, 1981).
Califia, Pat, *Macho sluts* (Boston, 1988).
Carrington, Leonora, 'The sisters' in *The seventh horse and other tales* (London, 1989).
Cowlin, Dorothy, *Winter solstice* (London, 1991).
Crow, Christine, *Miss x or the wolf woman* (London, 1990).
Cruikshank, Margaret, ed., *New lesbian writing* (San Francisco, 1984).
Dane, Clemence [pseudonym for Winifred Ashton], *Regiment of women* (London and Toronto, 1966).
Daniels, Sarah, *Neaptide* (London, 1986).
Dee, Mandy, 'Shy – fragments' in Sheba Collective, pp. 37–8.
DeLynn, Jane, *Don Juan in the village* (London, 1991).
Duffy, Maureen, *Illuminations* (Glasgow, 1992).

————, *The microcosm* (London, 1989).

————, *Collected poems 1949–1984* (London, 1985).

————, 'Carmine veneriana' in *Collected poems*, pp. 245–51.

Dykewomon, Elana, 'The fourth daughter's four hundred questions' in Torton Beck, pp. 148–60.

Faderman, Lillian, *Scotch verdict* (New York, 1983).

Fairbairns, Zoë, *Benefits* (London, 1983).

Fell, Alison, ed., *Hard feelings: ficton and poetry from Spare Rib* (London, 1979).

Field, Michael, *Works and days: extracts from the journals of Michael Field*, see Sturge Moore.

Fitzroy, A. T., [pseudonym for Rose Laure Allatini], *Despised and rejected* (London, 1988).

Forrest, Katherine V., *Murder at the nightwood bar* (London, 1987).

French, Marilyn, *The women's room* (London, 1977).

Gems, Pam, 'Aunt Mary' in Wandor, Michelene, ed., *Plays by women* vol. 3 (London, 1984), pp. 13–49.

Grahn, Judy, 'The psychoanalysis of Edward the dyke' in *The work of a common woman* (London, 1985), pp. 26–30.

Grosskurth, Phyllis, *Havelock Ellis: a biography* (London and New York, 1981).

Hacker, Marilyn, *Love, death and the changing of the seasons* (London, 1986).

Haden Elgin, Suzette, *Native tongue* (London, 1985).

Hall, Radclyffe, *The well of loneliness* (London, 1982).

————, 'Miss Ogilvy finds herself' in *Miss Ogilvy finds herself* (London, 1959) pp. 6–31.

————, *The unlit lamp* (London, 1934).

Hall Carpenter Archives Lesbian Oral History Group, *Inventing ourselves: lesbian life stories* (London and New York, 1989).

Halliday, Caroline, 'Trapeze' in Sheba Collective, eds, pp. 30–4.

————, *Some truth – some change* (London, 1983).

Hanscombe, Gillian E., *Between friends* (London, 1983).

H.D. [Hilda Doolittle], *Her* (London, 1984).

————, 'The walls do not fall down' in *Collected poems 1912–1944*, ed. L. L. Martz (Manchester, 1984), pp. 507–44.

Highsmith, Patricia, *Carol* (London, 1990).

Ishatova, Dovida, 'What may be *tsores* to you is *naches* to me' in Torton Beck, pp. 174–8.

Jastrzebska, Maria, 'Some orgasms I'd like to mention' in Sheba Collective, eds, pp. 14–15.

Kaye, Melanie, 'Some notes on Jewish lesbian identity' in Torton Beck, pp. 28–44.

Kazantzis, Judith, 'The bath' in Fell, p. 47.

Kleinberg, Seymour, ed., *The other persuasion* (London, 1978).

Klepfisz, Irena, *Different enclosures; poetry and prose of Irena Klepfisz* (London, 1985).

————, 'Resisting and surviving America' in Torton Beck, pp. 100–8.

Lavery, Bryony, *Her aching heart, Two Marias, Wicked* (London, 1991).

Leaton, Anne, *Good friends, just* (London, 1983).

Lehmann, Rosamond, *Dusty answer* (London: 1952).

Lorde, Audre, *Zami: a new spelling of my name* (London, 1990).

————, *Chosen poems – old and new* (New York and London, 1982).

Lynch, Lee, *Old dyke tales* (Tallahassee, 1988).

Mahyère, Eveline, *I will not serve* (London, 1984).

Manning, Rosemary, *A corridor of mirrors* (London, 1987).

————, *A time and a time* (London and New York, 1986).

————, *The Chinese garden* (London, 1984).

Mansfield, Katherine, 'Bliss' in *The collected short stories* (Harmondsworth, 1984), pp. 91–105.

Manthorne, Jackie, *Fascination ... and other bar stories* (Charlottetown, Canada, 1991).

Mars-Jones, Adam, *Mae West is dead: recent lesbian and gay fiction* (London and Boston, 1983).

McEwen, Christian, *Naming the waves: contemporary lesbian poetry* (London, 1988).

Mohin, Lilian, ed., *Beautiful barbarians: lesbian feminist poetry* (London, 1986).

Murdoch, Iris, *An unofficial rose* (London, 1962).

Nachman/Dykewomon, Elana, *Riverfinger women* (Tallahassee, 1992).

Neild, Suzanne, and Rosalind Pearson, eds, *Women like us* (London, 1992).

Nestle, Joan, 'A change of life' in Nestle, pp. 131–33.

———, 'I am' in Nestle, pp. 13–14.

O'Donovan, Joan, 'Johnnie' in Kleinberg, pp. 216–26.

Rich, Adrienne, *An atlas of the difficult world: poems 1988–1991* (New York and London, 1991).

———, *The fact of a doorframe: poems selected and new 1950–1984* (New York and London, 1984).

———, *A wild patience has taken me this far* (New York and London, 1981).

———, 'The images' in Rich, *A wild patience*, pp. 3–5.

Rule, Jane, *Memory board* (London, 1987).

———, 'Middle children' in Kleinberg, ed., pp. 340–45.

———, *Theme for diverse instruments* (Vancouver, 1975).

———, *Outlander: short stories and essays* (Tallahassee, 1982).

Russ, Joanna, *Extra(ordinary) people* (London, 1985).

———, *On strike against god* (Trumansburg, NY, 1980).

Sappho, *Poems and fragments*, trans. Josephine Balmer (London, 1984).

Schulman, Sarah, *After Delores* (London, 1990).

———, *Girls, visions and everything* (London, 1986).

Sheba Collective, ed., *Serious pleasure: lesbian erotic stories and poetry* (London, 1989).

Shockley, Ann Allen, *The black and white of it* (Tallahassee, 1987).

Stein, Gertrude, *The autobiography of Alice B. Toklas* (Harmondsworth, 1981.)

———, 'A sonatina followed by another' in Kostelanetz, Richard, ed., *The Yale Gertrude Stein* (New Haven and London, 1980), pp. 287–315.

Sturge Moore, T. and D. C., eds, *Works and days: from the journal of Michael Field* (London, 1933).

Torton Beck, Evelyn, ed., *Nice Jewish girls: a lesbian anthology* (Watertown, 1982).

Troubridge, Una, *The life and death of Radclyffe Hall* (London, 1961).

Vivien, Reneé, *A woman appeared to me* (Tallahassee, 1982).

Walker, Alice, 'Porn', in *You can't keep a good woman down* (London and New York, 1982), pp. 77–84.

Weldon, Fay, *Down among the women* (Harmondsworth and New York, 1973).

———, *Female friends* (London, 1975).

Wilhelm, Gale, *We too are drifting* (Tallahassee, 1984).

———, *Torchlight to Valhalla* (Tallahassee, 1985).

Winterson, Jeanette, *Oranges are not the only fruit* (London and Boston, 1985).

Wittig, Monique, and Sande Zeig, *Lesbian peoples* (London, 1980).

Wolfe, Susan B., 'Jewish lesbian mother' in Torton Beck, pp. 164–73.

Wollstonecraft, Mary, *Mary and The wrongs of Woman* (Oxford and New York, 1976).

Theoretical texts, literary criticism:

Abbott, Sidney, and Barbara Love, *Sappho was a right-on woman* (New York, 1972).
Abel, Elizabeth, Marianne Hirsch and Elizabeth Langland, eds, *The voyage in: fictions of female development* (Hanover and London, 1983).
Abrams, M. H., *A glossary of literary terms* (London and New York, 1981).
Andermahr, Sonya, 'The worlds of lesbian/feminist science fiction' in Griffin.
——, 'The politics of separatism and lesbian utopian fiction' in Munt, pp. 133–52.
Anon., 'What's yours called?' in *Bitch* (Sept. 1992), unpaginated.
Arditti, Rita, Duelli Klein, Renate and Shelley Minden, eds, *Test-tube women* (London and Boston, 1984).
Armitt, Lucie, ed., *Where no man has gone before: women and science fiction* (London and New York, 1991).
Atkinson, Ti-Grace, *Amazon odyssey* (New York, 1974).
Auchmuty, Rosemary, Jeffreys, Sheila and Elaine Miller, 'Lesbian history and gay studies: keeping a feminist perspective' in *Women and history* 1/1 (1992), pp. 89–108.
Auerbach, Nina, *Communities of women: an idea in fiction* (Cambridge, Mass. and London, 1978).
Barrett, Michéle and Mary McIntosh, *The anti-social family* (London and New York, 1982, 1991).
Barrington, Judith, ed., *An intimate wilderness: lesbian writers on sexuality* (Portland, 1991).
Beer, Gillian, *Darwin's plots: evolutionary narrative in Darwin, George Eliot, and nineteenth-century fiction* (London and Boston, 1983).
Belsey, Catherine, *Critical Practice* (London, 1980).
Benstock, Shari, *Women of the left bank: Paris, 1900–1940* (London and Texas, 1987).
Blackman, Inge and Kathryn Perry, 'Skirting the issue: lesbian fashion for the 1990s' in *Feminist Review* 34 (Spring 1990), pp. 67–78.
Brady, Maureen, 'Insider/outsider coming of age' in Jay and Glasgow eds, pp. 49–58.
Brittain, Vera, *Radclyffe Hall: a case of obscenity?* (London, 1968).
Butler, Judith, 'Imitation and gender insubordination' in Fuss, pp. 13–31.
——, *Gender trouble: feminism and the subversion of identity* (New York and London, 1990).
Cameron, Deborah, 'Old het?' in *Trouble & Strife* 24 (Summer 1992), pp. 41–5.
——, *Feminism and linguistic theory* (London, 1985).
Carpenter, Edward, *The intermediate sex: a study of some transitional types of men and women* (London, 1908).
Cartledge, Sue and Joanna Ryan, eds, *Sex & love: new thoughts on old contradictions* (London, 1983).
Case, Sue-Ellen, *Feminism and theatre* (Houndsmill, 1988).
——, 'Towards a butch-femme aesthetic' in *Discourse* 11/1 (1988–9), pp. 55–73.
Cavin, Susan, *Lesbian origins* (San Francisco, 1985).
Chodorow, Nancy, *The reproduction of mothering: psychoanalysis and the sociology of gender* (Berkeley and London, 1978).
Cixous, Hélène and Catherine Clément, *The newly born woman* (Manchester, 1986).
Cruikshank, Margaret, ed., *Lesbian studies: present and future* (New York, 1982).
Davis, Jill, '"This be different" – the lesbian drama of Mrs Havelock Ellis' in *Women: a cultural review* 2/2 (Summer 1991), pp. 134–48.
Douglas, Carol Anne, *Love and politics: radical feminist and lesbian theories* (San Francisco, 1990).
Duggan, Lisa, 'History's gay ghetto: the contradictions of growth in lesbian and gay

history' in Benson, Susan Porter, *et al.*, eds, *Presenting the past: essays on history and the public* (Philadelphia, 1986), pp. 281–90.

Ellis, Havelock, *Studies in the psychology of sex.* 2 vols (New York, 1942).

Faderman, Lillian, *Odd girls and twilight lovers: a history of lesbian life in twentieth-century America* (London and New York, 1991).

———, *Surpassing the love of men: romantic friendship and love between women from the Renaissance to the present* (London and New York, 1981).

———, *Scotch verdict* (New York, 1983).

Faludi, Susan, *Backlash: the undeclared war against women* (London, 1991).

Feminist Review 34 (Spring 1990): special issue on 'Perverse Politics: Lesbian Issues'.

Farwell, Marilyn R., 'Heterosexual plots and lesbian subtexts: toward a theory of lesbian narrative space' in Jay and Glasgow, pp. 91–103.

Findlay, Heather, 'Is there a lesbian in this text? Derrida, Wittig, and the politics of the three women' in Weed, Elizabeth, ed., *Coming to terms: feminism, theory, politics* (London and New York, 1989), pp. 59–69.

flyin thunda cloud, rdoc. 'x-tra insight' in Hoagland and Penelope, pp. 284–6.

Foster, Jeannette H., *Sex variant women in literature* (Tallahassee, Florida, 1985).

Freedman, Estelle B., Gelpi, Barbara C., Johnson, Susan L. and Kathleen M. Weston, eds, *The lesbian issue: essays from SIGNS* (London and Chicago, 1985).

French, Marilyn, *The war against women* (London, 1992).

Freud, Sigmund, *On sexuality*, Pelican Freud Library vol. 7 (Harmondsworth and New York, 1977).

———, 'Three essays on the theory of sexuality' in Freud, *On sexuality*, pp. 33–169.

———, 'Family romances' in Freud, *On sexuality*, pp. 219–25.

———, 'Female sexuality' in Freud, *On sexuality*, pp. 369–92.

———, 'Female homosexuality' in Freud, *Case histories II:* 'Rat man', Schreber, 'Wolf man', *Female homosexuality*, Pelican Freud Library vol. 9 (Harmondsworth and New York, 1984).

Frye, Marilyn, 'Lesbian "sex"' in Barrington, pp. 1–8.

———, 'Some reflections on separatism and power' in Hoagland and Penelope, pp. 62–72.

Fuss, Diana, ed. *Inside/out: lesbian theories, gay theories* (New York and London, 1991).

———, *Essentially speaking: feminism, nature and difference* (New York and London, 1989).

Gilbert, Harriet and Christine Roche, *A women's history of sex* (London, 1987).

Gilbert, Sandra M. and Susan Gubar, *No man's land: the place of the woman writer in the twentieth century*, vol. i: 'The war of the words' (New Haven and London, 1988).

Gilligan, Carol, *In a different voice* (Cambridge, Mass., and London, 1982).

Grahn, Judy, *The highest apple: Sappho and the lesbian poetic tradition* (San Francisco, 1985).

———, *Another mother tongue: gay words, gay worlds* (Boston, 1984).

Grier, Barbara, ed., *The lesbian in literature* (Tallahassee, Florida, 1981).

Griffin, Gabriele, ed., *Outwrite: popular/rising lesbian texts* (London, 1993).

Halliday, Caroline, '"The naked majesty of god": contemporary lesbian erotic poetry' in Lilly, pp. 76–108.

Hamer, Diane, '"I am a woman": Ann Bannon and the writing of lesbian identity of the 1950s' in Lilly, pp. 47–75.

Hanscombe, Gillian, 'In among the market forces?' in Barrington, pp. 216–20.

Hanscombe, Gillian and Virginia L. Smyers, *Writing for their lives: the modernist women 1910–1940* (London, 1987).

Hastie, Nickie, 'Lesbian bibliomythography' in Griffin.

Henderson, Lisa, 'Lesbian pornography: cultural transgression and sexual demystification' in Munt, pp. 173–91.

Hennegan, Alison, 'On becoming a lesbian reader' in Radstone, pp. 165–90.

Hermsen, Joke J. and Alkeline van Lenning, eds, *Sharing the difference* (London and New York, 1991).

Hinds, Hilary, '*Oranges are not the only fruit*: reaching audiences other lesbian texts cannot reach' in Munt.

Hoagland, Sarah Lucia, 'From *Lesbian Ethics*: Desire and political perception' in Barrington, ed., pp. 164–81.

Hoagland, Sarah Lucia and Julia Penelope, eds, *For lesbians only: a separatist anthology* (London, 1988).

Hobby, Elaine and Chris White, eds, *What lesbians do in books* (London, 1991).

Hollibaugh, Amber and Cherrie Moraga, 'What we're rollin around in bed with: sexual silences in feminism' in Snitow *et al.*, pp. 404–14.

Hull, Gloria T., Bell Scott, Patricia and Barbara Smith, eds, *But some of us are brave: black women's studies* (New York, 1982).

Hutcheon, Linda, *A theory of parody: the teachings of twentieth-century art forms* (New York and London, 1985).

Jacobus, Mary, 'Is there a woman in this text?' in Jacobus, *Reading woman: essays in feminist criticism* (London, 1986), pp. 83–109.

Jeffreys, Sheila, *The spinster and her enemies: feminism and sexuality 1880–1930* (London and Boston, Mass., 1985).

———, *Anticlimax: a feminist perspective on the sexual revolution* (London, 1990).

Jo, Bev, 'Female only' in Hoagland and Penelope, pp. 74–5.

Kennard, Jane E., 'Ourself behind ourself: a theory for lesbian readers' in Gelpi *et al.*, pp. 153–68.

King, Katie, 'Audre Lorde's lacquered layerings: the lesbian bar as a site of literary production' in Munt, pp. 51–74.

Kitzinger, Celia, *The social construction of lesbianism* (London and Beverly Hills, 1987).

Kitzinger, Sheila, *Woman's experience of sex* (London, 1983).

Krafft-Ebing, Richard von, *Psychopathia sexualis* (Munich, 1984).

Krieger, Susan, 'Lesbian identity and community: recent social science literature' in Gelpi *et al.*, pp. 223–40.

Kristeva, Julia, *Strangers to ourselves* (New York, London, Toronto, 1991).

———, *Desire in language* (Oxford, 1980).

Lefanu, Sarah, *In the chinks of the world machine: feminism and science fiction* (London, 1988).

Le Guin, Ursula K., 'Is gender necessary? Redux' in *The language of the night: essays on fantasy and science fiction* (London, 1989), pp. 135–47.

Lesbian History Group, *Not a passing phase: reclaiming lesbians in history 1840–1985* (London, 1989).

Lilly, Mark, ed., *Lesbian and gay writing* (Houndsmill and London, 1990).

Livia, Anna, 'Lesbian sexuality: joining the dots' in Barrington, pp. 193–8.

Lorde, Audre, *Sister outsider* (Trumansburg, NY, 1984).

Lovell, Terry, ed., *British feminist thought* (Oxford and Cambridge, Mass., 1990).

Lynch, Lee, 'Cruising the libraries' in Jay and Glasgow, pp. 39–48.

Magee, Bryan, *One in twenty: a study of homosexuality in men and women* (London, 1966).

Meese, Elizabeth, 'Theorizing lesbian : writing – a love letter' in Jay and Glasgow, eds, pp. 70–88.

Meigs, Mary, 'Falling between the cracks' in Jay and Glasgow, pp. 28–38.

Miller, Alice, *The drama of the gifted child* (London and Boston, 1983); rpt. as *The drama of being a child* (London, 1987).

Miner, Valerie, 'An imaginative collectivity of writers and readers' in Jay and Glasgow, pp. 13–27.

Mitchell, Juliet, *Women: the longest revolution* (London, 1966).

Mitchell, Juliet and Ann Oakley, eds, *What is feminism?* (Oxford, 1986).

Munt, Sally, ed., *New lesbian criticism* (New York and London, 1992).

Nestle, Joan, *A restricted country: essays and short stories* (London, 1987).

Newton, Esther, 'The mythic mannish lesbian: Radclyffe Hall and the new woman' in Freedman *et al.*, 1985, pp. 7–25.

Oakley, Ann, *The captured womb* (Oxford and Cambridge, Mass., 1984).

O'Sullivan, Sue, 'Mapping: lesbians, AIDS and sexuality – an interview with Cindy Patton by Sue O'Sullivan' in *Feminist review* 34 (Spring 1990), pp. 120–33.

Palmer, Paulina, 'The lesbian thriller: crimes, clues and contradictions' in Griffin.

———, 'The lesbian feminist thriller and detective novel' in Hobby and White, pp. 9–27.

Penelope, Julia, *Call me lesbian: lesbian lives, lesbian theory* (Freedom, CA, 1992).

———, 'Wimmin- and lesbian-only spaces: thought into action' in *Call me lesbian*, pp. 52–9.

———, 'Lesbian separatism: the linguistic and social sources of separatist politics' in Hoagland, S. and J. Penelope, pp. 44–49.

———, *Speaking freely* (London and New York, 1990).

Potter, La Forest, *Strange loves: a study in sexual abnormalities* (New York, 1933).

Potts, Billie Luisi, 'Owning Jewish separatism and lesbian separatism' in Hoagland and Penelope, pp. 149–58.

Radford, Jean, 'An inverted romance: *the well of loneliness* and sexual ideology' in Radford, Jean, ed., *The progress of romance: the politics of popular fiction* (London and New York, 1986), pp. 97–111.

Radstone, Susannah, ed., *Sweet dreams: sexuality, gender and popular fiction* (London, 1988).

Radway, Janice A., *Reading the romance* (London and New York, 1984).

Raymond, Janice, *A passion for friends: toward a philosophy of female affection* (London and Boston, 1986).

Redwomon, 'Freedom' in Hoagland and Penelope, pp. 76–83.

Rich, Adrienne, *On lies, secrets, silence: selected prose 1966–1978* (London, 1980).

———, *Blood, bread and poetry: selected prose 1979–1985* (London, 1987).

———, 'Compulsory heterosexuality and lesbian existence' in Rich, *Blood, bread and poetry*, pp. 23–75.; also in Snitow, *et al.*, pp. 212–41.

———, *Of woman born* (London, 1977).

Rivière, Joan, 'Womanliness as masquerade' in Burgin, Victor, Donald, James, and Cora Kaplan, eds, *Formations of fantasy* (London, 1986), pp. 35–44.

Rolley, Katrina, 'Cutting a dash: the dress of Radclyffe Hall and Una Troubridge' in *Feminist Review* 35 (Summer 1990), pp. 54–66.

Ruehl, Sonja, 'Inverts and experts: Radclyffe Hall and the lesbian identity' in Newton, Judith and Deborah Rosenfelt, eds, *Feminist criticism and social change* (New York and London, 1985), pp. 165–80.

Rule, Jane, *Lesbian images* (New York, 1975).

Russo, Mary, 'Female grotesques: carnival and theory' in de Lauretis, Teresa, ed., *Feminist studies/critical studies* (London, 1988), pp. 213–29.

Ryan, Joanna, 'Psychoanalysis and women loving women' in Cartledge and Ryan, pp. 196–209.

Sandoval, Chela, 'Comment on Krieger's "Lesbian identity and community: recent social science literature"' in Gelpi *et al.*, pp. 241–5.

Shaktini, Namascar, 'Displacing the phallic subject: Wittig's lesbian writing' in Gelpi *et al*, pp. 137–52.

Showalter, Elaine, *Sexual anarchy: gender and culture at the fin de siècle* (London, 1991).

——, *The female malady: women, madness and English culture, 1830–1980* (London, 1987).

——, *Women's liberation and literature* (New York, 1971).

Sinfield, Alan, ed., *Society and literature 1945–1970* (London, 1983).

Smyth, Cherry, *Lesbians talk queer notions* (London, 1992).

Snitow, Ann, Christine Stansell and Sharon Thompson, eds, *Desire: the politics of sexuality* (London, 1984).

Stanley, Liz, 'Epistemological issues in researching lesbian history: the case of romantic friendship' in Hinds, Hilary, Ann Phoenix and Jackie Stacey, eds, *Working out: new directions for women's studies* (London and Washington, 1992), pp. 161–72.

Stern, J. P. *On realism* (London, 1973).

Stimpson, Catharine R., *Where the meanings are: feminism and cultural spaces* (New York and London, 1988).

——, 'The androgyne and the homosexual' in Stimpson, *Where the meanings are*, pp. 54–61.

——, 'Zero degree deviancy: the lesbian novel in English' in Stimpson, *Where the meanings are*, pp. 97–110; also in Abel, Elizabeth, ed., *Writing and sexual difference* (Brighton, 1982), pp. 243–59.

——, 'What matter mind: a theory about the practice of women's studies' in Stimpson, *Where the meanings are*, pp. 38–53.

Strachey, Ray, *The cause: a short history of the women's movement in Great Britain* (London, 1978).

Textual Practice 4:2 (Summer 1990): special issue on 'Lesbian and gay cultures: theories and texts'.

Todd, Janet, *Women's friendship in literature* (New York, 1980).

Wandor, Michelene, *Carry on, understudies: theatre and sexual politics* (London and New York, 1981).

Warnock, Mary, *A question of life: the Warnock report on human fertilisation and embryology* (Oxford and New York, 1985).

Weeks, Jeffrey, *Coming out: homosexual politics in Britain, from the nineteenth century to the present* (London and New York, 1977).

——, *Sex, politics and society* (London and New York, 1989).

Weideger, Paula, *History's mistress* (Harmondsworth, 1986).

White, Chris, '"Poets and lovers evermore", interpreting female love in the poetry and journals of Michael Field', in *Textual Practice* 4:2 (Summer 1990) pp. 197–212.

White, Haydn, *Tropics of discourse* (Baltimore and London, 1978).

Whitlock, Gillian, '"Everything is out of place": Radclyffe Hall and the lesbian literary tradition' in *Feminist studies*, 13/3 (Fall 1987), pp. 555–82.

Wilson, Barbara, 'The erotic life of fictional characters' in Barrington, pp. 199–209.

Wilson, Elizabeth, 'Deviant dress' in *Feminist Review* 35 (Summer 1990), pp. 67–74.

——, 'Memoirs of an anti-heroine' in *Hallucinations: life in the post-modern city* (London, 1988), pp. 1–10.

——, 'Chic thrills' in *Hallucinations*, pp. 44–55.

——, 'I'll climb the stairway to heaven: lesbianism in the seventies' in Cartledge and Ryan, pp. 180–95.

Wilton, Tamsin, 'Desire and the politics of representation: issues for lesbians and heterosexual women' in Hinds, Hilary, Ann Phoenix and Jackie Stacey, eds, *Working out: new directions for women's studies* (London and Washington, 1992), pp. 74–85.

Wittig, Monique, *The straight mind and other essays* (New York and London, 1992).

————, 'One is not born a woman' in *The straight mind*, pp. 9–20.

Wittig, Monique and Sande Zeig, *Lesbian peoples: materials for a dictionary* (London, 1980).

Wollstonecraft, Mary, *Vindication of the rights of woman* (Harmondsworth, 1982).

Woolf, Virginia, *A room of one's own* (1928; rpt. London and New York, 1977).

Zimmerman, Bonnie, *The safe sea of women: lesbian fiction 1969–1989* (London, 1992).

————, 'Exiting from patriarchy: the lesbian novel of development' in Abel *et al.*, pp. 244–57.

————, 'What has never been: an overview of lesbian feminist criticism' in Greene, Gayle, and Coppelia Kahn, eds, *Making a difference: feminist literary criticism* (London and New York, 1985), pp. 177–210.

————, 'The politics of transliteration: lesbian personal narratives' in Gelpi *et al.*, pp. 251–70.

Index